WITHDRAWN
UTSA Libraries

PUERTO RICO

0

PUERTO RICO

Negotiating Development and Change

James L. Dietz

LYNNE
RIENNER
PUBLISHERS

BOULDER
LONDON

Published in the United States of America in 2003 by
Lynne Rienner Publishers, Inc.
1800 30th Street, Boulder, Colorado 80301
www.rienner.com

And in the United Kindgom by
Lynne Rienner Publishers, Inc.
3 Henrietta Street, Covent Garden, London WC2E 8LU

Library of Congress Cataloging-in-Publication Data
Dietz, James L., 1947–
    Puerto Rico, negotiating development and change / James L. Dietz.
        p.   cm.
    Includes bibliographical references (p.) and index.
    ISBN 1-58826-122-0 (alk. paper) — ISBN 1-58826-147-6 (pbk. : alk. paper)
    1. Puerto Rico—Economic conditions—1918–1952.   2. Puerto Rico—Economic
conditions—1952–   3. Puerto Rico—Economic policy.   4. Puerto Rico—Social
conditions—1952–   5. Puerto Rico—Social policy.   I. Title.

HC154.5.D543   2003
338.97295—dc21

                                                                    2003041370

British Cataloguing in Publication Data
A Cataloguing in Publication record for this book
is available from the British Library.

Printed and bound in the United States of America

    ∞   The paper used in this publication meets the requirements
        of the American National Standard for Permanence of
        Paper for Printed Library Materials Z39.48-1984.

    5 4 3 2 1

Contents

Tables

Puerto Rico

1

An Overview of Economic and Social Progress

Throughout the 1980s and the 1990s significant changes in Puerto Rico's economic and political environment transformed the edifice of the "Puerto Rican model of development."[1] Some of these were the consequence of trends evident in the international economy since the Bretton Woods era came to a definitive end in 1973. Other transformations were the product of peculiarities surrounding Puerto Rico–U.S. political, legal, and economic relations, a veritable albatross around the metaphorical necks of both polities. Puerto Rico at the beginning of the twenty-first century now finds itself searching for a new path to a higher level of development to meet the still unresolved needs of its citizens, needs that continue to be beyond the reach of the style of economic growth in place since the late 1940s.

Some of the changes affecting the economy and society since the 1970s have been of Puerto Rico's own making and were within the control of local political and economic actors. Other effects, perhaps the most significant ones, were the consequence of exogenous forces emanating from the dynamics of U.S. and international political economic forces outside the reach of Puerto Rican decisionmakers. Taken as a whole, unparalleled technological, economic, and political changes that have accelerated over the last two decades of the twentieth century have fundamentally altered the nature of Puerto Rico's position in the international economy, especially vis-à-vis the United States, just as some of the same forces have propelled other economies into new relationships at the world level. A more open international economy and "liquid" borders for both goods and finance flowing between most nations in the world economy—what many call the forces of globalization—have created an entirely different economic environment for Puerto Rico, just as for virtually every other economy. It is a radical change from the environment that existed up to the 1970s and has altered in crucial ways the so-called special relation that has bound Puerto Rico to the United States since it became a U.S. possession in 1898.

Political economist Emilio Pantojas-García (2000: 228, 232–233) believes that there has been an obsession by social scientists in focusing on Puerto Rico's past development model and its failures to the exclusion of better understanding Puerto Rico's place in the "transnationalized economic spaces" that have dominated the last quarter of the twentieth century. While there is some truth to this perspective, it is my contention that even in "dependent" economies such as Puerto Rico the particular development strategy chosen and pursued is exceedingly important for at least partly defining and determining what the place of that economy will be within these transnationalized economic spaces.

Pantojas-García's viewpoint tends to imply that Puerto Rico is completely subordinated within this transnationalized economy. One of the emphases of this work is to suggest that this need not be so with the proper economic policies, even without a change in Puerto Rico's political status. Puerto Rico has had much more freedom to define its economic path than has commonly been thought and certainly more than has been exercised. Even dependent economies and societies have room to maneuver in determining their path of development if those in positions of power wish to make changes and understand what needs to be done. Many smaller independent economies face similar forces in the more open and competitive world economy of the twenty-first century. Puerto Rico is not alone in facing challenges.

What has been the nature of the changes in the Puerto Rico–U.S. relationship? How have these changes impacted Puerto Rico's economic and social development? What external events have contributed to these transformations? How does the Puerto Rican growth and development experience compare to that of the Latin American economies and to the more successful East Asian economies over the same period of time? Is the Puerto Rican experience sui generis, or is it a recognizable strategy replicated in other developing economies? And perhaps most important, what does the future of Puerto Rico promise in terms of economic, social, and political progress for its nearly 4 million citizens?

These are the fundamental motivating questions to be examined in this and the following chapters. These are the questions that do and should engage the attention of policymakers and others seriously concerned with Puerto Rico's future. The objective of this book is not to rehash the past and restate well-known criticisms of Puerto Rico's development path. Rather, the intent is to understand this past as having set the stage for the present and for delineating possibilities in the future. The purpose of this book is to suggest how and why the economic strategy has been a partial failure for the majority of Puerto Ricans. It is of course possible to argue that the economic path followed has benefited certain sectors, especially external investors, but the focus here is global social welfare.

It is impossible to begin the process of altering Puerto Rico's future without starting with the opportunities and challenges of the present, and this present is a product of the past. In doing so, the past is viewed through the lens of recent debates and theoretical scholarship in the field of economic development that can illuminate not only where Puerto Rico faltered but also what needs to be done in the future.

Income Convergence and the
Gains from Operation Bootstrap

In 1950, just three years after Puerto Rico had initiated its development strategy directed at shifting the economy from its agricultural base to a more robust and dynamic system grounded in industrialization, per capita income had grown to $328 from about $150 in 1940 (Junta de Planificación 1981: tab. A-1).[2] By comparison, U.S. income per capita in 1950 was $1,935, nearly six times larger. In 1960, Puerto Rico's per capita income had risen to $723 and by 1970 income once again had more than doubled, reaching $1,857 per person.[3]

Relative to the United States, Puerto Rico's per capita income gained ground rapidly over the first two decades of the industrialization program. U.S. per capita gross domestic product (GDP) as a multiple of Puerto Rico's income at first fell to just four times larger in 1960 ($2,915) and then to only 2.7 times greater in 1970 ($5,050) (U.S. Bureau of the Census 1999: 861, 888). It was over this period, from 1950 to 1970, that Puerto Rico's strategy of "industrialization by invitation," dubbed Operation Bootstrap, was presented to other poor nations as a formula worthy of emulation. Per capita income figures such as these, which show significant gains in Puerto Rico's income compared to the United States and a tendency toward income convergence, often were noted as evidence of the wisdom of a Puerto Rican–type path of growth for other less-developed economies, one based on attracting foreign direct investment (FDI) to speed up the growth process.[4]

This story line of growth and income convergence by FDI did not continue unabated, however. By 1980, though Puerto Rico's income per person had risen in absolute terms to $4,549, income per capita in the United States remained 2.7 times larger at $12,226. The same was true in 1990; average income in Puerto Rico had grown to more than $8,713, but the average U.S. income per person of $23,215 remained 2.7 times as large. The gap between U.S. and Puerto Rican income thus remained virtually unchanged for more than two decades, from 1970 to 1990, with income in the United States averaging nearly three times that in Puerto Rico. The trend toward income convergence observed in the first two decades of industrialization failed to be maintained by the subsequent income growth that occurred from 1970 to 1990.

Since 1990, the tendency toward income convergence with the United States has reemerged. In 1995, GDP per capita in Puerto Rico rose to $11,713. It was $28,131 per person in the United States, or now just 2.4 times larger. In 2000, U.S. income of $36,174 per person was 2.3 times larger than Puerto Rico's GDP per person of $16,065 (Junta de Planificación 1988: A-1; 1999: A-1; 2002: A-1; U.S. Bureau of the Census 2001: 422). Interestingly, this trend toward convergence of income reappeared during the 1990s precisely when the federal tax law governing U.S. corporations in Puerto Rico was undergoing its most fundamental change and the Puerto Rican economy was being forced to find its own path of economic development with less federal intervention and more local initiative, as Chapter 5 will detail.

The relative income gap between the United States and Puerto Rico actually is worse than painted by the above statistics, however. The data used for comparing incomes were GDP figures, which shed the best possible light on the level of income in Puerto Rico. From 1950 to 2000, Puerto Rico's total GDP has grown faster—9.3 percent per year—than gross national product (GNP), which grew 8.3 percent per year over the same period. As a result, aggregate GDP is now nearly 50 percent larger than total GNP (Junta de Planificación 2002: A-1), the difference being due primarily to the large outflow of income repatriated to U.S. corporations by their subsidiary operations in Puerto Rico.[5]

If GNP per capita figures are used as the basis of comparison between the United States and Puerto Rico, then in 1970 the U.S. GNP per person of $5,101 was 2.95 times larger than Puerto Rico's income of $1,729 per person. In 2000, U.S. GNP per person of $36,158 was 3.32 times larger than Puerto Rico's GNP per person of $10,906, though this ratio had declined slightly over the 1990s.[6] Using GNP as the income measure for comparison reveals an even wider income gap between the United States and Puerto Rico, a divergence that again only began to be moderated somewhat in the 1990s.

In effect, almost all of the gains in income relative to the United States were made over the first two decades of Operation Bootstrap's efforts to promote growth and industrialization. It is quite likely that much of this gain in income was due to a onetime shift of low-productivity agricultural workers to higher-productivity industrial and service jobs as part of the fundamental structural change that takes place in the transformation of agricultural economies into industrial societies.[7] Once that shift in the labor force had taken place, further gains in income did not take place as quickly. As a result, from 1970 to the 1990s, the development strategy failed to maintain the income convergence of the first two decades of transformation.[8]

Whether the tendency toward some mild income convergence observed in the 1990s continues, only time will tell. What is of interest in terms of this study is that the reappearance of relative income convergence occurred precisely when the federal tax advantages for U.S. corporations operating within Puerto Rico underwent their most drastic changes and at the same time that new efforts to strengthen the local economy began to be implemented in an effort to counteract the expected negative effects of the changing federal tax laws.

Table 1.1 compares Puerto Rico's personal income per person with the two richest and the two poorest U.S. states in 1980 and 2000. In 2000, Puerto Rico's per capita personal income was equal to less than one-quarter of that in the richest U.S. state, Connecticut, and was less than one-half the income per person of Mississippi. Since 1980, Puerto Rico's personal income has not shown any tendency to close the gap with Mississippi, the poorest U.S. state. In fact, the relative difference in income was marginally greater in 2000 than in 1980, as Puerto Rico's personal income per person was only 47.2 percent of Mississippi's in 2000 compared to a slightly more favorable 48.8 percent in 1980. Relative to Connecticut, the richest U.S. state in 2000, income divergence also is evident between 1980 and 2000.

**Table 1.1   Income per Capita: Puerto Rico Versus Richest and
            Poorest U.S. States, 1980 and 2000**

	1980		2000
Alaska	$14,807	Connecticut	$40,702
	(23.3)		(24.2)
Connecticut	12,439	Massachusetts	37,704
	(27.8)		(26.2)
Arkansas	7,586	West Virginia	21,738
	(45.5)		(45.4)
Mississippi	7,076	Mississippi	20,900
	(48.8)		(47.2)
Puerto Rico	3,455	Puerto Rico	9,870

Sources: U.S. Bureau of Economic Analysis, Regional Accounts data available at
www.bea.gov/bea/regional/spi; Junta de Planificación 1990: tab. A-1; Junta de Planificación,
tab. 1 at www.prsdclead.gobierno.pr.
Note: Numbers in parentheses show Puerto Rico's per capita personal income as a percentage of each state's per capita personal income.

The weakness of relative income convergence with the United
States also can be observed more closely by examining the evolution of
wages over time. Hourly wages for all Puerto Rican workers in 1979
equaled 53 percent of the U.S. level. By 1989 the relative wage relation
had declined to 47 percent, as U.S. wage levels had risen faster than
those in Puerto Rico. This declining relationship was observed regardless of education level, age, gender, or sector of the economy except in
communications, which showed a 1 percentage point increase in relative wages compared to the United States. Interestingly, though troubling from a perspective of economic development and economic theory, the relative wage losses for Puerto Rican workers compared to
U.S. workers actually increased at higher levels of education and
human capital accumulation, so that those with postgraduate educa-
tions actually suffered the largest relative wage losses compared to U.S.
wages over time.

For example, whereas a postgraduate degree in 1979 provided U.S.
workers with a wage 50 percent larger than was received on average in
Puerto Rico, by 1989 the U.S. wage per hour was twice as large as in
Puerto Rico, effectively doubling the wage differential. Overall, Puerto
Rican wages relative to the United States would have fallen even further if Puerto Rico's average education level had not increased relative
to that of the average worker in the United States (Sotomayor 2000:
109–110, 125–126).[9]

Nonetheless, despite the slowdown in relative income growth from the 1960s to the 1990s compared to incomes in the United States, Puerto Ricans undeniably have enjoyed an improving quality of life since the industrialization program was introduced in the late 1940s. Absolute incomes—that is, the sum of dollars received each week or month—have grown rapidly, expanding the choices available to virtually every family. Most ended their dependence on agriculture for their livelihood and began to enjoy lives quite similar to those in other modern economies.

In many respects, Puerto Rico manifests the characteristics of more developed economies, especially on key social indicators as well as in terms of the apparent level of industrialization in contributing to total income. Homeownership is widespread. More and more cars are on the road as traditional ways of transportation more associated with low incomes (e.g., *publicos*) slowly disappear due to lack of demand. Leisure activities such as spending the day at the mall and eating at the food court have become as typical as they are in the United States or elsewhere. Nonetheless, there remain significant gaps and weaknesses in the economy that threaten future development progress if the cracks that have appeared in the underlying economic foundation are not addressed correctly.

Social Progress and Its Origin

A few key social indicators illustrating some of the central advances achieved in overall well-being are shown in Table 1.2, measures that confirm the substantive social progress attained since the 1940s and the beginning of the industrialization program. For the sake of comparison, the values for the same indicators for the United States are shown in parentheses when comparable data are available. The first two columns, crude birth rate (CBR) and crude death rate (CDR), show that by 1990 (actually by 1985 if individual years are examined) Puerto Rico had completed the demographic transition—that is, there had been a reduction of both the CBR and the CDR to below 20 per 1,000 of population. As a result, the natural rate of population growth ([CBR − CDR] / 10) fell from a very high 3.02 percent per year in 1950 to 1.15 percent in 1990 and to just 0.81 percent in 2000.[10] Completion of the demographic transition often is considered to be one indicator of a relatively high level of human development, capturing underlying desir-

Table 1.2   Selected Social Economic Statistics, Puerto Rico, 1940–2000

	CBR	CDR	IM	LE	PPP	UN	LFP
1940	40.1	18.4	109.1	46	—	15.0	52.2
	(19.4)	(10.8)	(47.0)	(62.9)		(14.6)	—
1950	40.1	9.9	68.3	61	—	12.9	53.0
	(24.1)	(9.6)	(29.2)	(68.2)		(5.3)	(55.7)
1960	33.5	6.7	43.7	69	1,139	13.1	45.2
	(23.7)	(9.5)	(26.0)	(69.7)		(5.5)	(59.2)
1970	25.8	6.6	28.6	72	759	10.3	44.5
	(18.4)	(9.5)	(20.0)	(70.8)		(4.9)	(59.4)
1980	22.8	6.4	19.0	73	539	17.0	43.3
	(15.9)	(8.5)	(12.6)	(73.7)		(7.1)	(63.8)
1990	18.9	7.4	13.4	74	349[a]	14.3	45.5
	(16.7)	(8.6)	(9.2)	(75.4)		(5.6)	(66.5)
2000	15.6	7.5	—	—	—	11.0	46.2
						(4.0)	(67.2)

Sources: Junta de Planificación 1981: A-26; 1989: A-61; 1994: 4, 7–10; 1999: A-36, A-37; 2002: tabs. 31–32; U.S. Bureau of the Census 1999: 874, 879; 2001: 367.

Notes: CBR = crude birth rate (number of births per 1,000 population); CDR = crude death rate (number of deaths per 1,000 population); IM = infant mortality rate (number of deaths of children less than age 1 per 1,000 live births); LE = average life expectancy at birth, in years; PPP = persons per physician; UN = unemployment rate; LFP = labor force participation rate. Values in parentheses are for the United States.

   a. 1988.

able changes in fertility rates, improved health statistics, better nutrition, an improved income distribution, higher levels of education, and a host of other characteristics embodied in low CBRs and CDRs. Infant mortality rates (IM) also have decreased dramatically and are close to U.S. values, another indication of broader-based development than might be indicated by income alone.

Life expectancy at birth (LE) in Puerto Rico rose from an average 46 years in 1940 to 61 years by 1950 and to 74 years in 1990, rivaling life expectancy in most already-developed countries. In the early years of Operation Bootstrap, Puerto Rico's life expectancy increased rapidly, even superseding U.S. average life expectancy for a time. Since 1970, Puerto Rico's increases in life expectancy have slowed, and the U.S. level is now slightly higher, but the gains are nonetheless quite impressive. The number of physicians has risen faster than the population, allowing a decrease in the ratio of persons per physician (PPP).[11] All of these measures suggest broad-based gains in living standards that have contributed to a better quality of life for the great majority.

Another critical measure of success for an economy is its unemployment rate (UN), which provides some insight into the range of opportunities being provided to the population within the economy. Looking at this as an additional social indicator and not purely an economic variable, the story is more mixed than for the previous measures considered. The unemployment rate fell with the initiation of Operation Bootstrap, but it has never reached single-digit levels. The 1970s marked the greatest reduction in unemployment by Puerto Rico's standards, with the minimum of 10.3 percent being reached in 1970 (and again in 2001).

By U.S. standards, the level of unemployment in Puerto Rico has been unacceptable. Though the unemployment rate came down slightly after 1950, it bottomed out after two decades and then began to rise again until the 1990s. Surely one of the benchmarks by which a development strategy can be judged is its ability not just to create higher average income but also to generate sufficient employment and opportunities for individuals to reach their full potential through their own efforts based on applying their human capital in the workplace. When more than one in ten workers are unemployed, their potential is being wasted, with both individual and societywide effects.

Labor force participation rates (LFP) in Puerto Rico also historically have been low, certainly compared to those in the United States, with recent LFP rates even below those achieved at the beginning of Operation Bootstrap. This is perhaps not surprising given the relatively high unemployment rates, as workers either have chosen not to enter the labor force at all due to the lower expectation of actually finding employment or have left the labor force after some period of time as "discouraged workers" unable to find positions. There is also the matter of large federal transfer payments to individuals in Puerto Rico, which given their size, averaging more than 20 percent of disposable personal income, may have biased the labor force participation rate downward as earned formal-sector income assumed somewhat less importance to total income.

One component of the economic and social growth story not considered in Table 1.2, but of great importance to Puerto Rico's history, has been the exodus of potential workers to the United States in search of employment. Large-scale migration is certainly consistent with high unemployment and low labor force participation. As U.S. citizens, Puerto Ricans can move to the mainland with relative ease, and they have done so in large numbers. From 1950, at the beginning of Opera-

tion Bootstrap, when encouraging migration was actually part of official policy, to 1970, net emigration totaled 605,550 persons, or 27.4
percent of the 1950 population (Dietz 1986: 286). From 1970 to 1990,
net emigration totaled an additional 182,384 persons moving to the
mainland (Rivera-Batiz and Santiago 1996: 23).

This circulation of workers between Puerto Rico and the United
States has been the focus of many valuable studies, and the need for
this "safety valve" surely must be noted as one of the glaring weaknesses in Puerto Rico's style of development, despite the undeniably
positive progress made in the social indicators in Table 1.2 (see Duany
1999 for an excellent overview and analysis of the migration dynamic,
as well as an extensive bibliography). From 1950 to 2000, more than
20 percent of Puerto Rico's population (measured by 2000 statistics)
migrated to the United States.[12]

The Foundations of Social Progress

With the exception of weakness in the unemployment numbers and
some serious concerns about labor force participation rates, important
and valuable social advances have been achieved in Puerto Rico since
the 1940s. These demonstrate that the period after World War II ushered in rapid and profound advances in living standards that greatly
improved the lives of the average person. To what can the gains in
social welfare shown in Table 1.2 be attributed? Were they due to the
industrialization program begun in the late 1940s and the development
it ushered in? Or were the social gains the result of local spending decisions to some extent independent of the specific path of economic
development?

An argument can be made for the emergence of a particular political conjuncture within Puerto Rico beginning in the late 1930s that led
to the extension of the benefits of a capitalist, albeit colonial, economic
structure to a growing proportion of the population. In this interpretation, it was not solely the initiation of Operation Bootstrap and the promotion and expansion of the private U.S. manufacturing sector and any
economic growth it generated that were responsible for the social
advances documented in Table 1.2, though undoubtedly rising income
and the larger government revenues that followed facilitated the funding that underlay this progress.

In other words, the particularly rapid pace of social progress over the first two and a half decades of Operation Bootstrap was not the simple result of some sort of automatic "trickle-down" economic growth effect operating via the market system that raised the average standard of living and boosted the social indicators. Instead, the rapid social gains shown in Table 1.2 were made possible by direct local government action targeted at improving social welfare on a wider scale, exceeding what would have been possible from economic growth alone at the time. What evidence, if any, exists for such an interpretation?

This account of the source of Puerto Rico's gains in social welfare is grounded on an understanding of the interventionist role of the Partido Popular Democrático (PPD, Popular Democratic Party) within the economy and society. The PPD, which was created, controlled, and guided by Luis Muñoz Marín from its inception in 1938, took fundamental steps to increase spending in the social welfare areas of housing, education, and healthcare and introduced initiatives to strengthen local labor laws from the time the party was first elected to power in 1940.[13]

The PPD's initiatives served to empower Puerto Rican citizens both politically and to some extent economically, while simultaneously improving the conditions of daily existence for the vast majority, most of whom still were quite poor in the 1940s and well into the 1950s.[14] It is also probably the case, as some analysts have argued, that these programs contributed to the ability of the PPD to control the direction of future economic and social progress with greater ease by controlling labor unrest and stifling dissent via a higher standard of living that muted criticism among the population. But the PPD's initiatives also served to improve overall living standards considerably.

Emerging from the New Deal era as the island's most eminent politician and its first elected governor in 1948, Muñoz Marín operated within an ideological framework that led him and the PPD to focus on the provision to a wide spectrum of the population an array of government-financed goods and services that ranged from essential infrastructure to education to healthcare and housing (Pantojas-García 1990: 93–94). Today, economists would consider many of those expenditures to be fundamental human capital investments that bestow significant positive external effects upon society and within the economy.[15]

At the same time, some of those same services—schooling, healthcare, housing—provided indispensable individual and familial welfare-enhancing benefits that contributed fundamentally to a higher and more secure standard of living for an ever larger proportion of the population. These benefits are reflected in the improvements in the social indicators noted in Table 1.2, and they undeniably have contributed to a wider variety of choices available to Puerto Ricans in their roles as workers and consumers.

The point is, however, that these social gains were at least partly the outcome of locally made political decisions to increase spending to directly improve individual and family living standards via education, healthcare, infrastructure development, and housing that were to some degree, though not wholly, independent of what was happening within the economy.[16] The level of development on key social indicators and on multivariate measures such as the UN Human Development Index thus have exceeded what would be predicted from the apparent level of economic progress as measured solely by income per person.[17] That these decisions to expand spending and benefits were able to be undertaken by local decisionmakers within the same colonial context that affected the economy is suggestive of what a broader vision of what was possible might have accomplished if the same determination had been directed toward the economic sphere as well.

Income Distribution: Absolute and Relative Income

Despite the unquestionable advances in living standards that reached deep into the fabric of all sectors of society, there did emerge a growing inequality gap in terms of absolute incomes over even the most successful early period of Operation Bootstrap. From 1953 to 1977 the differential in income between the first and tenth deciles of families rose from $5,301 to $23,022 (in constant prices; Irizarry Mora 1989: 70, 511).[18] The average income of the first decile of families in 1953 was $282, while that of the richest decile was $5,583; the average income of all families was approximately $1,890 in 1953.[19]

In 1977 the average income for the bottom decile of families was $1,894, meaning that over the intervening quarter of a century since 1953 the poorest decile of families had only succeeded in reaching the level of average family income attained in 1953. By comparison, the richest decile of families had an average income of $24,916 in 1977, while average income for all families in 1977 equaled approximately $9,020 (these figures are all in constant dollars—that is, they are corrected for inflation). The absolute income gap between the richest and poorest of Puerto Rican families thus widened dramatically over this period.

Of course, even though the gap between the poorest and richest rose, the actual incomes received by the poorest and the richest income recipients were rising over this period, adding to the economic welfare of most citizens. This is not denied. What was happening, however, was a widening of the disparity in total money income received. Whether a widening absolute income gap between the rich and the poor is an important issue when the income of all (or most) income recipients is rising depends on a variety of social and economic factors. Over long periods of time, such differences not only can breed social problems, but they also may have economic effects on incentives for lower-income recipients who perceive such an outcome to be unfair. Whether these adverse effects have occurred in Puerto Rico is a matter deserving investigation.

The trend in relative income inequality was a little more encouraging, as there was a shifting of income shares toward the bottom half of the income distribution over the entire period. In 1953, when the poorest 50 percent of the population garnered 21.6 percent of total family income, 78.4 percent of Puerto Rico's total income was in the hands of the richest half of families, while the richest 20 percent of families received 48.2 percent of total family income. In 1977 the poorest 50 percent of families had enjoyed an increase in their share of total family income to 23.2 percent. The richest 20 percent of families received 44.7 percent of total income in 1977, a decline in their relative share though their absolute level of income still rose.[20]

So while relative income inequality improved from 1953 to 1977, the absolute gap between income earners and between the average incomes of the top 20 percent of families and the bottom 20 percent widened considerably. All income groups experienced growth in income received over the entire period despite this widening of the absolute income difference. From 1953 to 1963, the income of the lowest decile of families, for example, grew by 25 percent, that of the second decile of families grew by 52 percent, while the income of the richest decile of families rose by 73 percent. From 1963 to 1977, when the income distribution became less concentrated, the income growth of the poorest decile of families expanded by 72 percent while the richest decile of families experienced 35 percent growth, helping to improve the income distribution in that latter period. In Chapter 5, the issue of

Puerto Rico's income distribution will be revisited in considerably more detail, for in the particulars lies an important story about the workings and beneficiaries of the island's economic structure over time.

From the evidence presented so far, it seems clear that by the 1970s the steam in the Puerto Rican model of accumulation had been exhausted as a means to continue to improve the average standard of living. From 1970 until the mid-1990s, Puerto Rico's relative per capita income remained stuck at about a third of the U.S. average, suggesting that the relative differential between U.S. and Puerto Rican living standards could be bridged no further with the prevailing economic strategy.[21] Despite the undeniable gains in income and the quality of life achieved during the first two decades of Operation Bootstrap, achievements that brought the majority of Puerto Ricans out of the worst ravages of poverty, it became increasingly apparent that diminishing returns to Puerto Rico's model of development had set in and might have reached a point of zero marginal gains by the mid-1970s.[22]

Something new was needed for the economy, a reality that was well understood by most observers, at least at some level. It was the question of what could and should be done that was the vexing issue, not whether or not something needed to be done. The basic problem was that the increasingly anachronistic political relation tying the United States and Puerto Rico together as unequals seriously complicated the search for reasonable answers to the complex dilemma of stalled economic and social progress, regardless of one's political position. And all the while, the world around Puerto Rico was changing, with one of the key transformations being the rapidity with which some East Asian economies had grown from relatively poor agricultural economies to significant players on the stage of international production. The leading East Asian economies, for example, had succeeded in bringing the living standard of their populations up to and then beyond what Puerto Rico had attained, and they had done so over a shorter period of time and in a world economy that was becoming increasingly integrated and more open.

Alternative Paths to Development

Despite efforts by the United States to "export" the Puerto Rican model of development to other countries in the 1950s and 1960s as a means to jump-start industrialization and foment the structural transformation of poor, fundamentally agricultural economies into more prosperous and productive industrial economies, the attempt was not particularly successful, certainly not on the scale to which the model had been applied in Puerto Rico.[23]

As is well known from a host of previous studies of Operation Bootstrap, almost all new investment funds in the basic manufacturing sector in Puerto Rico came from U.S. sources. The share of local financing for the industrial sector never exceeded 5 percent of total investment. More troubling than this dependence on external financing was that these external funds were not loaned or otherwise transferred to Puerto Rican entrepreneurs to be administered by them, nor were they used to strengthen the local manufacturing sector vis-à-vis nonlocal firms. Instead, this external investment was embodied primarily in U.S.-owned firms operating under one or another form of federal and Puerto Rican tax exemption, among other fiscal benefits extended by both the Puerto Rican and the U.S. federal government to qualifying enterprises.

The production of these U.S. manufacturing corporations was directed primarily to the U.S. market. Never was Puerto Rico's internal market a significant focus of sales for U.S.-based firms producing within Puerto Rico. The reason U.S. corporations chose to locate in Puerto Rico had nothing to do with penetrating a promising internal market. They had moved to Puerto Rico *not* for import substitution reasons, as had motivated a large number of foreign investors who had entered other Latin American economies as far back as the 1930s. Rather, U.S. corporations were in Puerto Rico almost exclusively to take advantage of the exceptional profit-enhancing opportunities offered by a potentially zero-tax milieu, where not so incidentally other costs—labor, land, environmental, and so on—also tended to be substantially below mainland U.S. costs, particularly over the early years of Operation Bootstrap. For U.S. firms choosing to operate there, Puerto Rico was essentially little more than an export platform offering unparalleled profit-making opportunities in an all-around low-risk political and economic environment.[24]

No other location in the world could extend to mainland U.S. investors what Puerto Rico provided. Thus, no other country in the world has had the near-domination of its manufacturing sector by non-locally owned industries as has characterized Puerto Rico's industrial development. Some countries, notably many Latin American nations, have permitted and even encouraged widespread multinational investment in their manufacturing industries as part of their development strategy, though generally such investments have been heavily concentrated in certain key sectors and often with the same sorts of adverse outcomes as have been manifested in Puerto Rico, as will be discussed more fully in Chapter 2.

Reliance on foreign manufacturing investment as the axis of a development strategy reflects a certain style of development, and one about which scholars have more information today than, say, fifty or even thirty years ago. Research on the East Asian economies and a comparison of their rapid growth and development compared with the largest Latin American nations have contributed to the identification, or better, the rediscovery of optimal and suboptimal sequencing of stages of modernization and of industrialization and of the role of foreign investment vis-à-vis domestic investment in this process.

In an increasingly complex and integrated world, it is recognized that successful and sustainable local development requires the nurturing and creation of an indigenous technological capacity. Realizing this objective of an economy-specific ability to understand, adapt, and shape the world pool of knowledge about how "to do" technology and how to apply this understanding to local production needs requires the very cautious handling and "unbundling" of the inputs to production accompanying foreign direct investment. Otherwise, the local learning curve for gaining the capacity to use, adapt, and implement technological know-how can be seriously compromised or even short-circuited.

The East Asian economies as a group restricted and shaped the role FDI could play within their local economies, leaving substantial and critically important space for local entrepreneurs, workers, scientists, technicians, and engineers to develop their own competency in technology to such a degree that world-class skill levels now have been approached and in some cases surpassed in many of those economies.[25] This skill and the efficiency level of these East Asian economies are reflected in the growing share of manufactured exports that these nations supply to the world market and are mirrored by the shrinking share of manufactured exports from countries that have followed inferior industrial phasing paths. For example, in 1965, Puerto Rico provided 30.1 percent of all U.S. clothing imports. By 1976 this share had fallen to but 9 percent. Over the same period, the share of clothing imported into the United States from Hong Kong, South Korea, and Taiwan jumped dramatically from 17.8 percent to 54.6 percent, a reflection of the increasing dominance of the East Asian economies in certain markets and for certain products based upon their technological competence (U.S. Department of Commerce 1979: 108–109).

The much larger degree of FDI penetration in the Latin American economies and even more so in Puerto Rico failed to contribute to a significant transfer of technology or to an expansion of local technological know-how that uncritical proponents of FDI often seem to believe to be nearly inherent in such investment. Consequently, the efficiency level of local entrepreneurs in Latin America and Puerto Rico as revealed by their capacity to export manufactured goods has been seriously compromised for decades, slowing down the economic progress of these economies relative to more successful late developers like the East Asian economies. The technological knowledge essential to long-term economic growth was not assimilated and applied in Puerto Rico, basically because Operation Bootstrap had formulated no strategy for transferring and then encapsulating this knowledge in local entrepreneurs, workers, scientists, and engineers, at least in part because of the lopsided focus of the overall development strategy on U.S. firms and U.S. expertise.

A powerful argument can be made that it has been excessive FDI that has tended to thwart the growth in Latin America of a sufficiently large local class of entrepreneurs, workers, scientists, technicians, and engineers with the knowledge, experience, and level of efficiency to perform the dynamic functions that such economic actors have achieved in the development process in the East Asian economies and, it should be said, in the developed nations before them. The reasons for such a systemic failure between the Latin American and other less developed nations to learn "to do" technology and to become more dynamic within the rapidly changing world economy differ in their specifics. As we shall see in the next chapter, the particular sequencing of the industrial development path is an essential part, if not the whole, of the story in each economy helping to explain this failure.[26]

Puerto Rico, the East Asian Economies, and Latin America

We already have seen that while Puerto Rico's income per person has increased in an absolute sense, on a relative basis the growth of Puerto Rico's income reached a plateau by the 1970s that persisted until the 1990s as the ratio of Puerto Rico's income per person to U.S. income per capita attained a limit of about one-third. Interestingly, though few development scholars were watching closely, at about the same time that Puerto Rico initiated its Operation Bootstrap strategy, the South Korean and Taiwanese economies embarked upon their own modernization and development projects—but with a quite different trajectory and outcome.

A comparison over time of Puerto Rico's income with that of South Korea and Taiwan is revealing. Table 1.3 shows that Puerto Rico's per capita income was roughly two times larger than either of the East Asian economies in 1955. However, as the numbers in parentheses below the income figures for South Korea and Taiwan suggest, the growth rates of per capita incomes in both of the latter economies accelerated relative to Puerto Rico's growth in income per person, particularly after 1970. Having begun in 1955 with per capita GDP equal to between 40 and 51 percent of Puerto Rico's per capita income, by 1989 South Korea's income per person had reached nearly 74 percent of Puerto Rico's, while Taiwan's per capita GDP was 83 percent of Puerto Rico's.

Table 1.3   Income (GDP) per Capita: Puerto Rico, South Korea, Taiwan, Mexico, and Brazil, 1955–1989

	Puerto Rico	South Korea	Taiwan	Mexico	Brazil
1955	$538	$217	$276	$637	$389
		(40.3%)	(51.3%)	(118.4%)	(72.3%)
1960	816	246	349	798	521
		(30.1%)	(42.8%)	(97.8%)	(63.8%)
1970	2,145	629	829	1,481	915
		(29.3%)	(38.6%)	(69.0%)	(42.7%)
1980	5,026	2,358	3,416	4,757	3,332
		(46.9%)	(68.0%)	(94.6%)	(66.3%)
1989	9,833	7,239	8,154	6,281	4,870
		(73.6%)	(82.9%)	(63.9%)	(49.5%)

Source: Penn World Tables, Alan Heston and Robert Summers data set, mark 5.6, available at http://datacentre.chass.utoronto.ca/pwt.

Notes: Values shown are for real GDP per capita in current international dollars. The percentage values in parentheses indicate the income per capita for each country relative to the income per capita in Puerto Rico for the same year. These values for Puerto Rico's GDP per capita differ from the values provided at the beginning of this chapter since the data in this table are presented in purchasing power parity (PPP) dollars, reflecting differences in the purchasing power of income in different economies due to variations in the prices of goods and services, particularly nontraded goods.

Puerto Rico's income growth relative to the two East Asian economies actually was quite rapid until 1970, much like income growth was rapid relative to U.S. per capita income growth over that same period as workers were being shifted from lower-income agricultural pursuits to higher-income industrial and service occupations as industrialization was initiated on an expanded scale. Since 1970, however, both South Korea's and Taiwan's income per person have been growing faster than per capita income in Puerto Rico, as the percentage values for income per person in these economies relative to Puerto Rico's income per person have risen, reflecting faster overall growth in income per person.[27]

The data also clearly illustrate how both Mexico's and Brazil's incomes have lagged relative to the incomes of the other economies, especially after 1980, due to the particular style of development followed by the Latin American economies. Puerto Rico gained relative to the Latin American prototypes until 1970; both Brazil and Mexico had faster income growth than Puerto Rico from 1970 to 1980, as the higher percentages below the income figures for Mexico and Brazil attest. This resurgence of income growth in Brazil and Mexico relative to Puerto Rico was at least partly due to the availability of international loans due to the oil price crisis during that period that artificially boosted Mexico's and Brazil's incomes relative to other countries that did not overindulge in debt. However, from the 1980s on, as a consequence of the readjustments imposed on Mexico and Brazil by the debt crisis beginning in 1982, some of the gains that had been made relative to Puerto Rico's income in the 1970s had been lost by 1989 as the realities of needed adjustments in those economies set in.

The Heston and Summers data set, from which the table was assembled, currently has no data for Puerto Rico's GDP beyond 1989. However, South Korea's 1991 GDP per capita equaled $9,358, suggesting near parity with Puerto Rico's GDP per capita. It is quite likely the case that by 1989, if not well before, both South Korea's and Taiwan's income per capita, if measured by GNP rather than GDP, would have been a third or more larger than Puerto Rico's per capita GNP.[28] Given that most observers would agree that per capita GNP is a better proxy measure of an economy's aggregate welfare than is GDP per person, it can be surmised that both these East Asian economies have succeeded in achieving rapid economic growth that has outperformed the existing Puerto Rican strategy over the period from the 1950s to the present, but particularly since the 1970s.

Table 1.4 shows the average growth rates of GDP per capita for the five economies examined above over the period 1955–1989. The slow-down in Puerto Rico's growth rate can easily be compared with the higher rates of expansion observed in the two East Asian economies. Compared with Mexico and Brazil, Puerto Rico's income per capita grew faster over the early years of Operation Bootstrap and again in the 1980s, with the 1970s being the atypical period when the Latin American countries grew faster than Puerto Rico, rivaling, for a time, East Asia's expansion rates. What is remarkable about the East Asian growth record is its sustained nature, extending to well over thirty years at or near double-digit rates of growth. As shall be considered in the next chapter, there are structural reasons grounded in the particular paths of industrialization that help to explain these differences in performance among the five economies.

Conclusion

After having begun to great fanfare and relative success in raising incomes and reducing unemployment rates and poverty levels, there is and has been for some time ample evidence that the Puerto Rican model of development had exhausted its potential—by the 1970s at least. Changes that were made to the strategy after that date, and these will be considered briefly in the next chapter, were mostly cosmetic and far too marginal to extract the economy and society from its mounting malaise. The shift, for example, toward capital- and knowledge-intensive production that characterized post-1960s development after the labor-intensive industrialization phase of the 1950s and 1960s altered the emphasis of the industrialization-by-invitation strategy but not its

Table 1.4   Average Annual Growth Rate of Real GDP per Capita: Puerto Rico, South Korea, Taiwan, Mexico, and Brazil, 1955–1989

	Puerto Rico	South Korea	Taiwan	Mexico	Brazil
1955–1960	8.7%	2.5%	4.8%	4.6%	6.0%
1960–1970	10.1	9.8	9.0	6.4	5.8
1970–1980	8.9	14.1	15.2	12.4	13.8
1980–1989	7.7	13.3	10.1	3.1	4.0

Source: Calculated from Table 1.3.

essence, which was the overreliance on nonlocal investment and non-local expertise. If anything, this modification in the development strategy in the 1970s away from textiles, clothing, and other similar production and toward the drug and pharmaceutical and other high-technology industries actually reinforced the weakest facets of Operation Bootstrap qua development strategy, as reflected in the anemic employment-generation capacity and the low level of technology transfer to domestic factors of production. One positive, if perhaps unintentional, shift in direction toward even more service production and employment initiated by a change in the federal tax law will be considered in the next chapter.

Observers often blame the economic failures in Puerto Rico since the 1970s on the ambiguous political relationship with the United States. There are very few who still fail to admit that this is a colonial bond and one that has changed very little, in substantive terms, since Puerto Rico became an unincorporated territory of the United States in 1898. Without denying that this tie has considerable economic and social implications and imposes constraints on actions by Puerto Rican decisionmakers, that is not the whole, nor even the majority, of the story for explaining the stalled economic progress after the 1970s. The colonial explanation places more blame than is warranted on the shoulders of the U.S. decisionmakers and not enough on responsible Puerto Ricans, from politicians to the universities to the private sector, for promoting economic progress.

For reasons explored in the next two chapters, those in a position to structure the economy after the 1940s chose to believe, and then to act upon that belief, that Puerto Ricans themselves could not provide the dynamic for future growth and progress in their own economy. Instead, U.S. investors and U.S. entrepreneurs were made the axis of the industrialization strategy with the result that few linkages, spin-offs, or positive externalities accrued to the local private sector, particularly in the manufacturing sector, the focus of the Operation Bootstrap strategy for most of its history. I will argue, by examining successful and unsuccessful experiences of other late developers, that this dependence on foreign knowledge, foreign finance, and foreign expertise embodied in an export-dominant strategy was a systemic failure that accounts for the inability of the economy to sustain the early progress shown by the Operation Bootstrap strategy. This failure was due to both limitations in economic knowledge, as well as ideological restrictions that delimited the viable range of policy options at the beginning of the industrialization program. However, over more than fifty years, it might reasonably have been expected that a learning process would have led decisionmakers to rethink the development-by-FDI strategy and begin to give more attention to stimulating local factors of production within the overall economic structure.

At no time from the initial implementation of the Operation Bootstrap development strategy until well into the 1990s, however, was there any significant attempt to fundamentally alter its direction away from nonlocal sources of financing and expertise, and little attempt was directed toward diluting the export platform bias of the model regardless as to which industries were being promoted. After the initial gains from the development-by-FDI approach had been exhausted, gains that were at least partly the result of a reallocation of labor from low-productivity agricultural pursuits to higher-level industrial and service production, further economic progress, at least relative to the United States and, just as significantly, relative to other late developers like South Korea and Taiwan, did not take place. In other words, subsequent productivity gains within what became an apparently increasingly industrial and service-oriented economy were unable to further close the income gap between Puerto Rico and the United States or to allow the Puerto Rican economy to keep pace with the late-developing East Asian economies that had started their industrialization at approximately the same time.

In the next chapter, the nature of Puerto Rico's industrial sequencing, or what might be called its "modernization" process, will be compared with what took place in East Asia and in Latin America in an effort to understand the nature of the systemic failure that has prevented Puerto Rico's style of development from fomenting significant relative gains in living standards after the 1970s. Chapter 3 examines the impact of the overreliance on nonlocal inputs in the development strategy, and Chapter 4 provides a look at some econometric analyses of the sources of growth in the economy. Chapter 5 details the end of federal tax exemption and the role of federal transfers in total income. Chapter 6 looks to the future, examining the dilemma of political status and the search for a new direction for the economy.

Notes

1. For a full discussion of the Puerto Rican economic development model from its inception until the early 1980s, see Dietz 1986, esp. chaps. 4 and 5.

Other valuable sources for gaining an understanding of the Puerto Rican model and its economic trajectory are Curet Cuevas 1976, 1986; De Jesús Toro 1982; Irizarry Mora 2001; Pantojas-García 1990; Villamil 1976; and Weisskoff 1985. Edgardo Meléndez (2000) has produced a remarkable bibliography of source material that anyone wishing to learn more about Puerto Rico will find indispensable.

2. This "structural transformation," in which lower productivity agricultural workers are shifted toward higher productivity industrial pursuits, is one of the fundamental changes that development economists believe to be required in all economies if they are to attain advanced levels of economic, social, and political development.

3. These income values are presented as GDP per person in current dollars—that is, without adjusting for price changes over the intervening years. Adjusting for inflation, the real value of GDP per person in Puerto Rico (in constant 1954 dollars) was: 1950, $383; 1960, $612; 1970, $1,132 (Junta de Planificación 1981: A-1). Thus, real income per capita rose by nearly 200 percent over this twenty-year interval at the beginning of Operation Bootstrap, for an impressive sustained average growth rate of 5.6 percent per year in income per person.

4. See, for example, Pantojas-García 1990: 88–89, for a discussion. Werner Baer (1959) was an early advocate of exporting the Puerto Rican strategy to other poor economies. There continue to be commentators who believe that the Puerto Rican strategy offers an alternative path for some less developed countries; see Baumol and Wolff 1996: 869, 882–883.

5. In the United States, GNP and GDP are nearly identical, typically being within 1 percent of each other, as can be observed from the similarity between the values of GDP per person and GNP per person.

6. Orlando Sotomayor (1998), in a sophisticated econometric analysis, examines wage and not total income convergence—which depends on wages and hours worked and other effects—between Puerto Rico and the United States. He finds divergence in spite of the increasing similarity of structural characteristics, such as education and experience, between workers in both economies. Some of the details of wage divergence are reviewed later in this section.

7. In 1950, 36.2 percent of Puerto Rico's labor force worked in agriculture and fishing. For each 1 percent of workers engaged in this sector, 0.48 percent of total GNP was produced. Industry, which in the early years included some cottage-industry needlework production, employed 17.8 percent of the labor force, with each 1 percent of the labor force adding 0.89 percent to total GNP. Each worker in industry was nearly twice as productive as each worker in agriculture, on average. By 1960 the effects of the transfer of labor from agriculture to industry due to the industrialization program were evident in the changing productivity levels in the sectors. Agriculture occupied only 22.8 percent of all workers in that year, with each 1 percent adding 0.43 percent to total GNP. The productivity of each 1 percent of the labor force in industry had risen to 1.3 percent of total GNP.

By 1970, only 9.9 percent of Puerto Rico's workers remained in the agricultural sector, producing only 3.4 percent of total GNP and 0.34 percent of GNP for each 1 percent of workers. On the other hand, 19.2 percent of the labor force was engaged in industry, creating 25.4 percent of total GNP value. Each 1 percent of the work force engaged in industry added 1.32 percent to total GNP.

What these numbers show is how Puerto Rico's GNP (and its GDP, by extension) was able to grow quickly in the early years of Operation Bootstrap as "surplus labor" was shifted from lower-productivity uses in agriculture, as revealed by the low value added per 1 percent of the labor force in contributing to total GNP, to higher value-added uses in industry, where each 1 percent of the labor force produced about four times the value added in agriculture by 1970 (Junta de Planificación 1981: A-3, A-7).

This shift of surplus labor from low-productivity agricultural production to higher-productivity industry (and services) is one of the basic structural transformations required if countries are to become more developed. The gains to such a reallocation of labor from low- to high-productivity uses were apparent in the early years of Operation Bootstrap, 1950–1970, when this transfer took place and income per person grew most quickly. However, once most of the surplus labor had been shifted away from the agriculture sector toward higher-productivity sectors in the economy, any further gains in income could only come from increasing the efficiency of labor in industry and services via the expanded application of greater knowledge to the production process—that is, from technological gains and from improvements in human capital. The early burst in income that Puerto Rico achieved from reallocating resources from agriculture to industry and services was in some sense the easy part of the economic growth story. Long-term economic progress, however, must go beyond the simple reallocation of labor to higher-valued uses. It requires improved efficiency in the use of these reallocated resources over time.

8. The growth rate of real income per person between 1970 and 1990 fell to 2.6 percent per year, less than half of what it had been during the first two decades of Operation Bootstrap, when the economy grew at a 6.1 percent pace (Lara and Villamil 1999: 46–47). Some might argue that there were extraordinary external changes in the 1970s, for example the Organization of Petroleum-Exporting Countries (OPEC) oil crisis, and in the 1980s, such as the world recession, that contributed to trending income growth downward after 1970. However, other countries succeeded in growing quickly despite facing the same external conditions over this latter period, as shall be seen later in this chapter.

9. The last two sentences may seem to be, but are not, in contradiction. Though better-educated workers in Puerto Rico in 1989 earned a wage that, compared to 1979, was a smaller percentage of the wage of an equivalently educated worker in the United States, better-educated workers nonetheless earned higher wages than did less educated workers in Puerto Rico. Thus in 1989, with an average level of education higher than in 1979 in Puerto Rico

and higher in 1989 than the average in the United States, the decline in the
overall ratio of the Puerto Rican wage rate to U.S. wages from 53 to 47 percent was smaller than it would have been if the education profiles of the two
economies had remained unchanged between the two years.

10. As a result, the time it would take for the population to double rose
from approximately 23 years in 1950 to almost 61 years in 1990 and to more
than 86 years in 2000.

11. For a comprehensive overview of health issues in Puerto Rico, see the
Pan American Health Organization's report on Puerto Rico at www.paho.org/
english/sha/prflpur.htm#asis.

12. On migration, see Bonilla and Campos 1981, Centro de Estudios Puertorriqueños 1979, and Rivera-Batiz and Santiago 1996.

13. Until 1948, Puerto Rico's governor was a presidential appointee and
until 1946, when President Harry S. Truman appointed Puerto Rican Jesús T.
Piñero as governor, always a mainland American. Luis Muñoz Marín had been
elected as senator in 1940 to the local legislature, which the PPD dominated.

In 1941, President Franklin D. Roosevelt appointed economist Rexford
Guy Tugwell as Puerto Rico's governor, an arrangement that proved most propitious for future social and economic change as he and Muñoz saw eye-to-eye
on many social, economic, and political issues. Their collaboration paved the
way for Muñoz's domination of the political scene for three decades (Tugwell
1947).

14. For example, the PPD-dominated government facilitated extremely
low-cost financing for the construction of cement houses to replace the
wooden and zinc structures in which most Puerto Ricans lived, as well as providing small lots *(parcelas)* for the building of such houses to many landless
families. Not only did cement houses help to reduce endemic health problems
from insect infestation and other air- and pest-borne illnesses that accompanied
life in permeable wooden structures, but cement houses were better able to
withstand the force of the hurricanes that are a part of life each autumn in the
Caribbean. Over time there was less damage to homes and property, and
greatly reduced loss of life and injury resulted when hurricanes did strike.
Homeownership spread rapidly, and owning a home became one of the enduring symbols of success for families at all income levels.

15. The importance of these human capital investments to economic
growth and development has been formalized, particularly for schooling, in so-
called endogenous growth models. We will be considering the importance of
such human capital investments and their contribution to the growth process in
Chapter 4.

16. Table 1.5 displays some of the changes to key commonwealth government fiscal variables that provide empirical support to this argument. From
the 1940s to 1970, commonwealth government spending for all purposes grew
faster than total GNP and faster than central government revenues. Government spending slowed down to an annual rate less than the change in total GNP
over the 1970s, after the Muñoz era and the absolute dominance of the PPD in

Table 1.5   Change in Commonwealth Spending and Revenues,
             1940–1980

	Annual % Change in Total GNP	Annual % Change in Commonwealth Expenditures	Annual % Change in Commonwealth Revenues from Local Sources	Annual % Change in Commonwealth Revenues from All Sources[a]
1940–1950	10.2	16.3	15.7	15.3
1950–1960	8.3	9.1	7.9	8.7
1960–1970	10.8	13.7	11.3	12.6
1970–1975	8.9	6.7	5.9	6.2
1975–1980	9.0	2.4	5.4	5.8

Sources: Junta de Planificación 1981: A-4, A-28; 1987: A-2, A-26.
Note: a. Commonwealth, federal, and other (e.g., customs duties).

politics had come to an end. This provides some evidence for the independence of the PPD's spending decisions from the economy, though obviously a growing economy and its higher income levels provided the resources to be mobilized by the commonwealth government for increased spending on education, health, and other key areas.

17. See Banco Popular 2000.

18. A decile is equal to one-tenth of the population, in this case equal to one-tenth the number of families. Each decile, from the poorest to the richest, has the same number of families within it.

19. These income values are for families, whereas the income levels introduced at the beginning of the chapter were per person.

20. Disaggregating from 1953 to 1963, income inequality worsened as the income share of the poorest half of the population fell to 20.5 percent of total income while the share of total family income of the richest 20 percent of families rose to 50.8 percent. By 1977, income concentration had eased somewhat. These changes in income distribution are evident in the Gini coefficient, which was estimated to be 0.412305 in 1953, 0.416826 in 1963, and 0.383041 in 1977 by one economist (Irizarry Mora 1989: 511–512), and 0.415 in 1953, 0.449 in 1963, and 0.397 in 1977 by another (Mann 1985). During this period the evolution of the Gini coefficient followed what one might argue was a traditional Kuznets inverse U-shaped path as the income distribution first worsened and then improved as economic growth took place. I am indebted to Orlando Sotomayor of the University of Puerto Rico, Mayagüez, for his insights on these and other issues.

21. Emilio Pantojas-Garcia (1999: 14) notes that in a 1975 report on the competitive position of manufacturing industries, Fomento recognized that the existing Operation Bootstrap strategy was in crisis. This report does not, however, seem to have had much impact.

22. Fernando Lefort (1997: 11–12) writes quite emphatically on the cessation of relative progress: "Puerto Rico showed an outstanding catch-up effect

in the early post-WWII period compared to the US, out-performing all other Caribbean and Latin American economies. However, since 1973 Puerto Rico's per capita output growth rate has decreased relative to other economies in the region, and there is no clear indication that it will ever be able to close the income gap with the US." This may be too strong a conclusion, effectively closing the door on alternative policies for improving economic performance. Lefort also writes (1997: 10–11): "Between 1955 and 1972, Puerto Rican per capita GDP moved from 22 percent to 45 percent of American per capita GDP. Per capita GNP follows a similar pattern although less pronounced, increasing from 19 percent to 30 percent. . . . [A]fter 1973, the catch up force has been practically non-existent when comparing GDPs, and it has been clearly reversed in terms of per capita GNP."

Lefort (1997: app. 2) provides a rigorous test of the income convergence hypothesis vis-à-vis U.S. income, finding that Puerto Rico's growth rate has been lower by at least 2 percent per year than would be expected from the economy's characteristics (e.g., investment level and human capital levels). Lefort argues that this is because Puerto Rico is not a state fully integrated to the U.S. economy, and his study provides some empirical support for such an assertion.

J. Thomas Hexner and Glenn Jenkins (1998: 1) are even more strident in their evaluation: "The Puerto Rican economy, contrary to the opinion of many, is not a model of economic growth. In fact, the economy has been beset with slow growth, high unemployment and little advance in productivity. The Puerto Rican economy has stagnated since the 1970's, after some successful growth in the 1950's and 1960's. Annual growth rates averaged only 1.7% from 1975 to 1984. . . . Puerto Rico and the US persisted with a development strategy based on government initiative and tax gimmicks long after it proved ineffective."

23. It might be argued that Puerto Rico's particular development model was important in providing the design for the policies of the Reagan administration in the early 1980s for the Caribbean Basin Initiative (CBI) and, in a wider sense, for the effort of the United States to create a hemispheric free trade area that would extend the North American Free Trade Agreement (NAFTA) throughout the Americas by 2005.

24. "A skewed economic composition has resulted, in which profits from manufacturing comprise a larger part of Puerto Rico's GDP than in any other US state [*sic*]" (Hexner and Jenkins 1998: 9).

25. There are differences of degree in the acceptance of FDI in the East Asian economies, with South Korea being perhaps the most restrictive. For more details, see World Bank 1993 and Amsden 1989.

26. Of course, there is more to successful development than optimal industrial sequencing. Institutional innovation, efficient public management, appropriate fiscal and monetary policies, management of exchange rates and the balance of payments, the creation of appropriate human capital, and a whole range of other policies also are essential. However, optimal industrial sequencing is likely to be complementary to, and perhaps contributes to, a suc-

cessful policy mix in other key areas of the economy and society (see Cypher and Dietz 1997: chaps. 9–16).

27. Readers who might object that comparing Puerto Rico with larger economies such as South Korea and Taiwan is unwarranted might wish, then, to make the comparison with Singapore, which in terms of population is roughly the same size as Puerto Rico. Per capita income in 2001 was more than double that in Puerto Rico (World Bank 2003: 235). Small and large economies have the ability to make use of the resources at their disposal within the institutional constraints faced. Puerto Rico's constraints are different from those of independent economies, but neither are they the same as an old-style, colonial relationship.

28. Using GDP per capita as the income criterion is not the best measure for comparing living standards among nations if the goal is to understand what is available for consumption and investment. The better measure of relative incomes and for assessing what residents have available to them is per capita GNP (and even better is to use purchasing power parity [PPP] GNP per person). This is particularly true when the gap between GDP and GNP is large and widening over time, as has been the case for Puerto Rico.

According to the Penn World Tables (Heston and Summers mark 5.6 data set), Puerto Rico's GNP relative to GDP was 97.8 percent in 1970, 83.5 percent in 1980, and only 68.0 percent in 1990 (down from 69.1 percent in 1989, showing how quickly the GDP/GNP gap has widened). By comparison, South Korea's GNP relative to GDP was 100.6 percent in 1970, 96.7 percent in 1980, and 99.3 percent in 1990. For South Korea and Taiwan, the gap between GNP and GDP is extremely small and does not show any systematic tendency to rise over time. The gap between Mexico's and Brazil's GNP and GDP also was relatively small in 1990 (GNP was 97.3 percent of GDP for Mexico and 95.4 percent for Brazil). Of the 132 economies in the data set, Puerto Rico is 131st in terms of the ratio of GNP to GDP, and the gap between Puerto Rico's GNP and GDP is many times greater than that for even the country 130th on the list. In many ways, the size of the GNP/GDP gap makes the Puerto Rican experience nearly unique.

Using data from the World Bank's World Development Indicators, by 1990 South Korea's GNP per capita was 110 percent of Puerto Rico's. Data for Taiwan are not available from a comparable source, but by 1990 it is also reasonable to assume that Taiwan would have passed Puerto Rico's average level of GNP per person as well, based on income growth trends.

2

The Development Path: A Comparison with East Asia and Latin America

The phasing of an economy's industrialization process and of its long-term structural transformation is an important determinant of its level of development and gives some idea about future growth prospects. Of significance for this study is a comparison of Puerto Rico's industrialization experience with the stylized industrialization and development paths followed by the East Asian and Latin American economies.

The per capita income data presented in Table 1.3 were suggestive of the impact of the development trajectories characteristic of the three prototype economies. This table showed that since 1970 both South Korea and Taiwan, as leading examples of the distinctly East Asian style of development, outperformed both Mexico and Brazil, as examples of the Latin American style of industrialization, as well as Puerto Rico. There definitely appear to be superior and inferior paths toward becoming more developed that are manifested in differential income outcomes and in other social and economic indicators of progress, and these diverse experiences are correlated with the industrial phasing followed.

Becoming more developed requires that an economy undergo essential structural change. Achieving developed economy status goes beyond just increasing the pace of economic growth as measured by the annual percentage change in gross national product or some other indicator of income. Poorer nations cannot just do more of what they already have been doing if they wish to become like the developed nations such as the United States, Canada, Japan, and the countries of Western Europe. Instead, they must fundamentally alter what is produced and how it is produced. What is exported—more manufactured goods and nontraditional exports, fewer agricultural, and other primary exports—and what is imported also must evolve in broadly predetermined directions if the development process is to move forward.

The skill and education levels of workers of all types must be upgraded and brought more in line with international standards. Efforts to become more technologically proficient and technologically autonomous also are essential to any successful development process and to the overall structural transformation. This contributes to greater efficiency in the use of inputs and resources of all types, allowing more income to be generated with less effort and at a lower cost. Just as important, there are a whole host of what can be called institutional changes that nations and economies on the road from lower to higher levels of development must undergo—altering the role of government and its efficiency level, changing the attitudes and value systems of rural and urban workers, challenging existing wealth-holding patterns, emphasizing human capital augmentation, upgrading managerial and entrepreneurial talents, strengthening and expanding banking and other financial markets, and a multitude of other transformations crucial to sustaining long-term economic and social progress.[1]

What differences distinguish the East Asian paths of modernization and development from the path that was adopted by most Latin American nations? How do both of these paths compare to Puerto Rico's trajectory of economic growth and development since the late 1940s? What impact does the sequencing and phasing of industrialization and economic modernization have on the long-term development prospects of economies? And can economies alter their sequencing and recapture "missed" stages if doing so could improve future prospects for economic and social expansion? These are the basic questions to be discussed and answered in this chapter.

East Asia's Sequencing of Industrialization and Development

Following the useful stylized models described by Ranis (1981), a framework that also has been used in a modified form by the World Bank (1993: chap. 1) in their comprehensive and influential study, the East Asian sequencing of economic modernization can be outlined as three stages.[2]

First Stage: Easy Import
Substitution Industrialization, 1953–1963

Easy import substitution industrialization (ISI) involves the initiation, or in some cases the expansion, of the domestic production of relatively simple, nondurable consumer goods—items such as clothes, shoes, some furniture, ceramics, toys, beverages, and so on—to replace, partially or wholly, imports of these same goods from the international market. In most less developed countries (LDCs), as it was in Taiwan, South Korea, Malaysia, and the other East Asian economies, this is the most common first effort to advance industrialization on an expanded scale and to initiate the fundamental structural transformation of shifting workers engaged in relatively low-productivity agricultural pursuits to higher-productivity industrial pursuits.[3]

Protective "infant" tariffs were imposed on imported products to shield domestic easy ISI producers from foreign competition by raising the prices to final consumers of imported nondurable merchandise. Such protection is typically necessary at the beginning of the easy ISI process in poor countries with little industrial experience due to the inevitable transitional inefficiencies encountered by new domestic firms beginning to produce import substitute goods for the first time or on an expanded scale. Underdeveloped worker and management skills, low levels of technological knowledge, faulty quality control, missing input supply networks, incomplete markets, inadequate infrastructure, weak financial markets, government red tape, and other inefficiencies in LDCs result in higher costs of production for domestic producers than is the case for comparable imports purchased from foreign firms with a longer history of producing goods for the world market, firms that already have reached the technological frontier in their production methods.[4]

The tariffs imposed by the state on imported consumer goods raise their prices in the local economy, thus allowing space for the growth of domestic production by permitting those with higher initial costs than foreign firms to be price competitive, something that would be impossible in head-to-head competition otherwise. This phase in the structural transformation of East Asia began to reshape its economies away from rural, agricultural societies toward urban, industrial economies, as the labor surplus in rural areas began to migrate to and work in the expanding urban, industrial regions. Further, and most important for the structural transformation and long-term economic growth, workers

were moving from lower-productivity agricultural jobs to more productive industrial employment, so that this labor shift added more to
total national output via the expansion of the industrial share in total
production relative to the production than was sacrificed by the loss of
workers in agriculture.

In the easy ISI stage, domestic entrepreneurs in East Asia were
given a chance to succeed against foreign imports, but not only because
of the existence of tariff protection imposed by the state that reduced
foreign competition. The East Asian governments went beyond this
fairly standard artificial "price wedge" and also subsidized domestic
firms via low-cost loans; state efforts to train workers and scientists and
improved education for society in general; subsidized access to technological knowledge through participation at international business
conferences, foreign consulting, and study abroad for managers, entrepreneurs, and scientists; and in a general sense by facilitating the acquisition by local human capital resources of the essential information
required for efficient production methods. These are but a few of the
array of state and private-sector joint initiatives utilized by the various
East Asian governments to help make their private sectors more efficient.[5]

In effect, in this stage of development the East Asian economies—
via state and private-sector cooperation—created, nurtured, and helped
bring to maturity a class of entrepreneurs and an increasingly skilled
work force in industry who could then form the base for future sustained progress. Importantly, this stage of industrialization, in which
simple nondurable consumer goods were being produced, also tended
to be quite labor-intensive, meaning it was labor-absorbing. As the production of import substitute goods expanded, these were able to provide sufficient urban industrial employment to absorb the flow of rural
migrants from the agriculture sector, workers who became increasingly
proficient at industrial production over time and who, not so incidentally, earned higher incomes in industrial employment than in the rural
jobs they had left behind due to the higher productivity of such employment.

During this stage of easy ISI the East Asian economies continued
to export the same array of primary products to the international market—that is, mostly unprocessed agricultural and fishing products—as
had been sold prior to initiating industrialization. The industrialization
process was at this stage still focused on the internal transformation of
the productive structure. The export profile of these increasingly more

industrial economies had not been altered by this "inward-looking" easy ISI process.

The import profile of the economies did, however, change. The income earned from primary product exports now were not needed to pay for nondurable consumer imports, as these were increasingly produced locally for domestic use and became less important over time as a share of total exports. Exports now financed the purchase of imported intermediate and capital goods destined for use in production in the rapidly expanding locally owned easy ISI sector. Besides these producer-good imports, durable consumer goods (e.g., autos, kitchen appliances) continued to be imported just as they had been before the initiation of easy ISI, but the overall import pattern shifted toward capital and intermediate goods used in the expanding industrial sector.

Second Stage: Easy Export
Substitution Industrialization, 1963–1972

The East Asian economies followed up their easy ISI stage of industrialization with that of easy export substitution. In this phase, they began to export to the international market some of the very same nondurable consumer goods being produced by the domestically owned and domestically controlled easy ISI industries, thus extending the market for these commodities beyond their own borders and the more limited demand of their local economies.[6]

Of course to have the ability to export toys, clothes, shoes, textiles, and other nondurable goods to the world market, East Asian firms needed to be price competitive and quality competitive with similar goods already being produced for the international market. The attainment of this level of competitiveness did not happen by chance or simply via the workings of the invisible hand of the market. Rather it was accomplished through two avenues of policy carried out during the previous stage of easy ISI.

First, the East Asian economies had phased out their infant-industry tariffs over a period of time, thus forcing domestic producers to compete or perish as the artificial protection provided by these tariffs from imports was progressively reduced. And second, in preparation for the removal of tariff protection, there had been explicit attention paid to the attainment of a greater technological capacity that would permit the easy ISI firms to compete on the world market at something close to the world-level technological frontier. This world-class level of skill was reached not only due to the efforts of the easy ISI firms themselves in anticipation of the end of tariff protection, though that "stick" of expected import competition was at work, but also because of explicit policy initiatives of the state, especially in South Korea, Taiwan, and Japan before them, to encourage more efficient production.

One fundamental goal of state industrial policy had been to assist the private sector in the acquisition and internalization of the "knowledge" component of production—that is, in the training of workers, managers, and skilled employees at the highest levels and of the attainment of world-class technological proficiency in the broadest sense. This was accomplished, as noted in the previous section, through the provision of loans, training programs, education of scientists and engineers, grants for international study, participation in international conferences, and a host of other initiatives large and small that contributed to the acquisition of essential technological skills. All of this took place during the easy ISI phase of industrialization, and the stage of export substitution would have been impossible without this having happened.

The easy export substitution stage of industrialization offered two further benefits beyond the substantial gains in efficiency and technological autonomy that the ability to export to the world market demonstrated, as basic as these would be to long-term progress in these economies. First, East Asia's primary product exports were progressively replaced by (hence the name *export substitution*) nondurable consumer manufactured-good exports, fundamentally altering the overall export profile of these countries in the direction of more manufactured products. Primary exports not only decreased in relative importance during this stage, but also in an absolute sense they began to wither away. Primary exports as a share of total exports dropped, trending toward zero.

Second, with the expanded production of labor-intensive manufactured goods—toys, textiles and garments, shoes, and so forth—for the world market, the East Asian economies were able to continue to absorb the flow of workers still moving from the rural agricultural sector toward the urban industrial sector in search of a better life. In this urban setting, government policies directed at providing housing, education, and healthcare also were more easily and effectively implemented because of the greater density of population, which reduced the cost of delivering such services, and the work force was able to further upgrade its human capital.

Third Stage: Difficult Import Substitution
with Difficult Export Substitution, 1973–Present

Ultimately, further pressures from the balance of payments, as well as reduced economic growth opportunities due to diminishing returns to the easy export substitution strategy, led to the next stage of industrialization for the more advanced East Asian economies. South Korea and Taiwan in particular began to undertake difficult ISI, that is, to produce for the domestic market consumer durables—from microwave ovens to computers to cameras to automobiles—and capital goods—machines and other tools destined for industrial and service-industry uses as inputs. Once again, tariffs on imports were required to allow domestic producers the time needed for learning to produce these more complex products for the local market without facing insurmountable competition from more efficient foreign producers. The East Asian governments continued to assist their domestic producers in achieving the goal of attaining world-class efficiency levels through both incentives and threats, as in the previous stages of easy ISI and export substitution, via what one keen observer of these economies has described as the "three Rs system": rules, rewards, and referees (Amsden 1989).

The manufacture of difficult ISI goods required a higher degree of skill and more knowledge than had been necessary to produce nondurable goods like suits, toy cars, and dishware.[7] This expertise—among workers, scientists and engineers, managers, and entrepreneurs—had been forged to a great extent during the easy ISI and easy export substitution stages of industrialization, and the skills and knowledge acquired in the prior stages of industrialization by domestic entrepreneurs and workers were at least partially transferable to the production of these new commodities. As workers were shifted from easy ISI production to the fabrication of these more complex goods, wages and family incomes rose, reflecting the higher productivity of such occupations.

After overcoming the transitional inefficiencies in producing these more complex goods, the East Asian economies began to do further export substitution, now replacing some of their simpler manufactured goods exports with these more valuable durable-goods export items. Once again, the export profile of East Asia was altered, with higher value-added manufactured exports substituting for lower-valued manufactured-good exports. Not only were the East Asian economies undergoing structural change internally via more complex industrialization, but the external sector profile was constantly being altered as well, as more sophisticated exports progressively replaced simpler exports. This transformation of the export profile, along with the internal industrial transformation focused on achieving world-class efficiency levels by domestic firms, is one of the distinguishing features of the East Asian path of development.

Latin America's Sequencing of Industrialization and Development

First Stage: Easy Import Substitution Industrialization, 1930–1950

Latin America's first stage of industrialization was the same as East Asia's, easy ISI. One difference, however, was the time frame for this stage. For the larger Latin American economies such as Argentina, Mexico, Chile, and Brazil, easy ISI was initiated on a limited scale as far back as 1890. However, easy ISI on an expanded scale began for all the larger economies at least by the 1930s as a consequence of the artificial protection from imports provided by the sharp drop in world trade during the Great Depression and then during World War II. During this crisis period, new industries were initiated and previously existing firms could expand given the near absence of import competition in nondurable consumer goods during those nearly twenty years of upheaval from 1929 to 1945.

After 1945, what had been imposed by necessity—domestic production of nondurable consumer goods, goods that could not be imported because of the collapse of the international trading system—then became explicit industrial policy as recommended by the UN Economic Commission for Latin America (ECLA), with state-imposed explicit protection in the form of infant-industry tariffs to replace implicit protection resulting from the interruption in world trade due to depression and war. This easy ISI stage of industrialization came to a conclusion in the larger economies by about the 1950s.

As was the case in East Asia, the Latin American economies had been primary product exporters prior to initiating easy ISI, and this pattern of exporting primary products—mainly unprocessed mining and agricultural products—was unchanged by the higher degree of industrialization internally. Easy ISI did further the fundamental structural change of shifting workers from agriculture and mining and other primary production to industry, but in this stage there was no impact on the export profile. Domestic entrepreneurs were allowed to prosper behind protective tariff walls, and the domestic capitalist class grew rapidly.

Second Stage: Difficult
Import Substitution, 1950–1970

Recurring balance of payments crises forced the larger Latin American economies to look for a new development strategy and to shift their efforts away from easy ISI to bring exports and imports back into balance, just as an external balance of payments problem had confronted the East Asian economies during their stage of easy ISI. To attempt to resolve this external imbalance, the larger Latin American nations moved in the direction of difficult ISI—that is, they chose to further deepen the import substitution process, unlike the East Asian economies, which in their second stage of industrialization had begun to export their easy ISI manufactured goods. This meant that, besides continuing with easy ISI behind protective tariff walls, now consumer durables—automobiles, refrigerators, stoves, and air-conditioning units—and producer goods—intermediate and capital goods—also were to be produced for the domestic market to replace some or all of the imports of these goods from the international market to help reduce import expenditures overall. This stage now required infant-industry tariff protection for these goods too, thus extending the coverage of infant-industry protection deeper into the entire industrial structure from nondurable to durable to intermediate goods.[8]

Unlike the East Asian economies, which initiated the difficult ISI stage of industrialization only after domestic entrepreneurs and domestic workers had become technologically proficient and had achieved success in exporting manufactured products to the world market, the Latin American economies were not prepared to undertake this step of industrialization on their own. Producing automobiles and refrigerators required a degree of technological know-how and skill levels beyond those that Latin American entrepreneurs and workers had attained during the easy ISI stage of industrialization. Partly this was due to the failure of the Latin American economies to have scaled back their infant-industry tariffs during the easy ISI stage of industrialization, as the East Asians had done. If this had been done in Latin America, it would have forced domestic entrepreneurs to attempt to overcome their transitional inefficiencies and begin to approach the world production possibilities frontier if they were to meet external competition. Instead, for a variety of reasons, infant-industry tariffs remained in place long after they should have been phased out.[9]

Decisionmakers in the Latin American economies realized that the only way they could initiate the production of these more sophisticated, technologically based import substitutes was to depend on foreign multinational corporations (MNCs) to manufacture these goods for the domestic markets. Thus when one thinks of a "Brazilian" or "Mexican" automobile, one thinks of a Volkswagen or a Ford or a General Motors car. The same cannot be said if one is asked to think of a "South Korean" or "Japanese" car, or of an "East Asian" microwave oven, for example. The East Asians did not let foreign investments dominate their industrial sector as did the Latin American economies in their heavy industries, where the supply of domestic factors of production with the skill levels appropriate to produce these products had not been forged in the previous stage of industrialization.

Latin America needed to depend on foreign MNC investment and foreign know-how to produce the more sophisticated manufactured goods characteristic of the difficult stage of ISI, leading longtime observers like Gustav Ranis (1981) to refer to Latin America's difficult ISI stage as "premature." Latin American entrepreneurs had not been prepared to produce the more sophisticated products characteristic of the difficult ISI stage, never having been forced to meet international standards of efficiency during the easy ISI stage, which comes from having to face international competition unmediated by tariff protection. Latin American scientists and engineers were not available in sufficient numbers—their training not having been a priority of state or private policy—to have mastered the knowledge required to produce at anything close to international quality and price standards in any but a few sectors.

The retention of infant-industry tariff protection during the easy ISI phase of industrialization long after such industries should have been expected to have overcome their transitional inefficiencies surely ranks as a major policy misstep in Latin America. Maintaining tariffs allowed industries to prosper without having to become technologically proficient. Thus, once the decision was made to move industrialization in the direction of difficult ISI with its higher level of sophistication and technological knowledge requirements, foreign MNCs were the only source of expertise and know-how required to produce these goods for the domestic market. Thus began the epoch of MNC dominance of key industrial sectors within the Latin American productive structure. In the process, MNCs began to substitute for what should have been local know-how, and the local learning process was further short-circuited by factor substitution as MNCs began to supersede or thwart the maturation of the local entrepreneurial class.

There was a further problem with this premature shift to difficult ISI beyond the abandonment of domestic entrepreneurs and other human capital resources. The more capital-intensive production characteristic of difficult ISI contributed to substantial employment-generation problems in the larger Latin American economies and to a growing bifurcation of incomes. The continuing migration of workers from agriculture to industry continued unabated. However, the job-creating capacity of each dollar of investment declined as the capital-output ratio for manufacturing difficult ISI goods such as automobiles rose compared to what had prevailed in firms producing easy ISI products.

For those workers lucky enough to secure employment in the difficult ISI sector, wages were significantly higher due to the greater productivity and higher value added of such jobs compared to the wages that could be earned in the lower-valued easy ISI sector producing commodities such as tee-shirts and women's shoes. The smaller number of jobs in the capital-intensive difficult ISI industries contributed to the emergence of a growing number of migrants arriving in urban areas who were unable to secure employment in the formal, industrial sector in either easy ISI or difficult ISI enterprises. As a consequence, slums formed around the major Latin American cities, and informal-sector employment grew dramatically as the only source of survival for a substantial proportion—averaging 30 percent—of the labor force in most countries.[10] Given the low incomes typical of informal-sector employment, the distribution of income in Latin America was adversely impacted by this premature shift to difficult ISI. By way of contrast, East Asia's easy export substitution second stage of industrialization, by virtue of its continuing labor-intensive character, allowed those economies to continue to absorb the flow of rural migrants into industrial production and formal-sector employment, thus avoiding the proliferation of a large informal sector of slums and of a widening income gap between workers.

Difficult ISI further transformed Latin America's internal industrial profile to an ever higher level. However, this changing and evolving internal industrial mix was not reflected in fundamental changes in Latin America's exports. The export profile of the economies failed to evolve toward including more complex commodities as occurred in East Asia. From colonial times through independence all the way through their easy and difficult import substitution industrialization, exports in Latin America were predominately agricultural and mining primary products. The problem of long-term declining terms of trade for such goods has been well-documented, and the obstacles to importing that result certainly contributed to the recurring balance of payments problems that have plagued most of the Latin American economies since the 1970s.[11]

Despite the creation of economies that were predominately industrial (and service) in nature, there was no transformation of Latin America's exports such that manufactured goods might begin to replace primary exports. Partly due to the continuing political and economic power of a small number of landed elites and the luxury provided by having abundant natural resources—the so-called resource curse—the Latin American economies and their governments were not forced to alter their export profiles as internal industrialization expanded. Primary product exports continued to predominate in total exports far beyond what would have been predicted from the degree of industrialization observed in these nations, particularly in the larger economies.

This failure to transform the export composition as the internal productive structure became more industrial is one of the major differences between the Latin American and East Asian paths of industrialization. This failure to develop the domestic capacity to export manufactured goods on an expanding scale was one of the major reasons for the underperformance of the Latin American economies after 1980 as efficiency levels within Latin American industries suffered vis-à-vis world standards.

Third Stage: Export Promotion, 1970–1982, and Open-Economy Liberalism, 1982–Present

Continuing balance of payments problems plagued most of the Latin American economies throughout the 1970s, though these were partly disguised by the easy availability of international loans after the first OPEC oil crisis in 1973. Some efforts to expand exports by adding manufactured goods on top of the primary export base took place over this period, as the need to export manufactured goods could no longer be ignored. However, unlike the East Asian economies, for which manufactured-good exporting became an integral activity and a substitute for primary product exporting, far too often manufactured-good exporting was not integral to the economic strategy as a means to enforce internal efficiency on firms but was a simple add-on to a primary product–dominated export structure.

With the debt crisis in 1982, and often as a condition of receiving loans from the International Monetary Fund (IMF) necessary to keep their economies afloat, most of the Latin American economies were forced to reduce the roles of central government in the industrialization process. State-owned enterprises were sold off. The private manufacturing sector was forced to face foreign competition for the first time on an expanded scale as tariff levels were dramatically reduced, leading to an inflow of imports. The larger Latin American economies do have a significant industrial base after decades of ISI, and since many of their larger enterprises are foreign-owned, the ability of some enterprises to meet outside competition has been easier than would have been the case if more firms had been local only with little experience in the world market. Nonetheless, the rapid opening to foreign imports devastated smaller easy ISI firms in many countries, further eroding the local entrepreneurial base.

The transition from what were essentially protected import substitution industrialization economies to more dynamic societies in which producers must become more efficient players on the world market has not been without its costs in Latin America. Part of the problem resides in the great inequalities in wealth ownership and political power that continue to plague most countries in the region. As a result, the benefits and costs of the transition to more efficient structures have been unequally shared. Progress, however, is being made, and the existing industrial base in the region is important, though the vexing issues of the large extent of foreign ownership of production, the need for domestically based technology acquisition, the search for the best mix of human capital accumulation, and the pressing necessity of reducing extreme inequality must be addressed if Latin America is to hope to move forward in a way that the East Asian economies have been able to do. One area that needs attention is the expansion of an efficient and competitive domestic capitalist class able to market locally made goods on the world market.

Puerto Rico's Sequencing of Industrialization and Development

Despite what may seem at first glance to be surface similarities to the stages of development of both the Latin American and East Asian economies, Puerto Rico's trajectory has had significant differences that have contributed to its specific form of path dependence.[12] From Tables 1.3 and 1.4, we know that the East Asian economies have had a longer period of rapid economic growth than those of either Latin America or Puerto Rico. East Asia's industrialization path contributed to the creation of a local economic structure that was enabled to mature and prosper, transitioning from producing for the local market and then for international markets, as local producers learned to be more efficient. Along this path, average incomes rose quickly, and the economies increasingly looked more like already-developed nations.

How did Puerto Rico's industrialization trajectory differ from the East Asian and the Latin American paths and with what effects? And just as important, what accounts for these differences?

First Stage: Intermediate Import Substitution Industrialization, 1942–1950

This stage of industrialization is somewhat sui generis. Rather than focusing on the production of consumer nondurable goods via easy ISI, the most common point of entry for initiating industrialization among late industrializers, Puerto Rico's efforts to promote industry primarily were directed toward producing intermediate inputs for the existing rum factories and inputs to an expanding local construction industry. There was a shoe enterprise and a textile factory producing nondurable consumer goods for local consumption that were encouraged in this early period, but these were only limited exceptions to the intermediate ISI focus of the other enterprises promoted during this stage. But even taking into account these exceptions, the overall effort to promote industrialization undertaken by the Puerto Rican government was extremely modest relative to the size of the Puerto Rican market at the time. Different, too, from the initiatives characteristic of the East Asian industrialization path was the fact that these intermediate ISI firms were not only promoted by the Puerto Rican state, but also they were owned and operated as state enterprises.[13]

These firms were created at least partly with the expectation of contributing to the accumulation of profits and investment funds within Puerto Rico, one of the usual motivations for initiating ISI anywhere, along with the shift of labor from low-productivity agriculture to higher-productivity industrial pursuits. In this way, it was hoped that expenditures that otherwise would have flowed to U.S. firms that had long been the supply source for intermediate inputs would now be retained within Puerto Rico rather than leaving the local economy as import expenditures. Additional income would be available to be plowed back into production as local spending rose, thus giving rise to the usual income and employment multiplier and accelerator effects associated with expanded reproduction in modern economies. Further, it was hoped that the establishment of these firms would help to stimulate backward and forward interindustry linkages that everywhere are characteristic of more advanced, dynamic, and articulated economic structures. Teodoro Moscoso (1980: 167–168), one of the pioneers in creating and overseeing the industrial development process, noted precisely these effects as goals, along with increasing employment, of the Puerto Rican agency Fomento, which was made responsible for furthering the industrialization process.

It is interesting to note, especially to understand the origin of this stage of industrialization, that the mission statement of the original industrial development agency, created in 1942, included as one of its objectives the stimulation of local capital and local entrepreneurs. This was justified as a means to avoid "the problems created by large-scale, absentee capitalism," which had been characteristic of Puerto Rico's agricultural phase of economic growth, though this viewpoint was not shared by all those who actually administered the industrialization program (for details, see Durand 1980: 180–184; Maldonado 1997: 27–31; and Pantojas-García 1990: 43–44).[14] The encouragement and training of local entrepreneurs and workers who would become efficient producers for the international market was an essential component in the overall success of the East Asian path of development, just as the failure to foster the continued expansion of domestic capitalists was a weakness of the Latin American strategy following the easy ISI stage. At least some of Puerto Rico's policymakers, though perhaps not those who most counted in the final analysis, would seem to have had this goal in mind of stimulating and expanding the class of local entrepreneurs, at least during this phase of the industrialization process.

This stage of intermediate ISI, however, was at best abbreviated and ultimately mostly unsuccessful. Compared to either the East Asian or the Latin American experience of initiating their industrial processes, this first stage of development cum industrialization failed to create either a domestic entrepreneurial class of any significant size or a central core of workers with modern industrial-arts skills. Only five new enterprises were created during this phase, hardly an industrial base of consequence, and one substantial and modern hotel (the Caribe Hilton) was constructed. Four of the new industrial firms were sub-sidiaries of the Puerto Rican government, which acted as a "collective" entrepreneur: the Puerto Rico Glass Corporation (1945) was formed to provide bottles to the local rum industry; the Puerto Rico Pulp and Paper Corporation (1946) was created to provide cardboard for the boxes to be used both by the Puerto Rico Glass Corporation and the rum factories for packing; the Puerto Rican Shoe and Leather Company (1947) was created to produce shoes for the local market;[15] and the Puerto Rico Clay Products Corporation (1947) was founded to provide bricks, tiles, and sewer pipes for local construction purposes.[16] Con-struction of the Caribe Hilton as well as a textile mill that came into operation (the one other easy ISI firm producing a nondurable con-sumer good for local use) were substantially financed by the govern-ment, though these ventures were operated by private entrepreneurs.[17]

The four government subsidiaries, as well as a fifth enterprise, the Puerto Rico Cement Company, another intermediate input-type ISI firm, were owned and operated as government corporations *(autori-dades)* under the direction of the Puerto Rico Development Company, itself an independent government corporation.[18] These firms had been planned since the early stages of World War II, when imports were dif-ficult to obtain from the usual mainland suppliers, thus providing the same sort of protection from import competition that had stimulated the expansion of easy ISI production in Latin America during the Great Depression and after.

However, once World War II was over and the artificial protection from imports ended, the Puerto Rican government did not have it in its power to provide tariff protection for these still-infant firms, since Puerto Rico's legal and institutional standing as an unincorporated ter-ritory within the U.S. legal system forbade such action. The future of these intermediate ISI firms, which had never been particularly prom-ising from their inception given fierce internal political and ideological resistance to them as publicly owned enterprises, was sealed. U.S.

imports reentered the Puerto Rican market, recapturing their former market shares and seriously compromising the future of these state-owned firms.

The decision soon was made that the four government-owned enterprises and the cement factory should be sold (the cardboard operation already had been shut down after continuously losing money). The wealthy Ferré family, who already owned Ponce Cement, the only other cement plant on the island, purchased them all. The shoe factory, which had been troubled from start to finish, eventually closed its doors after having been sold at a bargain-basement price to a U.S. shoe firm. The textile mill ultimately was privatized after operating into the 1950s as a joint venture between Fomento and Textron, Inc. (see Dietz 1986: 190–194 for a short look at this history, and Maldonado 1997: chaps. 5–7 for a fascinating insider view of the ill-fated history of these state firms).

Puerto Rico's first efforts to seriously promote any form of ISI came to an end in 1947 without having achieved the important benefits—development of a larger entrepreneurial class, technological learning, improved industrial efficiency, a more skilled work force—that can be acquired during this stage of industrialization. These advantages seem to be essential in forming the skills for future, self-sustaining progress, as the successes of the East Asian economies attest. Privatization of the state-owned firms resulted in a fundamental shift in the overall development process almost entirely away from promoting ISI of any type over the future. With privatization, the decision was made to rely in the future almost exclusively upon mainland U.S. financing and U.S. entrepreneurial expertise and knowledge as substitutes for Puerto Rican sources of financing and entrepreneurial talent, all without ever having made any concerted effort to grant preferences or to create incentives that might have promoted or expanded local sources of financial or managerial resources as part of a more comprehensive industrial program that could have enriched the local entrepreneurial and labor pool.[19]

As already noted, industrialization that can contribute to long-term sustained development would seem to demand the domesticated learning associated with the successful transition from the easy ISI stage of production toward the capacity to export manufactured goods by domestic firms (Dietz 1989: epilogue; also see Dietz 1990 for a guide to the literature). It was during the easy ISI phase of industrialization that East Asia and the developed countries before them were able to create and equip a local entrepreneurial class with the degree of technological competency required to compete on the world state, while honing the skills of industrial workers needed for sustaining economic growth over time. The attainment of these cutting-edge skills by local industrialists and workers was revealed by the capacity of domestic enterprises to export manufactured goods to the international market and via an expanding share of manufactured exports in total world exports.

Puerto Rico skipped the critical ISI phase of industrialization, unlike most Latin American countries, which overextended it by prematurely going from easy to difficult ISI. On the other hand, countries like South Korea and Taiwan began the process that would transform them from being easy ISI producers to becoming successful manufacturing-good exporters beginning in the 1950s, at roughly the same time that Operation Bootstrap began.

While it is true that Puerto Rico's smaller internal market would have placed some limits on the import substitution process, it is not the case that there were no opportunities for expanded production geared toward the local market.[20] This certainly was true for consumer nondurables imported from the United States, as well as a larger range of intermediate goods than Puerto Rico attempted to produce during its aborted stage of intermediate ISI. In a sophisticated input-output study completed by economist Richard Weisskoff (1985: 44–47), it was argued that if import substitution equal to but 20 percent of Puerto Rico's consumption and intermediate goods imports had taken place, a not unreasonable goal leaving 80 percent of domestic demand still to be met by imports, employment in 1970 would have been 31 percent greater than it actually was, while gross national product would have been 44 percent larger (based on calculations made from Junta de Planificación 1977: tabs. 1 and 25; and U.S. Department of Commerce 1979: 139). Given that the unemployment rate in 1970 was 10.3 percent and rising, such a contribution from ISI could have been as transformative in the Puerto Rican economy as it has been elsewhere.

In effect, no matter how strong Puerto Rico's actual aggregate growth record was in the early years of its development program, it could potentially have been significantly better with a sustained push for at least limited ISI. The economy also could have been allowed to grow in a way that might have reduced unemployment and migration and contributed to an increase in the labor force participation rate.[21] Dependence on external sources of financing also could have been reduced. The pace of economic growth achieved in the early years of industrialization might have been sustained beyond 1970, contributing to income convergence with the United States and greater parity with the East Asian economies.

The human capital, local linkage effects, and income gains characteristic of the labor-intensive ISI stage were foregone in Puerto Rico, and the cost to the economy of failing to expand its own industrial class of entrepreneurs and to stimulate technological learning among workers has been revealed over time by the slowdown in income growth, high unemployment, and migration.

Second Stage: Easy and Difficult
Export Substitution, 1945–1980

This phase of the industrialization program, which has two substages, overlaps the first stage of industrialization in Puerto Rico, perhaps suggesting a lack of focus of the industrialization strategy in its early years. It is in this stage that Puerto Rico invented its Operation Bootstrap approach.

In 1945, the Puerto Rico Industrial Development Company (PRIDCO) opened an office in New York to promote a new building subsidy program, known as Aid to Industrial Development (AID), to be marketed to mainland companies that might be swayed to relocate their operations to Puerto Rico. These were companies that would produce not for local production but for export to the United States. The hope of the AID promotion program was that badly needed employment would be stimulated by the inflow of these export-oriented enterprises. By 1949, sixteen companies had taken advantage of the rental subsidy provided by AID, though at least some of the enterprises—Red Cape Leather, Río Grande Artificial Flowers, Ponce Candy, and perhaps others—had been operating on the island before the program began and thus did not represent a net addition to the industrial base or the employment-generating capacity of the economy (Dietz 1986: 208–209; Perloff 1950: 107; Ross 1969: 84–95).

The employment impact of this building subsidy program soon was judged to be far too limited. There was a pressing need for more rapid structural transformation to convert Puerto Rico's rural labor force with ever more limited prospects in the sugar industry after the end of World War II into industrial workers with greater opportunities to find employment and to earn higher incomes. It was at this juncture,

beginning in 1947, that Puerto Rico created its famed Operation Bootstrap strategy of industrialization. The essence of this strategy was the
reliance upon U.S. financing and U.S.-owned enterprises to rapidly
forge a manufacturing sector geared to export to the United States
whatever was produced while offering expanding employment opportunities. This sector would become the "engine of growth" for the
entire economy.

With the embrace of Operación Manos a la Obra, as Operation
Bootstrap was called in Spanish, as the dominant vehicle for the promotion of industrialization, Puerto Rico entered in earnest upon a path
of outward-oriented development based on foreign direct investment.
The manufacturing sector of the economy became what would now be
called an export platform, in which production for external markets by
nonlocal enterprises became one of the chief activities of the economy.[22] Paradoxically, Puerto Rico's own internal market for manufactured goods continued to be serviced primarily through imports and not
via the production of these newly promoted firms, which sold an almost
inconsequential share of their output in the local market.

U.S. firms locating in Puerto Rico as a result of Fomento's promotional efforts were never envisioned by government planners as being
integrally tied to the internal market beyond the hiring of local labor.
They were promoted precisely because they could produce exports,
with the gains to Puerto Rico being primarily the employment and
labor income these new enterprises were expected to generate in the
local economy.[23] Puerto Rico was to become one link in the production
chain of U.S. multinational producers, enterprises that were in, but not
of, the local economy. As a result, the Puerto Rican economy did not
become more internally linked via supply networks, nor did it become
more closely integrated to the U.S. economy.

To be sure, local producers emerged in some industrial and nonin-
dustrial sectors to provide some of the inputs to production, especially
in construction, food, banking, and other services supplying inputs to
promoted firms. Some of the multiplier effects and backward linkages
did materialize to a degree in the local economy (Chapter 3 explores
these issues in more depth). As the East Asian experience has shown,
however, the easy export substitution stage of industrialization more
naturally follows the (easy) ISI learning phase of industrialization. In
no instance has a successful industrializer begun with a manufacturing
export orientation as the means for promoting the industrialization
process (Ranis 1981).[24] If the creation of a class of domestic entrepre-

neurs and locally owned enterprises on an expanding scale is judged to be an essential part of the development process, as it certainly was in East Asia and in the developed economies before them, then Puerto Rico seriously fails the test. On these grounds, Puerto Rico's industrialization trajectory is distant from either the optimum East Asian or even the suboptimal Latin American prototype.

The creation of Puerto Rico's industrial promotion program. Why did Puerto Rico's development path follow such an unconventional trajectory in which foreign firms would play such a large role and import substitution such a small part? Part of the explanation lies in the personalities, interests, and ideological dispositions of those who very early on became responsible for promoting industrialization, as well as the state of traditional development economics at the time. One of the key individuals in formulating policy was Teodoro Moscoso, who has been credited with the original concept of creating a development agency to promote industrialization based upon the model of Chile's Corporación de Fomento de Producción. Earlier efforts to promote industrialization in Puerto Rico reaching back to the 1930s had come to naught, but when Moscoso, by training a pharmacist but by avocation a political activist, was brought into the Puerto Rican government by Governor Rexford Guy Tugwell in late 1941, he very definitely had his own ideas about how to step up the pace of industrialization (Maldonado 1997: 25–31).[25]

Moscoso succeeded in getting the development agency he wanted via the intervention of senate president Luis Muñoz Marín, the PPD leader, with whom Moscoso worked closely. The Puerto Rican legislature approved and funded the Puerto Rican Development Corporation (PRDC) in 1942. Moscoso became a tireless promoter of Puerto Rico's industrialization, but he firmly believed that there were insufficient resources for Puerto Rico to industrialize itself, and he had no fears about "absentee capital," unlike others. The fact that the early efforts of the PRDC to jump-start industrialization had been concentrated on the state-owned enterprises discussed above reflected necessity due to World War II and in no way were a sign of any negative bias on Moscoso's part toward the private sector or a preference for state ownership.

In fact, Moscoso is reported to have told a U.S. senator concerned about the government-owned firms that "I will do business with the devil himself if he comes and establishes a factory in Puerto Rico"

(Maldonado 1997: 40). For Moscoso, the goal was ever more industry of whatever type and from any source to provide more employment. There seemed to him to be no other option than to depend upon U.S. investors and U.S. firms if Puerto Rico was to industrialize and if poverty was to be overcome. If foreign firms were a necessary vehicle for promoting and speeding industrialization, so be it.

What made Puerto Rico attractive to U.S. firms, however, was tax exemption combined with low wages and a relatively disciplined labor force (Suárez 2001). Puerto Rico's first local tax exemption bill was passed in 1947 (amended in 1948), providing complete exemption from local taxes for qualifying businesses for a fixed period of time (Dietz 1986: 209–210; Pantojas-García 1990: 69–71). A virtually identical bill actually had been passed the Puerto Rican legislature in 1944, but Governor Tugwell had vetoed it. In both instances, the initiative for the tax legislation came from Moscoso, and it was clear that the benefit was being extended to attract U.S. corporations to the island by complementing their existing exemption from federal taxes on earnings in Puerto Rico with complete freedom from local taxes as well (Dietz 1986: 209–212; Maldonado 1997: 49). In its outline and perhaps even in its substantive form what came to be called the "Puerto Rican model of development" had an indigenous origin within the Puerto Rico Development Company as conceived and shaped by its director, Teodoro Moscoso. Operation Bootstrap had the stamp of Puerto Rican policymakers on it from the start.

Still, it is important to keep in mind that Moscoso was not working in an intellectual vacuum. A large number of prominent economists and other social scientists had found their way to Puerto Rico in the 1940s and early 1950s, and their views undoubtedly helped to shape the policy debate.[26] Moscoso was an ardent student of these intellectual discussions even before entering public service. Harvey S. Perloff, author of *Puerto Rico's Economic Future* (1950) and an economist from the University of Chicago, for example, played an extremely important role in the economic planning debate in Puerto Rico in setting the agenda for future economic development and in refining the design of Operation Bootstrap (Santana Rabell 1984: 174ff.).

The División de Economía (Economics Division), created in July 1950 within the Junta de Planificación (Puerto Rican Planning Board), was directed by Perloff, who worked with other North American economists in collaboration with Puerto Rican economists and planners. It was this office, according to Teodoro Moscoso, that had the responsibility for shaping the development strategy that Fomento was to follow for nearly fifty years: "The industrialization program, in its current stage of development, was conceived and adopted in 1950 following the recommendations presented to the Governor by the Division of Economics of the Planning Board" (Moscoso 1954: 575).

Moscoso, perhaps, was being falsely modest in this evaluation of who had ultimate responsibility for shaping the Operation Bootstrap "industrialization-by-invitation" strategy. It was he, after all, who had pushed for the first complete local tax exemption law embodied in the Industrial Incentives Act of 1947. He certainly supported wholeheartedly the Perloff Plan, which codified, extended, and legitimized what already had been achieved. The support of "external" experts and their intellectual imprimatur was perhaps important to Moscoso and others in the Puerto Rican government for staving off criticism of the local tax exemption program and the promotion of nonlocal investments as the basis of the industrialization, a thrust that had begun even before the Perloff Plan was known.[27] Outside expert endorsement of Puerto Rico's strategy also may have been important in legitimizing the industrialization program for potential U.S. investors considering locating a facility in a land mostly unknown to them.

Whoever was ultimately responsible for conceiving Operation Bootstrap is perhaps unimportant. The facts are that Governor Luis Muñoz Marín, Fomento under Teodoro Moscoso, and the Junta de Planificación all lent their support to the outward-oriented, externally financed industrialization-by-invitation strategy, which became the model for Puerto Rico's economic future for nearly half a century. There was a widespread view, one that many of the foreign experts shared along with Moscoso, that locally generated investment funds and the efforts of local entrepreneurs and other local inputs would be insufficient to meet Puerto Rico's pressing needs and that there thus was no alternative to such an externally based approach if poverty was to be overcome in a reasonable period of time.[28]

The views and analyses of foreign economists would seem to have been important too in convincing Governor Muñoz Marín to accept the need for making accelerated economic development a matter of urgency for the PPD-dominated government. Whereas Muñoz Marín and the PPD had made social justice their highest priority when they first came to political power in the 1940s, the Perloff Plan ranked social justice objectives as the third and fourth priorities within the four planning tiers for Puerto Rico's future. The first and second priorities of the

Perloff Plan were directed to economic development and infrastructure, thus essentially turning the PPD's ordering of equity and growth on its head.[29] In his 1951 message to the legislature, Governor Muñoz Marín endorsed this fundamental change of emphasis in his personal politics and for the society and economy as a whole:

> The most essential economic lessons of the times are: it is essential to define and maintain a strict sense of priorities; that social justice attained at low levels of production may be honorable, but it is inefficient for achieving true well-being; that in the long run the only means to reach and sustain the highest level of social goals is by maximizing production. Our primary efforts when we began this decade were dedicated to legislation that would divide the little there was more justly among the growing number of Puerto Ricans. Soon, it was clear that we had to pay more attention to production. It is not possible to distribute that which does not exist. (quoted in Santana Rabell 1984: 1987)

This shift in the prominence given to economic growth, with social and economic justice becoming essentially "trickle-down" residuals that were to be achieved over time with greater economic growth, was certainly consistent with the mainstream of economic development thinking, at the time embedded in the concept of the inverted U-shaped Kuznets curve.[30] However, this does not explain fully the uninterrupted dependence over half a century of the Puerto Rican development strategy on the privileging of external factors of production over domestic inputs, including the essential local entrepreneurial factor of production, which was essentially excluded from the development equation by Operation Bootstrap.

Even if the initial full-scale industrialization-by-invitation plan in Puerto Rico can be attributed to the influence of Perloff and other North American economists and experts, their opinions coincided with the predisposition of many in Puerto Rico to accept not only the efficacy of U.S. capital markets but also the need for a near-complete reliance on U.S. corporations as the dominant investors. What is of great import is that local decisionmakers had to continue to accept the validity of this perception not only at the time the Perloff Plan was introduced but over the next five decades as well (Santana Rabell 1984: 195–197).

In his last official message in the Capitolio as governor in 1964, Muñoz Marín did express once again his concern over the replacement of Puerto Rican capital by foreign investment interests, a perhaps unintended but certainly unwelcome outcome of the economic strategy he and the PPD had long advocated and supported: "It is difficult for me to understand how a self-aware society does not have as a goal that its private sector increasingly predominate in decisions that affect that society" (quoted in Santana Rabell 1984: 229).[31]

Over the history of Fomento's promotional activities, this sustained and growing reliance on U.S. capital and expertise is difficult to fathom, particularly given the compelling evidence of the need for a new approach once economic growth had slowed by the late 1960s. The first stage of external promotions by Fomento (1947–1965) had resulted in the establishment of relatively labor-intensive, export-oriented light industries, like clothing and textiles, food processing, and leather and tobacco products. Until the early 1960s, promoted firms were generally small or medium-sized with relatively low levels of physical capital requirements, using fairly standard and commercially available technologies. Thus, at the same time that the bulk of U.S. direct foreign investment in other countries was increasingly concentrated in high technology and intermediate goods production in which large MNCs were most likely to dominate the technology, Puerto Rico's promoted foreign firms were at the low end of the MNC production spectrum and at the bottom of the product life cycle.

Extraordinarily, it would have been in precisely these same consumer, nondurable industries that a concentrated effort to expand locally controlled ISI production could have been most successfully mounted. The technological, financial, and entrepreneurial requirements of such production were relatively modest, while the potential learning effects for the incipient capitalist class and for the labor force were quite large, as the East Asian experience showed. Instead, U.S. firms began to produce in Puerto Rico for export to the U.S. market in precisely those industries that everywhere else have been the entry point for initiating ISI, and without substantive local participation in either ownership or control. After 1965 or so, in the second subphase of export substitution, Fomento's promotional efforts were aimed at attracting large, capital-intensive, external-oriented U.S. multinational investors in pharmaceuticals, chemicals, and electronics where local capital could have no comparative advantage.[32]

Whatever the deeper explanation for this failure of policy foresight, after 1947 Fomento clung to the decision that even partial ISI was impractical and that private Puerto Rican–owned firms and Puerto Rican entrepreneurs were unable to carry the weight of the industrialization project on even a limited, let alone an expanded scale. Whether or not it was believed initially by Puerto Rico's leaders that dependence on U.S. financing and U.S. firms was a short-term strategy in which it was imagined that U.S. investment could induce internal backward and forward linkages to Puerto Rican capital and entrepreneurs and effectively provoke locally controlled ISI is uncertain and ultimately unimportant.[33] What happened, happened, whatever the motivations and intentions of those involved in originally proposing the industrialization strategy.

It may be that at that juncture in time, and given the state of economic knowledge available to planners and decisionmakers about how to develop small economies, it would have been expecting too much for a more comprehensive, integrated planning process that would have involved the state in promoting local enterprises rather than nonlocal firms to produce manufactured goods. The fact that at nearly the same time Taiwan and South Korea were pursuing such policies may reflect the substantial ideological differences about "how to develop" that even today separate mainstream U.S. policy analysts from the views of economists and others in many Asian countries, especially Japan, who long have envisioned a larger arena for state and private-sector cooperation and integration in promoting equitable development in market economies. In East Asia, the idea that the market could be shaped and that the forces of international competition and international capitalism could be used to local advantage never seemed radical, let alone impossible. The success of the East Asian economies in shaping their destinies and in being able to mold market forces to their advantage suggests that there remains considerable space for countries, large and small, to shape their futures with the proper vision about the impact of policy choices, even within an internationalized economy dominated by the larger economies and their interests (see Amsden 1989).

Throughout its history, however, Fomento exhibited an undiminished emphasis—one is tempted even to say fetish—in promoting nonlocal investment as the driving force of industrialization. Fomento failed to conceive and impose positive or negative incentives that might have forced U.S. MNCs to create more local linkages. This policy lapse virtually doomed the creation of a local manufacturing sector of any increasing significance that might have supplied through backward linkages inputs to U.S. subsidiaries, let alone a local manufacturing sector that might have substituted over time for the need for promoting U.S. companies. Instead, the great bulk of Puerto Rico's fiscal incentives to industry were lavished upon foreign firms.[34] As a consequence, though the local manufacturing sector grew in absolute terms, foreign capital expanded nearly three times as rapidly, gaining a paramount absolute and relative position in the economy (the *Echenique Report* [see Comité Interagencial de la Estrategia de Puerto Rico 1976: chap. 6], was quite concerned about improving the *balance empresarial* in favor of Puerto Rican owners, but this all too evidently fell on deaf ears until quite recently; also see in Pantojas-García 1999: 17–19 the review of documents produced by the Governor's Council of Economic Advisers, which in the mid-1980s and after began to voice concern about the lack of local capital and entrepreneurs and put forward some recommendations to begin to remedy this weakness in the economic strategy).

As a consequence, U.S. investment became a substitute for Puerto Rican investment rather than a complement that might have helped the local manufacturing sector make fundamental progress. Fomento acted in its promotion activities as if local entrepreneurs and local finance capital were permanently moribund with no prospect of ever making more than a marginal contribution to the overall development project. And of course, to a great degree this result was predestined given the focus of Fomento's promotional activities. By dedicating such a large part of its promotional operations and funds to encouraging external investors to locate in Puerto Rico and maintaining the artificial federal and local tax advantage of such location decisions, Fomento and the PPD (with the collaboration of the U.S. government) anchored the development strategy upon the continued success of such outside promotion.

Having no central stratagem for phasing in locally owned and locally controlled production that could substitute over time for foreign firms or even act in a more complex complementary fashion via expanded interindustry linkage effects, the Operation Bootstrap development strategy actively re-created an enclave economy very much like the sugar economy, which had dominated Puerto Rico until the 1940s. Only now it was a manufacturing enclave, from which a major part of the value added in production—more than a third by the 1980s and even more in the 1990s—flowed outside the economy to external, primarily U.S. investors.[35]

Premature export substitution. The stage of export-oriented industrialization overlapped with the stillborn intermediate ISI strategy. And much like the second Latin American phase of industrialization (which, it will be remembered, has been called premature difficult ISI), Puerto Rico's second stage of industrialization might well be called premature export substitution. This is because, unlike East Asia's stage of easy export substitution and more like Latin America's premature difficult ISI, Puerto Rico had not yet developed the local industrial class of entrepreneurs and the local support base—financial, managerial, technological, scientific, and so on—with the capacity to compete in the United States or in international markets as exporters. Thus the superficial similarity of the Puerto Rican path of industrial phasing with the East Asian sequence—in that both focused on industrial exports in their second phase of industrialization—is just that, a surface semblance and little more.

Puerto Rico's industrialization path has in fact a greater resemblance to Latin America's failure in its second stage of industrialization to have nurtured its entrepreneurial class and to have created a domestic industrial base able to compete at world-class levels, but for different reasons. The result, however, of economic systems that are far from the cutting edge of world competition has been the same in both Puerto Rico and Latin America, resulting in a widening income and knowledge gap relative to the late-developing East Asian economies and even more compared to the already-developed economies like the United States.

The "showcase" sector in the second stage of Puerto Rico's development was undoubtedly that of chemicals, led by the drug and pharmaceutical producers. By 1982 the chemical industry produced more than 30 percent of manufacturing gross output, though it contributed only 10 percent to total employment in manufacturing. In the same year, only 16 percent of the chemical sector's gross income was paid as wages and salaries, the remainder being the return to capital resources. This lopsided effect of high incomes for U.S. owners of firms in this capital-intensive sector and limited total income and employment for workers in the local economy was one of the unintentional outcomes of the particular structure of federal and local tax laws and other incentives provided to attract these types of U.S. firms to Puerto Rico.

The growth and dominance of the drug and pharmaceutical and other high-technology corporations within the manufacturing structure—from a third of manufacturing output in 1980 to more than 60 percent by 2000—can be linked directly to the U.S. possessions corporation tax laws that provided special incentives to U.S. firms to transfer "intangible assets," such as patents and copyrights, to Puerto Rico, where the gross income earned on such assets could be attributed to the possessions corporation.[36] Then this income could be repatriated to the parent corporation free of federal taxes, though this loophole was partially closed once it was recognized. This tax benefit on income from intangibles in Puerto Rico provided an advantage over other possible locations outside the United States for certain types of corporations, most specifically U.S. drug and pharmaceutical companies and other research-intensive firms. This helps to explain their considerable presence in the manufacturing profile of Puerto Rico after 1970. In 1990, for example, nearly half of all manufacturing net domestic income was being produced by the chemicals sector, which is dominated by the drug and pharmaceutical companies. By 1998 this share had increased to nearly 60 percent (Junta de Planificación 1999: tab. 12, p. A-13). In 2000, drugs and pharmaceuticals alone accounted for 54 percent of all merchandise exports and for the equivalent of 91.4 percent of the positive trade balance with the United States (Junta de Planificación 2002a: tabs. 6, 10).

These operations were quite profitable both absolutely and relative to similar mainland operations. For high-technology possessions corporations, their operating income in 1980 as a percentage of assets ranged from 34.8 percent for rubber products to a high of 94.2 percent for electrical and electronics products (73.1 percent for pharmaceuticals). By comparison, for U.S. firms in the same industries, the rates of return on assets were 8.2 percent and 13.6 percent (16.0 percent for pharmaceuticals). Income per employee in the same industries was about five times greater for possessions corporations as for mainland enterprises. The greater returns to high-technology firms over lower-technology possessions corporations in Puerto Rico (though even these, too, exceeded the returns of mainland firms) suggests the importance of the tax laws in general and the marginally large importance of the tax-free possibilities on income from intangibles available to possessions corporations locating in Puerto Rico (U.S. Department of the Treasury 1983: 62, 65–66).

Puerto Rico failed from the beginning to provide the space for local entrepreneurs to flourish at higher levels in the manufacturing sector. Instead, efforts were focused on creating an industrial sector at virtually all costs,[37] and speeding the structural transformation of the economy from an agricultural base to manufacturing by almost exclusive reliance on FDI.[38] To some degree, these were policy choices, not mechanically predetermined outcomes based upon international or national forces out of Puerto Rico's control.[39] PRIDCO and later Fomento, as well as the leading political parties, could have recommended an intermediate path—a more judicious mix of U.S. and local investment and ownership, for example—or PRIDCO could have given greater priority to local finance and local ownership from the beginning, including financing for firms that could have been involved in export production for the U.S. market, as well as supplying the domestic market. Of course, this would have meant an industrial program quite different from that of Operation Bootstrap, but there is no logical or compelling economic reason why such a strategy could not have been envisaged or implemented. It is this failure of policy direction over decades—it might have been excusable in the early 1950s—that has contributed to the stagnation of the Puerto Rican development process since the 1970s and to the particular form of adverse path dependence from which the economy and society suffer at the beginning of the twenty-first century.

All economies—colonial and independent, large and small—face constraints on their sovereign and independent action. Sometimes these constraints are market-imposed, such as those forced on decisionmakers by their balance of payments or exchange rate movements. Sometimes these barriers are institutional, such as colonial or semicolonial bonds, another external constraint. Other institutional barriers are internal, such as weak or corrupt government bureaucracies or lopsided distributions of wealth that thwart economic, social, and political change. The existence of barriers, internal or external, however, does not mean there are no avenues for moving forward *if* there is the will to do so and an understanding that such changes are necessary. To believe otherwise is to accept the status quo as determined and to forgo even marginal change, let alone the possibility of substantive qualitative improvements that challenge the existing barriers and may even contribute to undoing them. By the 1970s at least, the argument that policymakers had no other choices available to them beyond the Operation Bootstrap model, an argument that perhaps had some truth to it at the beginning of industrialization, could no longer have been true. The economic and political pressures of the late 1940s and 1950s could no longer be blamed for the endemic policy failures repeated again and again from the 1960s onward.

Third Stage: High-Finance, High-Technology Strategy, 1980–1996

Emilio Pantojas-García (1990: chap. 5) has argued persuasively that the third phase of Puerto Rico's modernization should be viewed as a "high-finance" strategy and not a predominately industrial phase of transformation, though this may not have been the intended outcome of the transformations that ushered this stage into being (also see Baver 1993). To a degree, this change in economic strategy reflected deep political changes taking place within Puerto Rico, particularly the challenge of the prostatehood Partido Nuevo Progresista (PNP, New Progressive Party) to the two-decade dominance of the procommonwealth PDP. Interested in smoothing the transition to eventual statehood, the PNP was not averse to tinkering with the local tax exemption laws or in pursuing policies different from those that had been at the base of Operation Bootstrap from the late 1940s if it was thought that these changes would help to create greater parity with the United States. Nor was the PNP reticent to challenge the U.S. role in Puerto Rico as being both colonial and antidemocratic, a political stance that was anathema to most supporters of the PPD.

Looking at the challenge to the economic model only, it was during the administration of PNP governor Carlos Romero Barceló that a new Industrial Incentive Act (1978) was passed that eliminated the 100 percent local tax exemption for the first time. During the first five years of an exemption period for qualifying firms, 90 percent of local income and property taxes were excused; during years six through ten, the exemption fell to 75 percent and on down to only 50 percent exemption for firms with a full twenty-five-year exemption period (those operating in the island municipalities of Vieques and Culebra; Dietz 1986: 301–304).[40] Another innovative thrust of the PNP was directed toward extending tax exemption to export-oriented service enterprises of all types, from marketing to insurance to movies to tourism, and not just the manufacturing ventures that had been the focus of Fomento's promotions from its inception.

This shift in economic policy by the PNP reflected the realties of the "postindustrial" nature of the emerging economic structure within a changing international environment. One constant in policy, however, was that the major beneficiaries of these transformations continued to be nonlocal firms. The PNP's change in focus toward including service industries within its promotion efforts did not involve a reorientation of Fomento's activities in a way that might have tilted the balance of the economy toward local ownership and control and away from U.S. enterprises.

On the U.S. side, the major change in policy that facilitated the creation of the high-finance phase was the change in federal tax policy that replaced Section 931 of the U.S. Internal Revenue Code with Section 936. Section 931 had allowed qualifying U.S. businesses—called "possessions corporations"—located in Puerto Rico (and in other U.S. territories) to remit their profits to the United States free of any federal corporate income tax *only if* they shut down their operations.[41] Virtually every possessions corporation exercised this option at the end of their exemption period in Puerto Rico, "shutting down" and remitting their profits to their parent operation, only to reemerge as a "new" firm to qualify for a new exemption period in Puerto Rico (Dietz 1986: 209, 301–302). The incentive for such "ghost" liquidations was eliminated by allowing possessions corporations to operate under Section 936 of the federal tax code, which effectively permitted tax-free remittances of profits to the United States at any time during the qualifying tax exemption period of the enterprise.

The purpose of this change in federal tax legislation was twofold. First, it was designed to control how and where U.S. subsidiaries in Puerto Rico used any retained earnings. Under Section 931, a large proportion of the retained earnings of possessions corporations were held until the end of the exemption period in deposits outside of Puerto Rico, where the funds could be more easily manipulated for the parent corporation's benefit while it still remained true to the letter, if not the spirit, of the federal tax law. Under Section 936, though qualifying profits could be immediately repatriated with no net federal tax liability, the Puerto Rican government with the concurrence of the U.S. government imposed a maximum 10 percent "tollgate tax" on any repatriated earnings. However, this maximum could be reduced significantly (to 4 percent or less) if 936 corporations deposited their retained earnings within the Puerto Rican banking system in qualifying financial instruments for specified periods of time prior to remitting to the parent corporation. Thus the volume of potential loanable funds available to the local economy was expected to grow rather than leak out to other U.S. possessions and to the Eurodollar market as had been the case under Section 931.

And grow these deposits did, as Table 2.1 illustrates. By 1980, 936 funds accounted for one-third of all commercial bank deposits and more than 42 percent in 1985. There is no doubt that the 936 legislation contributed to the rapid growth of bank deposits within the local banking system up through the early 1990s, deposits that were available for local uses and that later would help to fund investments in the Caribbean basin as part of the policy of the U.S. government embodied in the Caribbean Basin Initiative.[42]

This growth in the banking system resulting from the expansion in local financial deposits was one of the consequences of the introduction of the Section 936 federal tax law change, a transformation not at all unwelcome given the new thrust to promote export-oriented service industries begun by the PNP. Such funds also contributed to growth in deposits in savings and loans and in brokerage firms, thus expanding the financial base of the economy in that direction as well (see Colón and Martínez 1999 for a comprehensive consideration of the financial sector including the significance of 936 funds).[43] These funds in 1987 were equal to some two-thirds of 936 deposits in the commercial banking system, totaling some $6.6 billion (Pantojas-García 1990: 164–165).

Intentionally or not, this change in the federal tax law helped to forge a shift in the local economy toward generating income in the service sector at a higher rate than in the manufacturing sector. This contributed directly and indirectly to the "high-finance, high-technology" strategy, though the industrial sector remained important to the local productive structure. While locally owned banks shared in the growth of 936 deposits and Puerto Rican bankers and others in the financial sector were important players in this sector, other local firms were dis-

Table 2.1 Deposits in Puerto Rican Commercial Banks, 1980–2000 (millions of $)

	936 Funds	Total Deposits	% of Total Deposits
1980	2,840.8	8,608.5	33.0
1985	6,403.7	15,159.9	42.2
1995	5,000.6	24,928.8	21.8
2000	2,304.8	44,845.0	5.1

Sources: Colón and Martínez 1999: 306–307; Junta de Planificación 1981: 147; 1987: VIII-14; 2001: III-8.

placed by foreign financial institutions that consolidated their positions within the local economy.

The expansion in the banking sector can be observed further from Table 2.2. The share of total income produced in the finance sector and in services rose from about one-quarter of all income in 1975 to nearly half in the mid-1990s. On the other hand, the contribution of manufacturing to total output fell throughout the period. This again illustrates the growing importance of services to total income as the high-finance strategy induced by the passage of the Section 936 tax legislation began to take effect and complemented the efforts of Fomento to stimulate services, particularly export-oriented services.[44]

The shift to this high-finance phase envisaged Puerto Rico as the gateway to Latin American and Caribbean markets, as a central airline hub for the region and as a more desirable tourist destination for higher-income travelers. Further, Puerto Rico would become the banker, the insurer, the marketing design center, trade entrepôt, and high-technology industrial partner to the rest of the region. U.S. capital would continue to be important and even dominant in Fomento's reorientation of its "postindustrial" efforts, but now in the service sectors. Still, within this new high-finance strategy there also was space for local capital and local firms to compete based on the comparative advantage of the relatively high level of education of the local work force, the large number of professionals at work, the language advantage in Spanish-speaking markets, and knowledge of regional markets and customs that foreign firms could not easily or cheaply acquire. This was expected to be an important opening for the future.

The accumulation of funds that made this high-finance phase possible was facilitated by the high-technology firms in the pharmaceuti-

Table 2.2 Manufacturing and Service Contributions to Income and Output, 1975–2000 (% of GNP)

	1975	1980	1985	1990	1995	2000
Manufacturing[a]	18.8	18.2	17.5	12.3	12.9	7.3
Finance, Insurance, and Real Estate	13.6	13.4	17.0	18.0	20.1	23.9
Services	11.2	11.6	12.2	13.9	16.6	15.7
Trade	19.2	20.5	21.1	21.9	21.0	20.3

Sources: Junta de Planificación 1990: A-17, A-18; 1999: A-10; 2002: A-10.
Note: a. For the particular methodology for calculating this share, see Table 3.3.

cal and drug industry, in electronics, and in scientific instruments, and by the extraordinary profits they earned and needed to place on deposit within Puerto Rico to minimize their tollgate tax burden on profit repatriations. These firms found ways to accumulate in Puerto Rico their earnings not just from local operations but also from their worldwide profits earned on patents and other such intangible property. This allowed them to shelter these earnings from federal taxes by making local 936 banking deposits. The coming together of capital-intensive, high-technology enterprises accumulating huge profits and local and federal tax legislation that rewarded deposits of these funds in local financial institutions combined to provide the financial base for the high-finance, high-technology phase of industrial-cum-financial development in Puerto Rico's economic growth process.

The high-finance, high-technology phase built on the tendency of modern economies to evolve from agricultural to industrial to service production, and it recognized the need for Puerto Rico to begin to be more dynamically adaptive to a changing external environment. However, in terms of deepening the base of local entrepreneurs, much more could have been done. Instead, foreign banks, financial institutions, consulting firms, brokerage houses, hotels, and so on were enabled to thrive in the "hothouse" of new fiscal incentives provided both by the local government and by the United States.

Even within a "high-finance" effort in which services are conceived as playing a more central role in the development project, industry will not and cannot wither away. Industry must remain an integral part of every economy's development path, even as the service sector expands. After all, what will all the Wal-Marts, the Home Depots, the Gaps, and the Barnes and Nobles of the world stock and sell if not manufactured goods? Puerto Rico can no more ignore its industrial sector today than it could in the 1950s and 1960s. Undoubtedly the industrial sector has changed, and it will continue to do so, but so too will the service sector. More will be said about these issues in the final chapter, where policy initiatives for the future are explored.

Comparing Development Trajectories

Table 2.3 presents a summary and comparison of the stages of structural transformation of East Asia, Latin America, and Puerto Rico. From the description of these stages of industrialization in this chapter

Table 2.3   Stages of Economic Transformation

	East Asia	Latin America	Puerto Rico
I	Easy ISI	Easy ISI	Intermediate ISI
II	Easy export substitution	Difficult ISI	Easy and difficult export substitution (with two subphases)
III	Difficult ISI with difficult export substitution	Export promotion and open economy liberalism	High-finance, high-technology post-936 transition
IV	High-finance, high-technology?	?	New development strategy?

and from the evidence presented in the first chapter on the evolution of income per capita of these three cases, it is not surprising that many economists conclude that in most respects the East Asian sequencing of industrialization stages has been optimal. Both the Latin American and Puerto Rican industrialization provided suboptimal outcomes compared to what was possible. One way in which this difference in industrial phasing optimality can be observed is in considering total factor productivity (TFP) levels among countries and regions.[45]

Over the period 1960–1987, total factor productivity in the East Asian economies was responsible for 28 percent of the 6.8 percent annual increase in total output over that period. In Latin America, on the other hand, 0 percent of the annual 3.6 percent increase in total output could be attributed to greater efficiency (World Bank 1991: 43, 45). The only way the Latin American economies were able to sustain positive levels of economic growth over this period was by adding more inputs of labor and capital to production. The East Asian economies combined both more inputs with greater efficiency in the use of those inputs to increase even more rapidly their total output and total income than would have been possible from expanding the use of inputs to production alone. Over that nearly thirty-year period from 1960 to 1987, East Asia's total income was able to grow nearly eightfold due to combined TFP and input expansion, while Latin America's income grew only by a factor of about three, as there was no TFP growth at all. (Puerto Rico's TFP growth is considered in Chapter 4.)

In some ways, the larger Latin American countries, which at least contributed to the initial growth of their domestic entrepreneurial classes during the easy ISI stage, have a broader base for future industrial progress than does Puerto Rico. There are indications that in some countries, such as Chile, Brazil, and Mexico, the local industrial class is learning to compete at world-class levels in a variety of sectors, from basic manufacturing to telecommunications to new areas of expertise, such as wine production, shrimp cultivation, and other nontraditional exports, as their economies have been forced to be more "open" to international competitive forces since the 1980s.

In Puerto Rico, the domestic class of entrepreneurs has operated in a more limited fashion since the 1950s, and there is more work to be done to foment and deepen the core of entrepreneurs, scientists, and skilled workers in both industry and services that can move Puerto Rico down a path of more independent and sustainable growth and development, a path that calls for less economic dependence on the United States. The nature of this dependence is not only in the financing of investment; it also extends deeply into the fabric of the economic structure through the provision of incomes via federal transfer programs, as will be examined in detail in Chapter 5, and in the knowledge component of production (see Del Valle 1999 for an excellent overview of the issue of technology as it applies to Puerto Rico). What Puerto Rico *does* have as an advantage is a relatively well-educated labor force, and this human capital base may prove to be the most important resource of all, as it has in other economies, if it can be better utilized.

Will there be a fourth phase of transition and modernization for East Asia, Latin America, and Puerto Rico? Undoubtedly there will be, as all existing development strategies evolve and reach diminishing returns. There is evidence that the East Asian economies already are moving in the direction of their own high finance, high-technology services to complement the diversified industrial economies they have forged. Puerto Rico is in search of a new development strategy that may go beyond the high-finance phase and build up both services and local industrialization. For Latin America, the nature of any fourth phase is not yet fully apparent.

Conclusion

All economies and societies are subject to what is called path dependence. The concept simply is a way of reminding us that the present is the consummation of decisions made in the past. Economies and societies are shaped and molded by their history. This past not only fixes the present, but it also simultaneously imposes constraints and offers possibilities for the future. An economy's and a society's path dependence can be "virtuous" or it can be "adverse," depending upon its particular history, the policies and decisions made by government and individuals over that past, and of course, due to exogenous and endogenous forces of all sorts from wars, droughts, changes in technology, changes in tastes and demand, institutional innovations, ideological factors, and so on. Virtuous path dependence is a "history" that is favorable to future progress; adverse path dependence is a past that burdens the present and makes future progress more difficult and costly to achieve, though not impossible.

Part of the history that shapes an economy's present and conditions its future possibilities is the particular industrial sequencing it has followed. This phasing creates a particular industrial, agricultural, and export and import "present," among other given characteristics derived from the country's evolving history.[46] The Puerto Rican model, as opposed to the superior East Asian path of structural transformation, created a subordinate form of adverse path dependence that has proven to be a barrier to continued progress beyond the early gains in living standards achieved in the 1960s and 1970s, and not even all of those advances can be attributed fully to the growth in the government-promoted export-oriented manufacturing sector, as argued in Chapter 1. Nor can the more modest income gains accruing to individuals since the 1970s be fully attributed to the Operation Bootstrap development strategy, as Chapter 5 will make abundantly clear.

The results of the Operation Bootstrap model of industrialization provided the illusion of growth, development, industrialization, and modernization in Puerto Rico. In fact, the overall impact of the growth strategy in contributing to sustained and articulated economic growth and to rising living standards always has been more modest than its more fervent proponents proclaimed.[47] In the process, this externally oriented strategy created a particular institutional, social, and economic history underlying the economic model, one that has engendered large-scale migration, high unemployment, idleness, and crime, among other tangible and intangible costs, which have imposed burdens on large numbers of individuals and families, costs that need to be compared with the measurable benefits in income growth attained from pursuing the Operation Bootstrap strategy. One can ask, even if rhetorically, if the outcome of such a full benefit-cost analysis would resonate in favor of the Operation Bootstrap path of industrialization.

Notes

1. André Hofman (2000: 2) refers to this latter broad and somewhat nebulous category of institutional factors as the "ultimate causes" of economic growth. These shall be examined in greater detail in Chapter 4 when considering the sources of growth in Puerto Rico from the viewpoint of modern growth theory.

2. For a fuller analysis of these stylized stages of industrialization and their costs and benefits for structural transformation beyond the brief discussion provided here, see Cypher and Dietz 1997: chaps. 9–10.

3. The theory explaining this transformation was formalized by Sir Arthur Lewis in his famous model of "surplus labor," but such a transformation is implicit in all the classical economic writings from Adam Smith to Karl Marx, which examine the dynamics of the capitalist growth process from the perspectives of both history and theory.

4. In general, an infant-industry tariff is required because of the existence of some form of what economists call market failure. In the presence of market failure—for example the absence of a banking system with perfect foresight that might make loans to potential industrialists based on their prospective profits—action by the public sector, in this case to impose tariffs, may be the only means to achieve greater efficiency in the economy and to accelerate economic growth by utilizing surplus labor in higher-value employment. In such cases, government intervention is necessary to improve the efficiency and operation of the private sector, and in the absence of such a correction, the private market system will underperform compared to its potential.

5. See World Bank 1993 for details of these state initiatives in various countries in support of the private sector's attainment of technological competency.

6. The reason for a shift to a new stage or phase of development (as in the shift from easy ISI to easy export substitution in the East Asian economies) is typically required to rectify a problem in what economists call the external imbalance—that is, to escape from the difficulties presented by a persistent current account deficit in the balance of payments that must be financed by external borrowing. Typically, correcting a current account imbalance requires that export income (X) and import expenditures (M) be brought into equilibrium (such that $X \geq M$), from a situation where import expenditures have exceeded export earnings (i.e., $X < M$).

The expansion of industrial exports not only helped the East Asian economies to begin to correct their current account imbalance by increasing their export earnings relative to their import expenditures, but such an evolution toward manufactured good exports also helped to counteract the problem of long-term declining terms of trade, which afflicts most primary exports and primary product-exporting nations over the long run.

7. Of course, these earlier industries were not fully replaced and did not wither away as the new stage of industrialization evolved.

8. Contrary to the East Asian strategy, then, when confronted with a persistent current account deficit emanating initially from having export earnings less than import expenditures (i.e., $X < M$), the larger Latin American economies attempted to resolve the imbalance by further reducing the right hand side of the inequality—that is, by further reducing import expenditures, M, as had been done previously during the easy ISI stage. The East Asian economies, in their second stage of industrialization, however, had opted instead to expand the left-hand side of the $X < M$ inequality—that is, to expand their export earnings, X, by beginning to export simple consumer nondurable manufactured goods. This difference—export expansion versus import compression—is a major dissimilarity in the paths of industrialization of East Asia and Latin America, and one with significant consequences for their future development and income.

9. Such reasons—which range from the "resource curse" explanation to a failure to implement fundamental land reform to the continuing dominance of rent-seeking political elites that dominated economic policy—are considered in Ranis 1981.

10. Informal-sector work is often low-paid and low-productivity and is frequently a substitute for scarce formal-sector employment. While the informal sector does include illegal activities (drugs, prostitution, arms sales), most informal-sector employment is not technically illegal: domestic workers, sidewalk and street vendors, home repair work, neighborhood bars, home-based food service, begging, and so on. The expansion of this sector is correlated directly with the beginnings of the difficult ISI stage of industrialization in Latin America.

11. The terms of trade for a country are determined by the terms of trade index, which is equal to $(P_X / P_M) \times 100$, where P_X is the price index for exports (X) and P_M is the price index for imports (M). Basically, the terms of trade index is a measure of the purchasing power of exports to buy imports. Since 1900, there has been a long-term trend for the terms of trade index for primary products to decline at the rate of between -0.52 and -0.84 percent per year (with the exception of tropical drinks, such as coffee and tea, for which the terms of trade have shown a tendency to rise at a rate of 0.63 percent a year). What declining terms of trade means is that the quantity of exports sold must increase over time to be able to buy the same quantity of imports—that is, importing becomes more expensive in terms of exports sacrificed over time as the purchasing power of one unit of export decreases (Grilli and Yang 1988).

12. Details on Puerto Rico's early efforts to promote industrialization beginning in the 1940s can be found in Curet Cuevas 1976, 1986; Dietz 1986,

1989: chap. 4; and Pantojas-Garcia 1990: chap. 3. The phases of industrialization discussed later, while common to the literature on the Puerto Rican economy, have been based on notional conceptions of fundamental switch points. In their study of productivity in Puerto Rico, economists José I. Alameda Lozada and Alfredo González Martínez (2000: tab. 6, p. 19) confirm the existence of four distinct development phases similar to those noted here.

13. It was also the rum industry that indirectly provided the source of funding for establishing the state-owned, intermediate industries, as well as for other government-owned agencies such as water, electricity, the development bank, the public housing authority, and even for the development agency itself. Over the 1941–1946 period, some $160 million in federal excise taxes collected on rum sold in the United States was returned to the Puerto Rican treasury by the U.S. government, as required by federal law. These rebated taxes were more than five times larger than the 1940 budget of the Puerto Rican government, giving some sense of the significance of such rebated taxes to local government spending (Tata 1980: 1).

14. A. W. Maldonado (1997: 31) points out, however, that this restriction on absentee capital was added as an amendment to the bill creating the industrial development agency when it reached the floor of the Puerto Rican senate. It was not something that Teodoro Moscoso, who was responsible for the creation of the Puerto Rico Development Company, apparently wanted included. Moscoso accepted the amendment only to ensure that the industrial legislation funding the industrial promotion program would be passed.

15. This was one of the exceptions to the intermediate ISI thrust of this phase of industrialization; it was a traditional-style, easy ISI industry producing a consumer nondurable, as in East Asia's and Latin America's first stage of industrialization.

16. All dates refer to the year in which production of the firms ultimately was initiated, not when planning for these enterprises began. Initial construction and production of these enterprises was delayed due to federally imposed wartime restrictions on building that applied not just to the United States, where such restrictions perhaps made sense given the alternative uses for resources contributing to the war effort, but also to Puerto Rico, where such substitute uses did not really exist (Maldonado 1997: 39–43).

17. The Caribe Hilton was a huge success for both Puerto Rico and the new international operations of the Hilton chain. Under the agreement hammered out, Puerto Rico received two-thirds of the income of the hotel (Maldonado 1997: 123).

18. The cement company had been founded in 1936 by the Puerto Rican Reconstruction Administration (PRRA), an agency formed by President Roosevelt in 1935. The operations of the PRRA were taken over by a new organization, the Puerto Rico Development Company, which had been fashioned along with the Government Development Bank to promote the industrialization process. The Puerto Rico Development Company became the Puerto Rico Industrial Development Company (PRIDCO) in 1945, and in 1950 PRIDCO

became a subsidiary of the Economic Development Administration (Administración de Fomento Económico), or as it is more popularly called, simply Fomento.

19. Note, however, that there was an existing entrepreneurial pool in Puerto Rico, which the sale of the government-owned firms to the Ferré family confirms. There were other existing and certainly potential entrepreneurs who could equally have benefited from government efforts to promote and support their activities as well. Many entrepreneurs operated in the service sectors of the economy in retail establishments, construction, and other areas. The base for developing a core of industrial entrepreneurs existed and could have been broadened and deepened if that had been thought to have been important.

20. One should not be too quick to underestimate the size of Puerto Rico's internal market. In 1986, South Korea's GNP per capita of $2,370 was approximately half of Puerto Rico's income of $4,828 per person. South Korea's population was roughly thirteen times larger than Puerto Rico's, so neglecting income distribution issues (which would have slightly favored Puerto Rico at the time), South Korea's internal market was roughly about six times larger than Puerto Rico's. Compare this difference in size with that of the U.S. internal market in 1986, which was forty-two times the size of South Korea's (Junta de Planificación 1989: A-1; World Bank 1988: 222–223). If South Korea had ISI possibilities vis-à-vis the United States, so too did, and does, Puerto Rico compared to what South Korea attained.

Teodoro Moscoso (1980: 167), the head of Fomento, had argued that ISI possibilities were quite limited in Puerto Rico. This view, however, makes the common error of positing ISI and an export orientation as if they somehow are polar opposites. The East Asian countries created their ISI industries to service first the domestic market and then external markets as domestic production reached more efficient levels. If import substitution is viewed as part of the process of creating a predominately domestically owned and dominated manufactured-goods exporting sector after first learning how to do such production in the domestic market, then the possibilities for expanding easy ISI—with an eye on eventually exporting—are very much larger than might be supposed, particularly for countries that can fill the manufacturing niches that producers in more developed economies have left behind. ISI possibilities are certainly more extensive than those that, as an adjunct of its export promotion, Fomento tried to create over most of its history (Economic Development Administration 1986: 12–13).

There is still much to be learned from the *Informe Echenique* (see Comité Interagencial de la Estrategia de Puerto Rico 1976: chap. 5) on the possibilities for import substitution for Puerto Rico. Also see the more skeptical but rigorous report by the Economic Development Administration (1986) that also errs in posing ISI and exporting as if they are exclusive rather than complementary activities. This report does at least suggest a continuity of thinking within Fomento, albeit flawed from the perspective of modern development theory (p. 16).

21. As noted in Chapter 1, one of the enduring problems since the beginning of Operation Bootstrap has been inadequate employment generation. The unemployment rate reached its high in 1983, an incredible and deplorable 23.5 percent, at the same time that the labor force participation rate was at its lowest level, with only 41 percent of those eligible to be in the labor force actually working or looking for work (i.e., unemployed).

Breaking down unemployment by age shows that male teens aged 16–19 averaged 50.0 percent unemployment in 1980 and 53.9 percent in 1990 (female teens had even higher rates of unemployment, 51.9 percent and 61.9 percent). Males aged 20–29—that is, those of prime labor force participation age—had unemployment levels of 19.6 percent in 1980 (females, 18.7 percent) and 24.3 percent in 1990 (females, 29.4 percent). The age group with the lowest average unemployment rates tended to be workers aged 40–59 (Rivera-Batiz and Santiago 1996: 96).

The other face of employment inadequacy and high unemployment has been the migration to the United States of at least a third of the Puerto Rican people over the past century. The estimated unemployment rate in 1970 without migration would have been 22.2 percent (and not the 10.3 percent attained) and above 20 percent for all years, illustrating once again the importance of migration to the ability of the economy to function without severe social stress (Dietz 1986: 288).

22. In 1950, exports were equal to 33.7 percent of all tangible output and services, including government; in 1960, exports rose to 37.2 percent of all output; in 1970, the figure was 34.8 percent; in 1980, 49.3 percent; and in 1988, 49.1 percent of all output was exported, with the bulk of the production being goods manufactured by Fomento-promoted firms (Dietz 1989: 262, 308; Junta de Planificación 1989: tabs. 1, 16, 23). If government services were factored out of the total output figures, exports of privately produced goods would be a greater proportion still of total private-sector output.

23. There were always, of course, some sales by promoted firms in the local market, but the overwhelming bulk of goods for local consumption were imported (Dietz 1989: 309–312; Weisskoff 1985: 69). It is important to recognize, though, that there were limited sales by outward-oriented foreign firms in the local market, which is again suggestive of the larger possibilities for a more expanded local orientation via import substitution (Pantojas-García 1984: 2, 9).

24. In thinking about an export orientation and its likelihood of contributing to accelerated development, it is important to remember that all of the Latin American countries—and Puerto Rico followed this pattern as well until Operation Bootstrap was begun—long had been distinguished by an agricultural and mining export orientation. This primary product export orientation had begun with colonization, and primary product export profiles still dominate in some of the economies. The episodes of forced ISI in Latin America had been designed explicitly to deepen and diversify internal economic structures that had stagnated as a consequence of this disarticulated export structure inherited from the colonial past, one that was technologically backward, low in

value added, subject to adverse terms of trade fluctuations, and disproportionately controlled by foreign interests.

Some of the periods of most rapid economic growth for the major Latin American countries occurred precisely during ISI, which contributed to fundamental shifts in Latin America's social and productive structures compared to their histories as primary export economies, even taking into account the failures of the economies to improve efficiency and expand manufacturing exports (Alexander 1990). Exporting per se cannot be linked inextricably with progress. In fact, one of the more important lessons of the East Asian economies is the importance of the ISI stage as a predecessor to the success of manufactured-goods exporting. It is the capacity to export manufactured goods by domestic firms that is one of the hallmarks of successful development.

25. A bill to create the Insular Industrial Development Corporation had failed to be approved in 1937 by the Puerto Rican legislature, and in 1939, when it finally was approved, U.S. governor Blanton Winship vetoed the legislation (Maldonado 1997: 27).

26. Wassily Leontief, John Kenneth Galbraith, Ben Dorfman, Simon Ruttenberg, Harvey Perloff, Eric Wolff, and Sidney Mintz are just a few of the leading social scientists who worked in Puerto Rico and who often were closely involved in policymaking.

27. Criticism of tax exemption arose both from the left and the right of the political spectrum. The left objected to tax exemption on the basis of its implications for the distribution of income and other class issues, while others with more conservative agendas, including economists, objected to the "distortions" to the economy that would be caused by tax exemption, which would "artificially" promote some activities over others by reducing their costs. For some of the flavor of the opposition to Puerto Rico's own tax exemption program as a development strategy, see Maldonado 1997: 46–49, 99–101.

28. This view of Puerto Rico as being "too small" and too poor to generate the needed financial resources for the level of investment deemed necessary to boost employment and initiate the structural transformation toward greater industrialization persists to this day among many analysts. The influential Kreps report (U.S. Department of Commerce 1979: vol. 1, p. 5) repeated this refrain while lamenting, at the same time, the lack of linkages in the local economy promoted by nonlocal capital. Puerto Rican economist Eliézer Curet Cuevas (1986: 223, 192–196) would still seem to hold to this perspective of Puerto Rico as "too small," though he too finds it regrettable that there has been such a heavy price to pay for this dependence on foreign finance.

There is the issue of the rate of savings to be considered in thinking about whether Puerto Rico could have financed its own industrialization. The personal savings rate has long been negative, or at times slightly positive, as Table 2.4 shows. Typically, though, families have exceeded their disposable personal income in spending on consumption. This has required an increase in personal debt and the use of prior accumulated savings to finance the shortfall between income and expenditures. Personal debt in Puerto Rico has risen rapidly over

Table 2.4 Personal Savings Rate, 1940–2000

	Savings Rate
1940	−8.0
1950	−3.9
1960	−4.8
1970	−5.1
1975	0.3
1980	−6.2
1985	−10.3
1990	0.4
1995	−1.3
2000	−3.2

Source: Junta de Planificación, various years: A-1.
Note: Savings rate = (disposable personal income − personal consumption expenditures) / disposable personal income.

the past half century as a result of this imbalance, but interestingly and importantly, so have total savings.

Why are savings so important? Savings release real resources for uses other than consumption, in particular for investment purposes. If personal savings are negative, where do the funds come from to finance domestic investment? Part of the answer is that they can come from business itself, via retained earnings, which are plowed back into investment. Savings can also be generated or mobilized by government. And of course, domestic savings can be supplemented by nonlocal sources of savings that enter the local economy.

Those who insist that the negative rate of personal savings constituted a barrier to local financing of the industrialization program may have a partial point. However, external financing could have been mobilized to finance local industry. It was not predestined that such financing needed to be embodied in nonlocal firms. Financing and control of investment are separable issues. Further, with incentives (via income taxes, for example), personal savings might have been increased, thus adding to the pool of local funds available for local use. Just because savings have typically been negative does not mean they needed to have been negative. With a different economic strategy, one that generated more rapid economic growth and less unemployment, saving might have become positive, thus self-financing the promotion efforts to stimulate local industry.

29. What is here called the Perloff Plan can be found in the Puerto Rico Planning Board 1951. Muñoz also had been jolted by the pessimistic report of U.S. economist Ben Dorfman on the limited possibilities for economic progress under different political status options, a report that may have contributed to the rapidity with which Muñoz accepted the Perloff Plan's priorities (Maldonado 1997: 49–55).

30. The Kuznets inverted U-shaped curve is sometimes said to suggest that greater equity and social justice may only be able to be achieved once a

sufficiently high level of income per person has been reached in an economy. In other words, some degree of increasing inequality may need to be tolerated as a cost of economic growth, at least until the threshold level of income is reached, after which an economy apparently can "afford" to pay attention to equity issues.

Recent analysis on the relation and the dynamic between economic growth and equity has stressed the complementarity of the two goals of equity and growth, not their pure substitutability. Not all economic growth need lead to greater inequity, and not all efforts to promote equity (for example, expanded educational opportunities) need slow economic growth—in fact, quite the contrary. Contemporary research suggests that the traditional Kuznets curve is more a statistical and historical artifact than an inexorable economic law. Government policies on both growth and development can be effective in improving both, even at low income levels. See Birdsall, Graham, and Sabot 1998; and Solimano, Aninat, and Birdsall 2000.

31. This is an echo of what Muñoz had said in 1949 before the Puerto Rican legislature: "Production to serve what class of life? Economic productivity merely to produce, without an objective of life to guide it, can only lead in this modern world to greed for property and a twisting of the spirit. . . . People do not exist for industrialization. Industrialization exists for the people" (quoted in Maldonado 1997: 77).

32. For an insightful analysis of these transformations, see Pantojas-García 1990: chap. 4. Nine of the ten leading prescription drugs sold in the United States were being manufactured in Puerto Rico.

33. Teodoro Moscoso (1980: 167) indicated "with little capital available and given the lack of trained managers and entrepreneurs required to create an industrial structure as quickly as circumstances demanded, Puerto Rico had to depend at the *beginning* on foreign private investment" (emphasis added), which would seem to suggest, in a generous interpretation, that the dependence on foreign capital was not an aim in itself, but a conjunctural necessity only, and that with time Puerto Rican investment and entrepreneurs would play more active roles. One might also impute this view to Governor Luis Muñoz Marín based on his previous criticism of U.S. capital's dominance in the Puerto Rican sugar industry and his early socialist political leanings.

34. This is not to say, of course, that there were no local capitalists or local manufacturing firms, many of which also received Fomento's incentives. In the late 1960s, however, nonlocal firms generated about 70 percent of the employment, wages, value added, and sales in the manufacturing sector. There is no indication that this overall share has diminished since then; in fact, the relative position of foreign capital probably had deepened somewhat by the mid-1980s (Dietz 1989: 262–267). See Chapter 3 for a fuller discussion of these issues.

35. As discussed in Dietz 1989: 264, 275–277, 334–335, the share of total income produced in Puerto Rico that has been repatriated to foreign investors rose from (a minimum of) less that 1 percent of gross national product in 1960

to more than 30 percent in the early 1980s, and to more than 40 percent at the end of the decade (Junta de Planificación 1989: chap. 4, tab. 9, p. A-1). See Chapter 3 for a fuller discussion of this matter.

36. See Chapter 5 for details on Puerto Rican and U.S. tax laws.

37. Such a strategy in which there is the rapid creation of an industrial sector in many directions at the same time is reminiscent of the "Big Push" and "balanced growth" theories proposed by early theoretical development economists such as Paul Rosenstein-Rodan and Ragnar Nurkse in the late 1940s and early 1950s. Both of these strategies, however, require resources far beyond the capacity of less developed nations and were never taken very seriously, except in the classroom and, perhaps, in Puerto Rico.

38. It might be objected that it is a misnomer to refer to U.S. investment in Puerto Rico as FDI—that is, as *foreign* direct investment, given that Puerto Rico is an unincorporated territory and legally a part of the United States. However, the use here may be taken as "nonlocal versus local" if the FDI designation is objectionable, and this is the usage adopted in Chapter 3.

39. One observation about the failure to change Operation Bootstrap's fundamental orientation is perhaps in order. The independent economies of East Asia and Latin America typically were forced to rethink their industrialization strategies in the face of balance of payments crises in which foreign exchange shortages could no longer be financed via the normal international borrowing channels. Puerto Rico, however, as an unincorporated territory of the United States, has no independent balance of payments position, no independent currency, and hence no real external balance of payments problems to be confronted or financed in the usual sense of those terms. Instead, what would be external balance problems in independent nations are revealed as *internal* balance problems in Puerto Rico, and these imbalances have been manifested as unemployment, low labor force participation rates, and migration. Given that migration to the United States was unobstructed and that federal transfer payments to Puerto Rico helped to artificially boost incomes regardless of the weakness of incomes generated from production, the pressures to alter an ailing economic strategy were weaker than they would have been for an independent country facing binding external balance constraints in thinking about its economic policy choices.

The importance of "safety valve" options for Puerto Rico, while often commented on as mitigating social pressures, thus were equally if not more significant in reducing the necessity for fundamental reforms to the economic development strategy by obscuring and easing the underlying systemic dysfunctionality. Much as abundant resources in an economy can result in the seeming paradox of the resource curse that holds back progress, the safety valves of migration and federal transfer payments had the same effects for the Puerto Rican economy by not imposing binding constraints on state action that would have required fundamental changes in economic policies.

40. The move to partial tax exemption was also motivated by a severe fiscal crisis facing the Puerto Rican government that had resulted in increasing

amounts of external debt. In 1976, three out of every four industrial firms in Puerto Rico were exempt from taxes, amounting to more than 1,500 enterprises (Dietz 1986: 302). In 1970, the public debt of the commonwealth government, including that of publicly owned corporations, was $1,542.3 million; in 1975, gross public debt equaled $4,923.5 million; and in 1980 it was $6,812.4 million (Junta de Planificación 1981: A-33; 1989: A-58). Increasing the local tax base and government revenues was essential if this debt was to be serviced and Puerto Rico's bond rating preserved.

41. The reason for permitting tax-free operations in Puerto Rico (and other territories) in the first instance and the details of these changes in federal tax law are considered in Chapter 5.

42. While commercial bank assets grew by 83 percent from 1978 to 1988, their net income surged by 1,245 percent (Pantojas-García 1990: 161). The phasing out of the 936 tax exemption, discussed in Chapter 5, accounts for the decline in the importance of such deposits by 2000, but total bank deposits had grown substantially, making 936 deposits less important.

43. In 1980, the statehood-dominated legislature passed Law 26 to facilitate the creation of an international banking center in Puerto Rico, giving a further boost to this financial redirection in the economy.

44. Maximum tax exemption for export-oriented services was set at 50 percent. When the PPD returned to power, however, it passed the Puerto Rico Tax Incentives Act in 1987 (the first to not be called an "industrial" incentive), which partially reversed the PNP's policies. While the new law did not reintroduce full local tax exemption—it provided for a uniform 90 percent exemption over the full qualifying period of exemption—there also was no decreasing exemption, and qualifying service enterprises had their exemption increased from 50 to 90 percent (Pantojas-García 1990: 157).

I owe much of my thinking on the importance of the high-finance strategy to discussions with Emilio Pantojas-García (for a summary of his views, see Pantojas-García 1990: 149–166, and Pantojas-García 2000 for a more critical statement).

45. Total factor productivity measures any economic growth unexplained by increases in quantity of the physical inputs to production. In a broad sense, TFP is a measure of a country's intensive economic growth—that is, economic growth resulting from greater efficiency, regardless of the source of that efficiency, be it due to better education, healthcare, technology, the legal system, managerial techniques, learning-by-doing, and so on.

46. The institutional evolution of an economy and society is an extremely important aspect of its specific pattern of path dependence. This process entails the creation and the nature of basic infrastructure complementary to the process of economic growth from banking, to schools, to the state and its civil service, to the class structure, interclass mobility, and even ideology. These institutions are "given" in the sense that they have been shaped by the needs of the economy and society on its specific growth trajectory to that point in time. They are not "given" in the absolute sense of being immutable. Future deci-

sions are nonetheless both bounded by path dependence at the same time that such decisions are potentially transformative of that past as the economy and society evolve into the future.

47. In particular, the large and growing gap between gross domestic product and gross national product is an important indicator of the lack of articulation of the externally owned manufacturing sector and the remainder of Puerto Rico's domestic economy. The growth of rate of GDP was 7.7 percent per annum over the period 1980–1998, while the growth rate of GNP was a smaller 6.6 percent per year, and even that is somewhat misleading due to the size of federal transfers to Puerto Rico, which are added to GNP (Junta de Planificación 1989: A-1; 1999: A-1).

3

Dimensions of Ownership and Control

From the discussion of industrial phasing in Chapter 2, we know that Puerto Rico's strategy of development lacked a focus on the systematic support or the fostering of local entrepreneurs and local sources of finance, unlike the more successful East Asian path of industrial growth and development. Our review of the stylized paths of industrialization highlighted the central role of domestic entrepreneurs, skilled workers, and the technological learning that underlies sustained economic progress. These components have been instrumental to the industrialization and development success of the East Asian economies in recent decades and of the now-developed nations like the United States, Germany, France, and the UK long before them. The relative weakness of the Latin American economies in creating a dynamic core of domestic entrepreneurs, scientists and engineers, and skilled workers capable of shifting from producing manufactured goods for domestic use to export markets also helps to explain the more limited progress they attained compared to the East Asian economies.

In this chapter, the details of the local and foreign ownership question in Puerto Rico are examined in greater depth. We shall discover that while "foreign" manufacturing firms certainly have dominated in those sectors of the economy privileged by the promotion activities of the Puerto Rican government, there remain substantial areas of operation for local entrepreneurs whose activities and knowledge provide a base for future growth not only in manufacturing, but in other sectors of the economy, especially the provision of services with international trade potential.[1] The supposed lack of viability of local ownership and financing, at least in the manufacturing sector, motivated the Operation Bootstrap strategy from its inception. In any new development strategy, can local entrepreneurs and local financing reasonably be expected to provide a viable base for the economy?

We also shall be obliged to reconsider another key issue that typically lurks just below the surface of discussions about Puerto Rico's development path: Are there realistic opportunities for import substitution industrialization that might allow Puerto Rico to begin to retrace the more optimal path of development followed most recently by the East Asian economies and by the United States and other already-developed economies before them? Or is the Puerto Rican economy so small that import substitution is not a realistic possibility, meaning that an export orientation is the only alternative industrialization choice for the economy, thus validating to a degree the Operation Bootstrap strategy? This issue is separate from the local versus nonlocal question of *who* does the producing.

And somewhat more complexly but of equal importance, what precisely is the role of industrialization in an economy where already more than half of all output is produced in the service sector and approximately three of every four jobs are service-type jobs from fast food to retail trade to marketing, consulting, and public-sector employment? Is the industrial sector now, at best, secondary to the development trajectory of the economy? Is there a postindustrial reality facing Puerto Rico?

The first two issues—local versus nonlocal ownership and the possibility for import substitution—are separable concerns. Can local ownership of productive resources be increased, independent of the particular industrialization and development strategy pursued? And detached from the ownership question, can significant import substitution opportunities be identified that would help to drive the economy forward in a way that increases long-term sustainability? The issue of Puerto Rico's service sector and its potential contribution vis-à-vis industry will be considered later in the chapter.

Nonlocal Versus Local Wealth Ownership

In 1928, when Puerto Rico's economy still was dominated by the sugar industry and there was but minimal industrialization beyond the sugar *centrales* and small-scale needlework production, it was estimated that 27.1 percent of the economy's total wealth in the form of assets of all types, both productive and nonproductive but excluding labor, was nonlocally owned.[2] By 1974, some twenty-five years after the beginnings of industrialization and modernization, the share of Puerto Rico's total wealth of all kinds that was nonlocally owned had more than doubled, reaching 55.9 percent of all nonlabor assets (Clark et al. 1930: 418; Dietz 1986: 109, 266). Unfortunately, the statistics required to bring this asset measure up-to-date are no longer collected in the same manner, so extending this precise measure is not possible.

Using a somewhat different measure of wealth, however, economist Edwin Irizarry Mora (1989: 214–219) has carefully enumerated both the level of direct nonlocal investment and the evolution of national net worth over time. In 1950, three years after the start of Operation Bootstrap, total reproducible physical productive assets equaled $1,743.9 million, of which $107.0 million represented nonlocally owned direct investment (NLDI).[3] Puerto Rico's national net worth—after subtracting NLDI and debt owed to creditors outside Puerto Rico from total assets—was estimated to be $1,419.2 million. Table 3.1 shows the estimates for total assets, NLDI, nonlocal debt, and net worth over the period 1950–1980.

In 1950, the equivalent of about 6 percent of Puerto Rico's total reproducible physical productive assets were in the form of nonlocally

Table 3.1   Estimates of Puerto Rico's Wealth Distribution, 1950–1980 (millions of $)

	Total Assets	Nonlocal Direct Investment	Total Debt and Nonlocal Investment[a]	Puerto Rico's Net National Wealth
1950	$1,743.9	$107.0	$324.7	$1,419.2
		(6.1%)	(18.7%)	(81.4%)
1960	3,764.9	671.7	1,554.8	2,210.1
		(17.8%)	(41.3%)	(58.7%)
1970	11,556.8	3,038.8	7,109.1	4,447.7
		(26.3%)	(61.5%)	(38.5%)
1980	33,648.1	14,757.0	25,898.8	7,749.3
		(43.9%)	(77.0%)	(23.0%)

Source: Irizarry Mora 1989: 214–219.
Notes: Values in parentheses show the ratio of that item to total assets.
a. Total debt and nonlocal investment includes the nonlocal direct investment subcategory.

owned direct investment. By 1980, this figure had risen to 44 percent, and by 1984 to 57 percent, according to other research by Irizarry not shown in this table (Irizarry Mora 1989: 239, 241). Whereas in 1950 more than 80 percent of Puerto Rico's total reproducible physical productive assets were locally owned and only about 19 percent of these assets were encumbered to nonlocal owners (as either NLDI or debt), by 1980 the shares were virtually reversed, with 77 percent of assets being owned by nonlocals either as direct investment or via debt, while but 23 percent of total physical reproducible assets were under the control of local owners.

The degree to which nonlocal ownership increased relative to local wealth is disconcerting, but it reflects the result, if not necessarily the intent, of the Operation Bootstrap strategy of investment by invitation directed at U.S. sources of finance, entrepreneurship, and technology. To give some perspective, it is sobering to realize that in 1970, U.S. investments in Puerto Rico accounted for about 20 percent of all U.S. direct investment in all of Latin America, and in 1980 to almost one-third of such investments (Meléndez 1994: 242). Nonetheless, on the positive side, the above figures do show that there is a degree of local ownership that represents a substantial absolute amount of productive wealth in the hands of Puerto Rican owners, wealth that grew by more than five times from 1950 to 1980. This demonstrates that there has been a substantial core of entrepreneurs whose operations have expanded over time, though relative to nonlocal investment it grew at a much more modest pace.

In fact, looking at particular industries in 1978, and just by counting the number of establishments, nearly two-thirds of the ownership of the food products industry (113 firms) was in local hands, as was half of the rubber and plastics firms (33). A third of all firms (355) in the industries surveyed were locally owned (Pantojas-García 1990: 115). And while these firms had smaller shares of the total output value than their headcount share among firms in their respective industries, the numbers do indicate that there always have been a substantial number of local entrepreneurs who were able to finance their activities and to operate within a policymaking milieu that was not always particularly favorable to their interests vis-à-vis those of promoted U.S. enterprises. Entrepreneurs, Puerto Rico has had; policies to privilege their interests, however, have been a missing ingredient in the development strategy that underestimated the possibilities for even greater locally controlled and locally dominated production.[4]

The Effects of Nonlocal Capital
on Local Productive Structures

Three decades ago, economist Albert O. Hirschman (1971) hypothesized that there was a regular pattern of effects of nonlocal finance and capital on a host economy like Puerto Rico.[5] Initially, outside sources of finance and any net additions to the total capital stock of a nation might reasonably be expected to confer net benefits on the host in the form of increased employment, income and production, perhaps foreign exchange earnings, technological learning, and other potential spin-off advantages. However, over time, diminishing returns to further increments in the foreign capital stock might reasonably be expected to set in for the host economy as foreign exchange outflows to pay repatriated profits grew and as nonlocal capital swelled in certain sectors.[6]

There was a danger, Hirschman conjectured, that relatively easy access to foreign savings in the form of nonlocal capital over too long a period would result not in the stimulation and expansion of local sources of savings and investment but in their atrophy. In those cases where nonlocal capital began to dominate in keys sectors and when an economy failed to force foreign firms to "unbundle" their productive inputs, many of which were imported from abroad, the negative impact on local factors of production—especially on entrepreneurs, skilled workers, finance, and technology—from nonlocal capital flows could be devastating, unless aggressive action by government was taken to prevent this from occurring.[7]

It is not, then, that foreign sources of saving or finance or even multinational corporate investment should be eschewed completely. Hirschman was no doomsday zealot. Rather it was a matter of a host economy being attuned to its own long-term interests and of having in mind that nonlocal capital and nonlocal sources of savings should be seen, at least partly, as just one more mechanism to augment and encourage the expansion of local investments and local sources of savings and finance. Nonlocal capital should serve to stimulate and encourage the spread of local capital and local ownership via learning and linkage effects. When outside sources of finance and nonlocal firms begin to substitute for, rather than acting as a complementary means to jump-start, local finance and local capital, host economies need to undertake measures to right the balance between local and nonlocal capital or the negative effects of "too much" nonlocal capital will become all too apparent. This is what happened, it will be remembered, in the stage of premature difficult ISI in Latin America (see the discussion in Chapter 2), and this factor atrophy effect, it can be argued, also has been the result of the Operation Bootstrap strategy in Puerto Rico.

As evidence of this, in an empirical study of the effects of nonlocal investment on a number of economic variables, David Carroll's research (1993) tends to confirm this Hirschman-like pattern of, at first, generally positive effects from outside investment during the Operation Bootstrap period of promoting U.S. investment. Nevertheless, after about twenty years of industrialization, the negative effects of nonlocal capital in Puerto Rico began to dominate more and more, ultimately erasing the positive early effects of the nonlocal capital inflows, just as Hirschman had predicted.

For example, Carroll (1993: 208–209, 250, 287–288) found that over the 1951–1973 period, nonlocal capital contributed positively to the expansion of domestic production linkages, thus helping, seemingly, to create a more articulated and internally dynamic economic structure. However, over a slightly longer time period, to 1983, the effect of nonlocal capital on local linkages had turned sufficiently negative—that is, further inflows of more nonlocal capital led to a reduction in local backward linkages—so as to make the overall effect of nonlocal capital on production linkages negative over the entire period, 1951–1983, of his study.[8] The first subperiod (1951–1973) examined by Carroll, when some production linkages were stimulated, roughly coincides with the labor-intensive export phase of Operation Bootstrap, and the latter period, when the linkage effect was reversed, coincides with the capital-intensive stage of promotions in pharmaceuticals, the drug industry, and oil processing.[9]

This positive-then-negative diminishing returns pattern of nonlocal capital hypothesized by Hirschman also was observed in the effect of capital inflows on employment and, most significantly for this chapter's focus, on the level of local investment (Carroll 1993: 212–213, 223–224, 253–254). The infusion of nonlocal capital in the early stage of Operation Bootstrap initially helped to increase local employment as it contributed to an expansion in the level of local investment through linkages and other positive spin-off effects. In other words, in the early years of Operation Bootstrap nonlocal capital functioned as a complement to local capital formation. However, as the total stock of nonlocal capital continued to expand and the development focus shifted toward capital-intensive production in the 1960s, the effect of these capital inflows from the United States on employment and on local investment eventually turned negative as the optimum level of nonlocal capital was exceeded.

In its effect on local investment over time, Carroll's findings thus tend to support the argument that long-term inflows of nonlocal capital begin to replace local factors of production, including local investment sources, as the factor atrophy effect predicted by Hirschman began to dominate any initial positive catalyst effects of nonlocal investment on local production linkages, employment, and other variables.[10] Intriguingly, Carroll (1993: 293) did find that nonlocal investment in those few firms geared to the local market—that is, in import substitution industries—tended to encourage the expansion of local linkages throughout the entire period. When investment, even nonlocal, was geared to the local market, this contributed to creating a more articulated and vibrant local production structure with overall positive effects.

For example, Santos Negrón Díaz and Jose García López (1992: 150–151) found that all of the output of the local meat processing and canning industry was sold locally in 1988, with almost 90 percent of the output distributed via local retailers or wholesalers. More than 78 percent of the output of locally processed and canned fruits was destined for the local market. In both these industries, further opportunities for the expansion of local production existed to replace imported goods. Backward linkages were particularly strong in the meat processing and canning industry, with 65.7 percent of value added coming from local inputs. In particular, the local production of chickens was an especially important backward link to the processing and canning industry.

These findings support what we know from Chapter 2 about the importance of successful import substitution industrialization in the case of the East Asian growth process. They also are suggestive for Puerto Rico's future decisions about promoting further industrialization, because even though the economy is dominated by service activities, industry will always have a place within the overall productive structure, and the positive impulse provided to local linkages from import substitution is well documented by Carroll's research.

One variable that did respond positively to the expansion of nonlocal capital investment over time was the share of nonlocal income in Puerto Rico's total income (Carroll 1993: 222, 260), though this can hardly be considered a benefit to the local economy. In fact, quite the contrary is true.[11] Such a finding is, however, consistent with the view that "too much" nonlocal capital generates adverse effects in the host economy. One significant effect of the growth of nonlocal income to total income was a declining share of wage income within the total income created by the manufacturing sector. In 1967, 18.1 percent of all income created in manufacturing was received as wages; by 1994, this share had fallen to only 8.0 percent, even as the sector's total income grew. The reverse side of this decline in the share of wage income in total manufacturing income is, of course, the increase in the income share received by owners of capital, who in the manufacturing sector are predominately nonlocal owners (Castañer and Ruíz Mercado 1997: 30).

We shall examine further evidence of this growing share of nonlocal income later in this chapter as revealed by the growing GDP/GNP gap and the net effect of the manufacturing sector on total income. What is uncontestable, though, is that as nonlocal capital investment increased its reach in the economy throughout the Operation Bootstrap period, a larger and growing share of the total income created in Puerto Rico has belonged to nonlocal income recipients.[12] The U.S. Government Accounting Office (1997: app. 2, 34) reported on the situation in the following manner:

> Income from the direct investment of nonresidents grew between 1982 and 1996, both in total amount and also as a share of all income from investments owned by nonresidents. The income from direct investment increased from $7.6 billion in 1982 to $15.7 billion in 1996, growing at an annual rate of 5.3 percent. This income also increased as a share of total income from investments owned by nonresidents from 87.4 percent in 1982 to 92 percent in 1996.

That nonlocal capital was acting as a substitute and not a complement to local capital is further confirmed in the negative effect of nonlocal capital on the total income of local owners of capital reported by Carroll. Combined with the relative decline over time in the aggregate share of local investment as nonlocal investment expanded, Hirschman's fears about the adverse impact of nonlocal capital on a host economy, when allowed to swell over time beyond its optimal level, largely are corroborated in Carroll's study of Puerto Rico.[13] In his conclusions, Carroll summarizes (1993: 397–398) these adverse outcomes:

> Foreign investment appears related to decreases in: job creation per investment dollar, local employment, wages as a percent of total

income, per worker share of wages/GDP, the percentage of total income that is invested in the domestic economy (in the post-1970 period), and an increase in the percentage of total income accounted for by foreign-owned firms.

Much as Latin America's stage of premature difficult import substitution industrialization sapped the strength of the local industrial class with its overreliance on nonlocal capital to produce import substitutes in the second phase of industrialization, Puerto Rico's particular form of export industrialization and its dependence on nonlocal capital also had the same effect on the growth of the local entrepreneurial class and on skilled workers. Too few local entrepreneurs were given the opportunity or the institutional support to reach a level of competence such that, in local enterprises, they might have been able to dominate, or at least participate to a significant degree, in contributing to employment and income via the export of manufactured goods to the United States and to the world market.

Local enterprises tended to be relatively small-scale with relatively few employees, as Fomento's attention was geared to attracting and promoting larger-scale U.S. enterprises. In something of a self-fulfilling prophecy embedded in the Operation Bootstrap strategy, the belief that local capital and local entrepreneurs could not be at the center of the industrialization and development process led to decisions that effectively dictated that conclusion, leaving local entrepreneurs, especially in manufacturing, to operate at the margins of the industrialization process.

Local Industry and Local Entrepreneurs

There are and always have been local entrepreneurs and local industry in Puerto Rico, of course, as a look at some of the quantitative measures of import substitution industrialization later in this chapter will reveal and as Table 3.1 above and the impact of nonlocal capital on local capital in Puerto Rico already have suggested (see Aponte 1999 for interesting details of local versus nonlocal corporations).[14] Nonetheless, the Operation Bootstrap strategy, qua industrialization strategy, never gave prominence or priority to the encouragement or to the establishment of local producers as the base of the local economy, as the discussion of the rise of Fomento, Moscoso's initiatives, the

Perloff Plan, and the formulation of the Operation Bootstrap strategy in the previous chapter underscored. Nor, apparently, were nonlocal capital and nonlocal sources of finance seriously viewed as functioning primarily as a complementary force to local capital formation and to the growth of local finance in the manufacturing sector. If that had been the case, then nonlocal sources of finance and entrepreneurship would have been less and less necessary with time as local sources of finance and ownership would have blossomed and made nonlocal capital less essential.

At best, the local industrial sector played a distant second role within Fomento's overall industrialization strategy, when the sector was even targeted at all.[15] Nevertheless, for some time now, the local manufacturing sector, small though it may be relative to the U.S. subsidiaries that dominate, has been a more reliable source of economic stability in the local economy than has been the nonlocal sector, and that role cannot be underestimated, especially as Puerto Rico looks to the future.

For example, between 1981–1982 and 1991–1992, a period of slow economic growth, new local industrial operations (both startups and expansions) was responsible for creating an additional 11,294 jobs. Over the same period, however, 4,658 jobs lost were in that sector due to the closing of local firms for any variety of reasons, for a net employment gain of 6,636 jobs attributable to local industry over that ten-year period. Even this contributed to only a modest increase in manufacturing employment of less than 700 net jobs per year from local firms.

Looking at nonlocal, primarily U.S. firms over the same period, 9,647 additional new job positions were created. However, the shutdown of nonlocal firms reduced employment in that sector by a total of 14,933 posts, for a net loss of 5,286 jobs in the nonlocal industrial sector over the same ten years (Marqués Velasco 1994: 4–5). Thus, all of the anemic gains in manufacturing employment in government-promoted firms over the 1981–1992 decade, gains almost so small— 1,350 net jobs or 135 per year—as to be unbelievable from a sector so heralded by its supporters, came from the net expansion of employment in local firms relative to employment in nonlocal enterprises supported by the government's promotion efforts.

This is a first indication of the potential significance of the local industrial sector for the future and of the full importance of putting local entrepreneurs at the center of any future development strategy, be they in industry or services. Locally owned firms have been a more reliable source of economic expansion and job creation over the long term, whether by virtue of their smaller size and more labor-intensive nature or because of the stronger linkage effects such firms have within the local economic structure.

Carroll's analysis (1993: 300–301) of domestic linkages and the impact of nonlocal capital confirmed the importance of local capital over the entire Operation Bootstrap period. An expansion of domestic linkages, which means a more integrated local economy, contributed to net employment gains even as over time the net impact of nonlocal capital on employment was negative. In fact, without the creation of new domestic linkages due to local entrepreneurs meeting the needs of unserved niches in the economic structure, the overall impact of nonlocal capital on employment would have been even more negative, as the growing inflow of nonlocal capital investment tended to generate fewer linkage effects over time, thus further reducing its impact on job creation (Carroll 1993: 301–305).

By the mid-1960s, Fomento had reoriented its industrial promotion focus away from the lower-wage, labor-intensive industries, such as textiles and clothing, that had characterized much of the early phase of Operation Bootstrap, as firms in that sector either closed or began to move their operations elsewhere, succumbing to the unavoidable effects of a changing and more competitive world economy.[16] In Fomento's second phase of promotions, capital-intensive industries, especially pharmaceuticals and other drug and chemical companies (and for a short ill-fated time, oil refiners), were the industries most receptive to the federal and local tax incentives that motivated industrial relocation to and expansion in Puerto Rico.

Fomento targeted these producers on the rationale that, having a large and costly physical capital commitment, such firms would be more stable investors at the same time that they paid higher wages for the more productive jobs such firms would provide. However, the job-creating capacity of each additional dollar of investment fell over time in the nonlocal manufacturing sector as these more capital-intensive firms with high capital-labor ratios took the place of the shrinking labor-intensive firms in the apparel and textile industries, which tended to hire more workers per dollar of fixed investment.

The relatively limited job-creation capacity of manufacturing compared to other sectors of the economy can be seen in Table 3.2, which

**Table 3.2   Employment Generated per $1 Million Increase in
             Income, 1992**

Sector	Additional Jobs
Agriculture, forestry, fishing	138.58
Mining and construction	21.29
Manufacturing	10.51
(Food and kindred products)	(7.47)
(Drugs)	(8.76)
(Other chemical products)	(22.12)
(Machinery)	(20.35)
(Professional and scientific instruments)	(16.87)
Transportation services	41.56
Communications	35.91
Public utilities	13.52
Wholesale and retail trade	37.58
Finance, insurance, real estate	6.34
Personal services	55.39
Business services	37.84
Repair services and auto rental	15.18
Amusement and recreation	70.59
Government	52.78
Total	25.49

Source: Ruíz 1994: 65.
Note: For manufacturing, more detailed sector multipliers are shown in parentheses.

shows the number of jobs created for each $1 million increase in
income in the economy. The relatively low employment-generation
capacity of manufacturing—on average about eleven workers per $1
million of extra income in the economy—at least partly is the consequence of the capital-intensity of the industry and the higher level of
wages paid. The low-employment effect also reflects the lower degree
of local linkages associated with the manufacturing sector due to the
Hirschmanian diminishing returns effect of having "too much" nonlocal investment relative to the optimal level of such investment within
the total investment profile of the economy.

The structural shift of the industrial program from labor-intensive
to more capital-intensive production helps to explain much of the net
loss in employment in the nonlocal manufacturing sector. The effect of
a rising capital-output ratio on employment creation can be seen indirectly in how the number of jobs created per dollar of final demand
changed over time in Table 3.2. For example, each $1 million of final
demand was estimated to generate 101.00 jobs in 1967, 72.55 in 1972,

54.26 in 1977, 49.32 in 1982, and 42.36 in 1994. Looking at the jobs created from the export of manufactured goods, which gives a better idea of the effect of changes over time in the capital-output ratio in manufacturing, every $1 million of manufactured exports generated 82.06 jobs in 1967, 45.07 in 1972, 24.71 in 1977, 27.67 in 1982, and 19.52 in 1994 (Castañer and Ruíz Mercado 1997: 25). Of course there are more effects at work than just a rising capital-output ratio that affect employment generation, such as rising worker productivity and fewer linkages, but the numbers are suggestive of the nature of the underlying problem associated with rising capital-output ratios as the industrial structure of the economy evolved and fewer workers were employed per dollar of expenditure.

While depending on nonlocal capital and nonlocal firms as the base of the industrialization process, Puerto Rico could have done little to thwart the shift in the locus of production toward capital-intensive producers, as all export-oriented firms needed to both think and operate globally in increasingly competitive markets if they were to survive. As tariffs and other barriers to the movement of goods and capital fell rapidly around the world in the 1960s and 1970s, the attraction of lower wages and fewer restrictions on production in other countries meant those multinational firms that were labor-intensive would move from Puerto Rico to other relatively low-wage locations.[17] Add to this the fact that U.S. federal minimum wage legislation was made applicable in Puerto Rico, thus creating a wage-push effect, and it is understandable why profit-maximizing international firms with large labor costs as a share of total costs relocated from Puerto Rico to lower-wage locations such as the Dominican Republic and Asia. This was inevitable and, from Puerto Rico's viewpoint, in many ways desirable. Better-paying jobs were, and should have been, a goal of the development program all along.

At the same time, and as a reflection of these global production shifts, local producers had begun to expand into what can be called "fragmented industries" (Marqués Velasco 1994: 5–6)—for example, food products, printing, cement, lumber, cardboard, and other niche areas not being served adequately, or at all, by nonlocal producers in the changing global economic structure. Local industries with the greatest value added in production were chemicals, food products, electric products, instruments, construction materials, and printing (Aponte 1999: 363). Many of these local firms were producers or suppliers of nonstandardized products that, while not quite nontraded goods in the usual sense, were goods that do seem to have some of the characteristics of such commodities in that there is some degree of protection from import competition for reasons of product specificity, size of the market served (that is, lack of significant economies or diseconomies of scale), time of delivery considerations (e.g., in printing), or other characteristics that reduced external competition.[18] Many of these same products that local producers began to manufacture were also, it is important to note, traditional ISI products around which other nations have initiated their industrialization takeoffs.

In the past, local manufacturers could find little competitive space for contending with producers of traded goods, from clothing to leather goods to packaged food to televisions to computer parts, which were primarily imported from the United States, making import substitution based on head-to-head competition without some kind of protection difficult for startup companies. But over time, there increasingly emerged arenas for local producers to begin some degree of import substitution for traded goods (e.g., bagged cement and, from there, expanding into ready-mix; furniture; rubber and plastic goods; and clothing, such as printed tee-shirts) and quasi-nontraded goods (e.g., fresh and frozen chickens, fresh and canned milk, and other food products, like pasta) where, in relatively short time periods and with some assistance, reasonable levels of efficiency could be reached in these industries. In fact, it could be argued that many of these were products that always had offered a degree of import substitution possibilities in Puerto Rico but that had been ignored as building blocks for sustained development from the start of the industrialization program.[19] Some of the firms in these industries owed their existence to assistance from Fomento. For others, their existence suggests that, with effort and with a different vision by Fomento, the expansion of these industries could have played a much larger role in the overall development and industrialization project.[20]

At least a part of the slowdown in growth in the Puerto Rican economy beginning in the 1970s was due to changing international forces that impacted high- and low-tech and labor- and capital-intensive firms alike, wherever they may be located. With the dual and seemingly opposing tendencies for both "downsizing" and mergers of large national and multinational firms, there has emerged a consolidating process that has tended to benefit the balance sheet of the larger and more adaptable multinational corporations, but often at the expense of employment and incomes for workers and economies where those firms operate, including Puerto Rico (Colón 1994: 39–46). Economies that are going to be successful in this new, more open environment are going to be those economies that demonstrate a capacity to adapt quickly to changing external conditions within this more fluid environment. But they also are going to be economies that have a solid base of local production, including locally owned manufacturing and services that, to some degree, provide insulation from the buffeting forces of international production and its inevitable ups and downs and uncertainties.[21]

It is sometimes thought that the Economic Development Administration (Fomento) has promoted only nonlocal enterprises and has neglected the local sector entirely. This, however, is incorrect, at least in terms of the total number of enterprises supported by Fomento. From 1982 to 1996, Fomento promoted a total of 2,856 businesses. Of these, 61 percent were local enterprises. In fact, over the entire 1982–1996 period, local promotions exceeded nonlocal businesses promoted in almost every year.

On the other hand, looking at the investment commitment of enterprises promoted by Fomento and not just the raw number of promotions, the story looks more familiar, as nonlocal investments dominate the totals.[22] Over the 1982–1996 period, all promoted firms promised to invest $2.6 billion and to pay wages and salaries totaling $2.2 billion. Looking at Fomento's promotion from this angle, it was nonlocal enterprises that had the lion's share of the totals, with $2.2 billion of promised investment (84.6 percent of the total) and $1.5 billion (68.2 percent) of total committed wages and salaries.

Local enterprises did commit to more employment *relative* to the size of their investments than was the case for nonlocal investment. Again, this demonstrates the potential importance of a more substantial effort to promote local investments. The impact on employment per dollar of investment tends, on average, to be larger in local enterprises than for nonlocal investments. Of a total of 173,195 projected jobs, nonlocal enterprises committed to hiring 111,206 employees or 64 percent of the total despite the fact that their investment commitments totaled nearly 85 percent of all investments. Local firms, on the other hand, committed to providing 36 percent of the total jobs with only about 15 percent of projected investment (U.S. Government Accounting Office 1997: app. 3, 39–44).

The Manufacturing Sector's Importance
to the Economy: Myth and Reality

One near truism among those who analyze the Puerto Rican economy, and certainly this has been the perspective of the Puerto Rican government, has been that the manufacturing sector is the most important branch of the economy. This "truism," however, like many axioms perhaps, is less accurate than it seems on the surface. Just how important and how significant to the economy has been the manufacturing sector, which has been the focus of Operation Bootstrap's most intense efforts since the late 1940s?

If one looks at the contribution of the manufacturing sector to Puerto Rico's gross domestic product (*producto bruto interno* in Puerto Rico's national accounts), then it is true that its share of production and income has been the largest for some time. However, as a share of gross national product *(producto bruto)*, which is the relevant measure of income when considering the potential welfare of income to residents, the story is quite different (see Dietz 1986: 245–246, 255–259 for an earlier discussion).[23]

Table 3.3 provides some of the details relevant to better understanding this issue. The view that manufacturing is the most significant sector of the economy is derived from looking at the contribution of the manufacturing sector to total GDP. Since 1980, manufacturing has contributed more than a third of total GDP, rising by 1990 to almost 40 percent of GDP. In 2000, the manufacturing sector was responsible for nearly 40 percent of total production taking place within the economy. In 1980, the second most important sector was trade, which contributed 15.7 percent of GDP, a bit more than a third of the contribution of manufacturing. In 2000, the trade sector had slipped slightly to third in importance (with 13.8 percent of GDP), as the FIRE (finance, insurance, and real estate) sector rose to second in importance (16.2 percent), followed by other services (10.6 percent). By these measures, the manufacturing sector has been anywhere from two to three or more times as important as any other sector in contributing to Puerto Rico's total GDP, and it is from looking at such a comparison, based on the contribution of different sectors to total GDP, that the claim for the dominant importance of the manufacturing sector to the Puerto Rican economy is derived.

Table 3.3 highlights the large and growing GDP/GNP gap in the economy, reflecting the outflow of a large part of the income created that actually belongs to nonresidents, primarily owners of the U.S. cor-

Table 3.3   The GDP/GNP Gap and Manufacturing's Share of Output, 1960–2000

	GDP[a]	GNP[a]	GDP – GNP[a]	GDP – GNP as % of GNP	Manuf. as % of GDP	Net Manuf. as % of GNP[b]
1960	1,691.9	1,676.4	15.5	0.9	21.7	17.4
1970	5,034.7	4,687.5	347.2	7.4	23.6	16.7
1980	14,480.0	11,073.8	3,406.2	30.8	36.8	18.2
1990	30,603.9	21,619.1	8,984.8	41.6	39.6	12.3
2000	61,044.9	41,441.7	19,603.2	47.3	38.3	7.3

Sources: Dietz 1986: 244, 246; Junta de Planificación 1981: A-4; 1986: A-4; 1999: A-1, A-10, A-12; 2002: A-10, A-12.

Notes: a. In millions of current dollars.

b. Manufacturing income less proprietor's income repatriated outside Puerto Rico, as % of GNP.

porations operating in Puerto Rico. By 2000, this net outflow was equivalent to nearly than half (47.3 percent) of Puerto Rico's total GNP. The net outflow of $19,603.2 million (the GDP/GNP gap) meant that of every $1 of income created within Puerto Rico in 2000, a minimum of $0.32 left the local economy to be received by nonlocal income recipients.[24]

The bulk of the income leaving came from manufacturing profits earned in, but not belonging to, the Puerto Rican economy.[25] In fact, a strong argument can be made that even the GDP figures are overstated as a measure of the actual production taking place in Puerto Rico. Due to the nature of the federal tax laws after 1976, corporations have been able to shift income actually earned elsewhere to Puerto Rico via transfer pricing and other mechanisms to appear as part of local production value. Puerto Rico's actual GDP as a measure of output produced within Puerto Rico's borders, especially from 1976 until 1996, was less than the reported amount, especially in the manufactured-goods sector (Hall and Jones 1999).

The last column of Table 3.3 calculates the net contribution of the manufacturing sector to GNP—that is, the contribution of the manufacturing sector to the income actually received by and available for consumption, saving, and government spending by Puerto Rican residents. By this measure, the manufacturing sector's contribution to Puerto Rico's income is decidedly more modest, though not insignificant, though it decreased from 17.4 percent of GNP in 1960 to about 7 percent in 2000.

However, never over the period of Operation Bootstrap has manufacturing added much more than 18 percent to total GNP, and in recent years the contribution of the sector to local income has fallen quite sharply at the same time that its contribution to GDP has risen. These two statistics are not in conflict; they are rather part and parcel of the same phenomenon and reflective of a fundamental problem that has plagued Operation Bootstrap since the 1970s at least. That the GDP/GNP gap grows wider at the same time that manufacturing's net contribution to GNP falls is indicative of the larger returns being earned by the owners of the nonlocal firms located in Puerto Rico relative to income received in Puerto Rico, returns received as repatriated profits, and dividends that are unavailable for use in the local economy.[26] These figures also echo the relatively small contribution to employment and local income generation made by these capital-intensive producers.

Looking at the contribution of the different sectors of the economy to GNP, and not to GDP, in 2000, we find the shares shown in Table 3.4. From this it is observed that transportation and public utilities; trade; finance, insurance, and real estate; other services; and the government sector all contributed a larger share to total GNP than did the manufacturing sector. And it is precisely in these sectors that local Puerto Rican entrepreneurial activity is most active.

What is clear from Tables 3.3 and 3.4 is that the claim for the overriding importance of the manufacturing sector in contributing to total income, if income is measured by GNP, cannot be sustained. Indeed, and in ways that have not always been fully considered or even under-

Table 3.4 Contribution to GNP by Sector, 2000

Sector	% of GNP	% of Employment
Agriculture	1.3	2.1
Manufacturing	7.3	13.7
Construction and mining	4.4	7.3
Transportation/public utilities	10.4	4.7
Trade	20.3	20.6
Finance, insurance, real estate	23.9	3.7
Other services	15.6	26.5
Government	13.2	21.5

Source: Junta de Planificación 2002: A-10, A-38. Total does not add to 100% because the statistical discrepancy item is not shown.

stood, it has been local productive activity and not the manufacturing export sector that has sustained the economy since the 1970s at least. Finance, insurance, and real estate provide more than three times as large a share of GNP as manufacturing, showing the importance of these services and supporting, to a degree, the view of those who believe that the shift to Section 936 tax exemption in 1976 was pivotal in stimulating the financial sector's dominance in the local economic structure over that of the manufacturing sector. While not all of the value in these activities is generated by local firms, it is in precisely the service sectors that local entrepreneurs have found substantial space for their operations.

In terms of employment generation, more than one in five employed workers are in the public sector (actually more, since the public utilities share of employment includes public employees too). The "other services" sector makes the greatest contribution to employment. In terms of job creation, manufacturing is but fourth in importance. Services of all types, excluding government, accounted in 2000 for 55.6 percent of all employment.

Comparing the share of employment to the share of income of the manufacturing sector is revealing too. It points to the relatively low output and income generation of the manufacturing sector per 1 percent of the labor force. The finance, insurance, and real estate sector, on the other hand, adds substantially more to income than it does to employment, indicating the greater productivity of each worker in that sector. Each 1 percent of the labor force employed in manufacturing produced 0.53 percent of total GNP in 2000. Each 1 percent of the labor force in finance, insurance, and real estate, by comparison, added 6.43 percent to total GNP. For all services, excluding government, each 1 percent of the labor force contributed 1.26 percent of total GNP, indicating, for local income generation, the greater efficacy of services than manufacturing.

What explains these differences in labor productivity in distinct sectors? At least in part these differences are due to the degree of linkages and internal articulation within the local economic structure. These disparities in output per worker reflect real productivity differences and local income-earning opportunities in different sectors of the economy. In the services sectors, more income created in the local economy remains within the economy due to ownership differences and the more labor-intensive nature of such businesses.

The Myth of Exports as the Engine of Development

Economists often point to exports as an "engine of development." By this it is meant that exports provide a means for an economy to "grow its GDP" rapidly by producing for demand beyond its own internal market. There is no doubt that the ability to export, if it is a capacity attained by local entrepreneurs with strong internal linkages in the local economy, can be an important component of an overall development strategy. The optimal industrial phasing of the East Asian economies summarized in Chapter 2 highlighted the gains to productivity, incomes, local linkages, and technology acquisition that can be attained from a successful import substitution and then export sequencing process. Such a staging of industrialization improves efficiency and worker productivity and contributes to increasing local incomes and living standards.

But exporting alone can rarely carry the weight of generating the majority of employment in an economy, and a country that exports, per se, is not necessarily exporting efficiently nor is it necessarily exporting the range of goods that might create the greatest local returns. All countries export goods and services. If exporting alone were the key to development, all countries would already be developed.

Exports in Puerto Rico, particularly manufactured exports produced predominately by the U.S. firms promoted by Operation Bootstrap, have not shown a tendency "to grow" the economy. In 1967, 20.3 percent of total employment was due to manufactured exports. By 1994, only 23.6 percent of total employment could be ascribed to exports of goods of all types, despite the growth of the manufacturing sector as a share of GDP. Over the same period, the employment generating effect of manufactured exports fell from 113.6 jobs per $1 million of exports to but 34.5 jobs in 1994, once again demonstrating the weakness of the job-creation capacity of the economy given the existing structure of exporting based on U.S. subsidiary companies (Castañer and Ruíz Mercado 1997: 25, 27, 30–31).

Measuring Local Economic Activity: Linkages and Articulation

For an economy to have hope for sustained growth over time, there are several key ingredients that must be present, in particular an appropriately educated labor force and the capacity for indigenous technological acquisition. These factor inputs, however, need to be part of a comprehensive strategy of what economists refer to as structural change, one of the components of which is the creation of backward and forward linkages in the local economy via import substitution industrialization or other strategic means to expand such linkages.[27] The optimal path of industrial industrialization followed by the East Asian economies examined in Chapter 2 is one example of how to achieve desirable structural change and an articulated and internally linked economy, one in which domestic productive structures become more efficient and more competitive on world markets.

One technique for analyzing linkages in an economy is to estimate sectoral multipliers. In a fascinating and comprehensive study of the impact of federal transfer payments, economist Angel Ruíz (1994: 63) estimated the value of sectoral income (output) multipliers at between 1.12 and 3.53 for 1992, with an average value for the entire economy of 1.49.[28] While these multipliers were calculated specifically to weigh the significance of federal transfers on Puerto Rico's income and output, they can be assumed to be reasonable proxy measures for the impact of any change in income in a sector, whatever the source, on the total income and production in that sector and, aggregating all sectors, on the economy as a whole. It is important to note that these multiplier effects are on Puerto Rico's GDP, however, not on its GNP.

What does a particular multiplier value mean? The closer the value of the multiplier is to 1, the fewer are the local linkages of that particular sector with the local economy. A multiplier of exactly 1 for a sector would mean there were no local linkages, either backward or forward, for that sector. That is, a multiplier of 1 means that a $1 change in income (say, from higher wages being paid) in a particular sector would have exactly zero secondary (indirect) effects on total income and output beyond the initial $1 change of income. In other words, the receipt of an additional $1 of income would not generate any additional income (or spending) beyond the original injection of the $1 of income, suggesting that all of this additional income "leaked" from that sector either into savings or out of the economy entirely. Such a sector is completely "unlinked" to, or disarticulated from, the rest of the economy.

A multiplier value greater than 1 indicates that there are secondary effects of the sector from the original $1 expenditure, and the larger the multiplier, the larger are these secondary effects and the linkages of that sector to the rest of the economy. Table 3.5 shows some of these esti-

Table 3.5   Estimates of Output and Income Multipliers, 1992

Sector	Output/Income Multiplier
Agriculture, forestry, fishing	2.78
Mining and construction	3.53
Manufacturing	1.59
(Food and kindred products)	(1.29)
(Drugs)	(1.12)
(Other chemical products)	(2.93)
(Machinery)	(2.61)
(Professional and scientific instruments)	(1.55)
Transportation services	1.77
Communications	1.85
Public utilities	1.50
Wholesale and retail trade	1.14
Finance, insurance, real estate	1.35
Personal services	1.87
Business services	1.73
Repair services and auto rental	1.96
Amusement and recreation	1.66
Government	1.45
Total	1.49

Source: Ruiz 1994: 63.
Note: For manufacturing, more detailed sector multipliers are shown in parentheses.

mated multiplier values for key sectors of the economy. The largest multiplier was in the mining and construction sector. The impact was especially strong in construction, as additional income in the sector led to more home building, purchases of new houses, purchases of materials, government construction, and so on, resulting in multiple rounds of additional spending and income from the original injection of extra income. The relatively large multiplier value suggests that a significant part of the inputs to construction activity, especially residential construction, were locally provided or produced in 1992 via contractors, ready-mix cement, hardware stores *(ferreterías),* etc., so any increase in income was spent again and again in the economy through these induced linked effects.[29] In effect, an additional $1 million of income initially spent in the mining and construction sector would generate an additional $2.53 million in income and output for the economy via this sector beyond the initial injection, for a total change in income of $3.53 million from direct (the original $1 million) plus the indirect (the induced $2.53 million) income effects.

The income/output multiplier for the pharmaceuticals sector, virtually all of which is nonlocally owned, was 1.12, the lowest in the table.[30] Each $1 of additional income in the sector generated only an additional $0.12 in induced income in other parts of the local economy. For the manufacturing sector as a whole, the multiplier was 1.59, indicating that an initial injection of $1 of income into the manufacturing sector would generate a further $0.59 in indirect income (output) for the economy beyond the initial $1 direct increase in spending. This somewhat low multiplier value is at least partly due to the structure of the sector and its external orientation, which results in most inputs being purchased from the United States and most outputs being sold in the overseas market, thus reducing the extent of backward and forward linkages in the local economy. It also reflects the small share of the wage bill of these firms and the indirect impact that any additional spending by workers from their labor income earned in that sector would have on the rest of the economy, as most of the income created in manufacturing leaks from the local economy.

It is necessary to be a bit cautious in interpreting these multipliers, however, since the absolute effect of a sector depends upon the interaction of the multiplier value with the actual amount of new spending that gets introduced into that sector. To illustrate this point, let us ask the following question: What would be the impact of an increase of $500,000 of income in the economy as a whole? The overall impact, using the aggregate multiplier calculated by Ruíz, would be an ultimate growth in total income and output equal to $745,000 (1.49 × $500,000).

However, the contribution of each individual sector to this growth in total output and income depends upon the importance of each sector to total production—that is, it is dependent on the prevailing structure of production as well as existing linkages. Table 3.6 illustrates this point by estimating the impact for each sector of an additional $500,000 of income in the economy (the total is not exactly equal to $745,000 due to rounding to three decimal places in the "Sector Share" column). Thus, even though the mining and construction sector has a large multiplier value, indicating something important about the degree of linkages of that sector to the local economy, the relatively small structural importance of the sector to the total income of the economy compared to total output means that only a total of approximately $15,885 of the economy's total income would be generated in this sector, equal to 2.1 percent of the total income resulting from the hypothetical injection of $500,000 additional income into the economy.

PUERTO RICO

Table 3.6   Sectoral Contribution to Total Output (GDP) from a $500,000 Change in Total Income, 1992

Sector	Sector Share[a]	Total Contribution[b]
Agriculture, forestry, fishing	0.014	$19,460
Mining and construction	0.008	15,885
Manufacturing	0.303	240,885
(Food and kindred products)	0.095	(61,275)
(Drugs)	0.026	(14,560)
(Other chemical products)	0.006	(8,790)
(Machinery)	0.010	(13,050)
(Professional and scientific instruments)	0.008	(6,200)
Transportation services	0.024	21,240
Communications	0.016	14,800
Public utilities	0.072	54,000
Wholesale and retail trade	0.165	94,050
Finance, insurance, real estate	0.209	141,075
Personal services	0.014	13,090
Business services	0.062	53,630
Repair services and auto rental	0.024	23,520
Amusement and recreation	0.003	2,490
Professional and other services	0.070	42,000
Government	0.016	11,600

Source: Calculated from Ruíz 1994: 62.
Notes: a. Share of each $1 of extra income spent in each respective sector.
b. Equal to $500,000 × sector share (column 2) × output multiplier for the sector (from Table 3.4). For example, for "Agriculture, forestry, fishing": $500,000 × 0.014 × 2.78 = $19,460.

On the other hand, the manufacturing sector's current structural importance to producing GDP (but not GNP) means that its absolute contribution to total output is large, even though it has a smaller multiplier value than mining and construction. Thus, of the $500,000 new income, $151,500 (0.303 of the total) would be estimated to be spent in the manufacturing sector in the first round of spending. Given the multiplier in manufacturing, the indirect effects of this initial injection of spending in manufacturing would be estimated to be an additional $89,385 of spending/income/output in the rest of the economy for a total impact, equal to direct plus indirect spending, of $240,885 for that sector. Thus, even though manufacturing has a smaller multiplier effect on the economy than some other sectors, the relatively large size of the sector in total GDP means its absolute effect from any change in total spending remains large.

Again, it needs to be emphasized that these multipliers are for effects on GDP. If the multipliers for GNP were to be calculated, the overall impact of manufacturing to GNP would be substantially lower due to the leakage of income from Puerto Rico to the owners of the U.S. subsidiaries that dominate the manufacturing sector.

What this exercise indicates, however, is not only the significance of the particular value of the multiplier for each sector on the economy but also the importance of the structural characteristics of the economy, particularly the relative size of the sectors to total income generation when compared to total income and total output. Either a relatively larger mining and construction sector with the same multiplier value or a manufacturing sector more articulated and linked with the local economy would contribute to a larger increase in total income and output for the economy as a whole from any change in income, thus helping to increase total and average incomes more rapidly, at least as measured by GDP. Further, greater articulation would also mean a smaller GDP/GNP gap over time.

We already have seen from the research of Carroll (1993) that backward linkages have decreased over time, especially with the advent of the drug and chemical industries. In a study done by Fomento staff members John Stewart and Saúl Chico Pamias, and again using the Puerto Rican Planning Board's input-output tables as Ruíz did, it was found that backward linkages decreased after 1977, having increased over the period 1963–1977 (Stewart and Pamias 1990, cited in Carroll 1993: 186–187). These time periods roughly correspond with the positive/negative pattern that Carroll (1993) found in his more comprehensive study. Thus any expectation that the multiplier values in manufacturing might rise to match the structural importance of the sector will require that there be a refocus of investment within the economy designed specifically to expand these local linkage effects so as to reap their positive benefits.

Possibilities for Import Substitution

Any discussion about optimal and suboptimal industrial sequencing, about skipped and premature stages of industrialization, about the expansion of backward and forward linkages or of the importance of expanded local ownership of manufacturing, would be substantially beside the point if Puerto Rico never had and did not now have realistic opportunities to do more import substitution industrialization as was done in East Asia or in Latin America. As already noted in Chapter 2, there always have been skeptics who believed that Puerto Rico's relatively small population size meant an internal market that was much too limited for ISI. As a general statement, this must be patently incorrect.

Whether or not ISI is feasible depends upon the particular industries being considered and their characteristics, including the optimum *firm* size and *not* industry size for attaining economies of scale in those industries.[31] It is obviously easier to approach the optimum level of production and thus be able to take advantage of economies of scale which reduce per unit costs of production for a relatively labor-intensive producer of, say, tee-shirts or eggs or milk, than it is likely to be for capital-intensive, high-fixed-cost producers of automobiles or air-conditioning units or kitchen appliances (U.S. Department of Commerce 1979: vol. 2, pp. 91–106).

The relevant cost comparison for potential ISI firms is to contrast production costs in Puerto Rico (ATC_{PR}) with the full per unit cost of imported goods (ATC_M), where the latter includes per unit shipping, insurance, and other nonproduction costs which act as a form of protection for local industries, shielding them from the full effects of unfettered import competition at the net cost of production.

In thinking about ISI, it also is necessary to look to the future, and that future can well include, in fact it should include, the exporting of at least some of the output of the domestic ISI firms to international markets, as occurred in South Korea and Taiwan and other East Asian economies (and in Japan before them) during their phase of easy export substitution following easy ISI. It is thus important to ask which ISI industries might also be likely candidates for export substitution expansion to the United States and to world markets at some point in the future. Then the issue of the size of Puerto Rico's internal market becomes somewhat moot. Exporting can allow further economies of scale not yet exploited in the home market as enterprises become more efficient and are able to compete with existing international producers by expanding beyond their always more limited domestic market.

Puerto Rico's import coefficient, which is a measure of the share of total income spent on imports, rose during the capital-intensive phase of industrialization. An increasing percentage of each $1 of income was spent on imports, rising to $0.89 in 1990, though this had fallen to about 83 percent of GNP by 2000. This large share of income spent on imports is suggestive of potential import substitution possibilities. Such a large import coefficient means that most income in Puerto Rico tends to leak from the local economy primarily to the United States to pay for imported goods rather than remaining in the local economy to stimulate local production as would be the case in a more linked economic structure. The low multiplier values shown in Table 3.5 are related to the relatively high import coefficient values presented in Table 3.7, the last column of which shows the share of income being spent on consumer goods imports. The bulk of imports are intermediate and capital goods, many of which are destined for the U.S. subsidiaries promoted by Fomento. This simply reinforces the point that any import substitution in consumer goods most certainly will have to target not just the local market but, as for the East Asian economies, export markets as well, if they are to reach maximum efficiency. But these figures also are suggestive of the possibilities for backward production linkages in supplying intermediate and input needs of existing enterprises.

Among consumer goods imports, nondurable consumer goods continue to constitute about three-quarters of the total, amounting to $4.5 billion in 2000 and 98 percent of all nondurable consumer good purchases. There would seem to be ample room for import substitution in at least some lines of these goods. There is a viable market for such goods that is now serviced primarily by imports.

It might be questioned whether Puerto Rico has the policy instruments to carry out an import substitution strategy. After all, when ISI is

Table 3.7   Import Coefficients, 1950–2000

	Import Coefficient[a]	Consumer Import Coefficient[b]
1950	46.4	22.9
1960	54.0	21.8
1970	53.5	18.1
1980	81.4	22.0
1990	88.8	19.1
1995	76.7	18.4
2000	82.9	16.2

Sources: Junta de Planificación 1981: A-1, A-17; 1989: A-1, A-52; 1999: A-1, A-29; 2002: A-1, A-29.

Notes: a. Total adjusted imports by value / GNP

b. Nondurable and durable consumer goods imports / GNP

pursued in most economies, as discussed in Chapter 2, it is typical to protect new firms with infant-industry tariffs that inflate the price of imported goods, making it easier for new domestic producers to succeed. Given the current political status, Puerto Rico cannot impose tariffs on its own. Is it reasonable, then, to expect new producers with their inevitable transitional inefficiencies to be able to emerge and succeed in head-to-head competition with imported goods?

As the next section suggests, ISI already has taken place in certain sectors that have what can be called "natural protection." But it is also the case that, even in the absence of the tariff policy tool, an equivalent policy instrument *is* available and that is a subsidy. A subsidy can be in the form of low-cost loans, tax and other fee exemptions, assistance with training costs and technology acquisition, and a whole host of specific actions designed to reduce the costs of production of local producers vis-à-vis the costs of imported goods.

In Chapter 6, one specific suggestion is made as to how the United States could provide funds to the Puerto Rican government derived from taxes collected on U.S. corporations in Puerto Rico to be used to finance desirable development projects, some of which could be for ISI in manufacturing or services. The commonwealth status and the lack of access to the traditional infant-industry tariff policy tool is thus not an insurmountable barrier to forging a more integrated, linked local economy where ISI is integral to the overall strategy.

Existing or "Natural" ISI

The fact that ISI has not been a part of Puerto Rico's official development strategy since the aborted state-owned intermediate ISI of the late 1940s does not mean that import substitution has been wholly absent from the economic scene since then. It just has not been a part of government policy to explicitly target or promote ISI. However, due to the "natural protection" from import competition provided by shipping, insurance, and other costs associated with importing,[32] as well as other factors (just-in-time inventory concerns, for example) that provide local producers with a potential market, there exists the possibility for producers in Puerto Rico to be able to sell at lower prices if ATC_{PR} is less than ATC_M in particular markets. What evidence is there for such a possibility?

In a comprehensive input-output study, Rivera Figueroa (1988: 72, 74) found quite a number of sectors and a large number of products for which, over the period 1963–1977, local inputs had replaced imported goods. Such "natural" ISI was observed in the finance sector, paper products, printing and publishing, primary metals, health services, furniture and wood products, soft drinks, electricity, some categories of machinery, textiles, and apparel, and some chemical products, to name just some of the sectors identified.

In paper products the change in the coefficient of total input demand from the input-output matrix was equal to 0.3913, while the change in local input demand was equal to 0.4208. Thus the change in the import coefficient in this sector was equal to –0.0295 (0.3913 – 0.4208), indicating that imports were being replaced by local production—that is, there was import substitution taking place in this sector.[33] Likewise in furniture and wood products, the change in total input demand equaled 0.1314 while the change in local input demand was 0.2410, giving a change in the coefficient of import demand in the sector of –0.1096, again demonstrating that import substitution was taking place (Rivera Figueroa 1988: 72, 74).

In other sectors, both local production and import demand grew together, indicating that, for some sectors at least, Puerto Rican production was competitive with imported goods or that Puerto Rican producers were able to find and serve particular niches that imported goods could not satisfy in particular industries. This complementary tendency for local inputs to grow alongside imports was observed in the following sectors: stone, clay, and glass; construction; some agriculture; transportation services; sugar refining and confectioneries; leather; and trade.

For example, in the stone, clay, and glass sector (goods destined primarily for construction purposes), the change in the coefficient of total input demand was 0.2409, while the change in the coefficient of local input demand was 0.1969. Thus, while local production grew in this sector, so too did import demand (0.2409 – 0.1969 = 0.0440). In agriculture, the coefficient of total input demand grew by 0.2019, that of local input demand by 0.1724 and of import demand by 0.0295, indicating that local production serviced more of the growth in local input demand than did imports (Rivera Figueroa 1988: 69, 71).

These trends are important, indicating first of all the capacity of the existing pool of domestic entrepreneurs to innovate and to achieve levels of efficiency comparable to those attained by U.S. producers. Local producers are selling in the local market or are serving niches unexplored by foreign exporters or in which they are not interested in supplying. Still, the aggregate impact of these trends in local production was less than it might have been. Over the 1963–1977 period, 76.2 percent of the change in total output in the economy was the consequence of a response to changes in final demand, while the remainder, 23.8 percent, resulted from changes in the productive structure, such as the expansion of backward linkages in production noted above (Rivera Figueroa 1988: 83). There *was* greater integration of the economy over this early period, however, and that is important to note, as the growth in local input production to meet final demand suggests. But there remained much more space for further internal articulation of the local economy and for more backward linkages that might have further extended the growth of the economy through more direct and indirect effects.

Most important, this growth in local input production was often of the import substituting variety, indicating that the potential for ISI already is there and does not exist only in theory. ISI in Puerto Rico need not be comprehensive any more than it has been in other economies. Depending on the nature of the industry and the size of the firm required for attaining competitive production costs, ISI can be, and has been naturally in Puerto Rico, marginal in its implementation. As already noted in Chapter 2, Richard Weisskoff (1985: 44–47) estimated that import substitution equal to but 20 percent of Puerto Rico's total consumption and intermediate goods imports (that is, 20 percent of the 53.5 percent import coefficient shown for 1970 in Table 3.7 above) would have increased employment in 1970 by 31 percent and GNP by 44 percent.

What Goods Might Be Candidates for Import—and Export—Substitution?

Though it is now dated, a study by the U.S. Department of Commerce (1979: vol. 2, pp. 96–106) identified possible import substitute possibilities based on goods and industry characteristics that are still worth considering. Different categories of commodities were identified, ranging from those consumer nondurables where there already was import substitution taking place due to particular product characteristics or other factors providing some degree of local advantage (e.g., local taste preferences for some food products) or natural protection (their "Group I and II" goods, such as baked goods, milk, and beer), to some intermediate goods and durable consumer and intermediate products

("Group V and VI" goods, such as yarns, cloth, glass, and paper products, as well as furniture).[34] Additionally, some of these goods, such as Puerto Rican beer and liquors, offered opportunities for export expansion and export substitution to the United States and other markets (U.S. Department of Commerce 1979: vol. 2, pp. 100–101).[35] One of Puerto Rico's rums, Bacardí, long has been an example of just how successful an import and export substitution focus can be for both the private owners of the company and the local economy as a whole.

Maribel Aponte (1999: 364–365) identified existing local industries with high value added per worker that could be expanded by judicious targeting. Perhaps surprisingly, it is precisely in the chemical sector that local firms generated the greatest value added per worker and at a level that is about 75 percent of what the nonlocal Section 936 chemical and drug industry was producing. The food sector at both the level of production and the level of retailing and wholesaling also would seem to offer substantial import substitution possibilities combined with significant linkages to the local economy.

New studies of import substitution possibilities obviously will be needed if Puerto Rico chooses an economic policy that is to conform more to the path followed by other, more advanced countries. New ISI possibilities need to be considered and weighed in importance and continually reevaluated. What is clear, though, is that there *are* ISI possibilities within the reach of local entrepreneurs, some of which might involve the expansion of local industry (chemicals, baking goods, milk, beer) and others (tires and inner tubes, for example) that would require new investments. However, future development cannot be all or only about industrial expansion. The economy already is dominated by service production and service employment, and much of the effort directed at strengthening incomes and securing a sustained prosperity for the future will need to involve a focus on the service sectors of the economy where import substitution possibilities also exist, as in finance, banking, real estate, insurance, and other areas.

As economies experience structural change and modernization and evolve from being primary-goods producers, both the industrial and the service sectors expand in terms of their contribution to output and employment. Puerto Rico is no exception to this trend. By 2000, more than three of every four employed workers was employed at some type of service job from insurance to retail sales to transportation, from teaching to government at all levels, and they were producing more than 80 percent of gross national product (Table 3.4). Excluding government, employment in services created four jobs for every one job in the heralded manufacturing sector in 2000.[36] Some of those jobs in retail trade, tourism, and food services were relatively low-paying; others, however, offer relatively well-paid positions, whether in consulting, computer services, banking, or advertising.

Interestingly and importantly for thinking about possible directions for the economy over the future has been this relatively strong impact of the service sector in stimulating output and employment. The growing importance of private-sector service jobs on total employment compared to the manufacturing sector already has been noted. But also important has been the rising employment impact of service exports. In 1967, service exports contributed just 15.6 percent of all employment from all exports (that is, of all goods and all services), while by 1994, 25.2 percent of employment derived from exporting could be attributed to service exports, showing in another way the growing importance of that sector internally and in international trade as well.

Puerto Rico has the ability to expand locally controlled exports in certain sectors, particularly some services, but also in niche manufacturing areas, such as the liquor industry. Further efforts in these areas will pay large dividends in stimulating local income and local linkages. There remains, however, a need to think creatively about generating more locally controlled import substitution in industry, particularly of those nondurable goods for local consumption that have likely export substitution possibilities, such as for beer, Puerto Rican–style food products, fruit drinks, sweets, and so on.

Notes

1. Already the service sector has come to dominate both employment and output. It is perhaps in the service sector that Puerto Rico's comparative advantage from its strong human capital base can provide the most viable foundation for sustained future development. That certainly is the argument of longtime observers of the economy such as Emilio Pantojas-García (1990). If we look back to the share of services (including trade, government, finance and real estate, and transportation) in GDP, we find that even before industrialization began, services dominated in total output: 1950, 61.0 percent; 1960, 62.7 percent; 1970, 65.6 percent; and 2000, 61 percent of total GDP was produced as services. Employment in services rose from 40.8 percent in 1950 to 59.5 percent in 1970 to an astonishing 84 percent of the total employed labor force in 2000 (Junta de Planificación 1981: A-1, A-5, A-27; 2002: A-10, A-38).

2. The issue is posed here as *nonlocal* versus local ownership rather than as *foreign* versus local ownership. The "foreign" designation when referring to U.S. finance and U.S. corporations in Puerto Rico seems to some observers inappropriate usage given the nature of the U.S.–Puerto Rican relationship, including the fact that Puerto Ricans have been U.S. citizens since 1917. To others, the fact that this citizenship was granted to Puerto Ricans within a clearly colonial arrangement makes the "foreign" designation seem quite apropos. To avoid taking sides, and given that "nonlocal" is a somewhat less charged term that could be utilized in any economy, independent or not, "nonlocal" will be used here in referring to all nonresident sources of finance and capital.

3. Reproducible physical productive capital excludes housing, autos, and other assets used for family and individual consumption purposes (by virtue of being nonproductive wealth), as well as land (nonreproducible wealth) and human capital (nonphysical wealth).

4. From 1954 to 1958, the number of local firms fell from 1,718 to 1,655 and to 1,502 in 1967. The number of local enterprises, even in manufacturing, has always been greater than the number of nonlocal enterprises, but it has been nonlocal enterprises that have dominated in terms of total value added and total employment. Puerto Rican enterprises have tended to be, on average, relatively small establishments (for some details, see Dietz 1986: 263–266).

5. Nonlocal capital and finance can be seen as a part of an economy's total "saving": $S = S_L + S_{NL}$, where S is total saving in the economy, S_L is local saving, and S_{NL} is nonlocal saving. In traditional economic analysis, saving provides the means for investment, so that in equilibrium, saving and investment are equal. This demonstrates the importance of total savings to overall economic growth from this perspective, since it is new investment in productive assets that results in economic growth over the future and the financing for such investment comes from saving. The question of consequence from the viewpoint of economic development is, ultimately, whether S_{NL} acts as a complement to S_L, thus stimulating local saving and local investment and increasing total saving, or whether nonlocal saving substitutes for and replaces local saving and local capital, thus slowing the growth of total saving and total investment. There is also the issue as to whether nonlocal saving can be used to expand locally owned investment.

6. In purely abstract and theoretical terms, one might imagine a standard graph in economics showing increasing marginal costs of nonlocal capital and decreasing marginal benefits associated with the level of nonlocal capital (with the level of total nonlocal capital shown on the horizontal axis). The level of nonlocal capital where the two lines intersect would of course be the optimal level of nonlocal capital for the host economy. Any additional nonlocal capital beyond the optimal level would result in a lower level of total net benefits ("a marginal loss") compared with the optimal quantity of nonlocal capital where net benefits are maximized.

7. By "unbundling the inputs," Hirschman meant the receptiveness of multinational firms to purchases of inputs from local suppliers; the hiring of

local managers and other skilled workers; the training and incorporation of local scientists and engineers into the firm's learning and creative process; and other avenues for "transferring" knowledge to the host economy and in stimulating local production linkages. Thus the larger question about nonlocal firms has to do with their general openness to the hiring and training of employees who might be able to encapsulate the knowledge that multinational nonlocal capital brings with it. To the extent that this happens, such knowledge might be utilized to create direct backward and forward linkages via spin-off industries, as well as affecting far-flung sectors of the economy with no apparent link to nonlocal capital via the general upgrading of the skill levels of local factors of production—that is, via positive technological externalities—that increase productivity and learning of workers and managers.

8. Why this negative effect on linkages might appear was suggested by the U.S. Department of Commerce report (1979: vol. 2, p. 95), which also was quite direct about what needed be done: "Vested in the present Puerto Rican economic system is another important factor that may impede the movement to improve backward linkage investments; i.e., the presence of a large number of U.S. subsidiaries in the island. To assure the uniformity of products produced in Puerto Rico and in other branches in the United States, these subsidiaries must, in most cases, purchase material and intermediate goods from their parent companies. This, plus the lack of confidence in the steady and on schedule supplies of local inputs may create a tendency to 'resist' the purchase of locally produced inputs. Government action is needed to discourage this tendency." Such government action never materialized.

9. The negative impact of the stock of nonlocal capital on linkages was observed to be statistically significant over the following subperiods of Carroll's study: 1966–1983, 1971–1983, and 1976–1983 (Carroll 1993: 250).

10. It is possible to see this in the shift in the share of total value added in manufacturing produced by local industry in 1954 (62.4 percent, $117,472,000) and in 1963 (38.6 percent, $239,815,000), with the remainder produced by foreign firms. The 104 percent increase in production value coming from local manufacturing firms was swamped by the 438 percent growth in value-added produced by foreign firms (Pantojas-García 1990: 74).

11. Another variable that was positively affected by the growth of nonlocal capital in Puerto Rico was wages per worker, though there were fewer workers employed as a result of the inflow of nonlocal capital via U.S. multinationals over time (Carroll 1993: 218). The net effect of nonlocal capital on the total wages bill turned out to be negative, as the adverse effect on total employment of nonlocal capital investment overwhelmed the positive effect of the higher wages per worker.

12. Edwin Meléndez (1994: 236) estimated that after 1976 the net inflow of nonlocal capital actually became negative, as the outflow of profits and interest exceeded the infusion of new investment from the United States, thus resulting in a net outflow of capital from Puerto Rico primarily to the United States.

13. Carroll (1993: 226, fig. 6.1) summarizes the results of the effects of nonlocal capital on the aggregate economy (as opposed to separable sectoral effects). For four of the variables he examines, the positive-negative Hirschmanian pattern is observed moving from the early period of Operation Bootstrap to the later period. For four of the independent variables, the effect of nonlocal investment is negative over both subperiods. For three variables (worker productivity, nonlocal income as a share of total income, and nonlocal profits and interest as a share of total income), the effects of nonlocal capital are positive in both subperiods examined. However, two of the latter three results can be taken as being negative outcomes from the perspective of the Puerto Rican economy, the one exception being increased worker productivity. Over the entire period of study, 1951–1983, for eleven of the thirteen aggregate variables examined, Carroll finds a negative effect on the Puerto Rican economy from nonlocal capital. Only wages per worker and productivity showed positive effects (from the viewpoint of the local economy) from nonlocal capital expansion over the full period investigated.

Carroll (1993: 239, fig. 6.2 summarizes his results) also measures the impact of nonlocal capital on individual sectors of the economy (agriculture, manufacturing, construction, transport, finance, services), but only for the 1953–1973 subperiod. Thus the results of that exercise are less robust than those obtained for the entire economy.

14. A list of names of wealthy and entrepreneurial families in the industrial, banking, and other service sectors would be familiar to most Puerto Ricans: Ferré, Moscoso, Carrión, Serrallés, Roig, and González, among others.

15. And there have been efforts to promote local industries, discussed later. For example, in promoting the local beer industry, a clear example of an easy ISI industry, Fomento used funds from the excise tax on beer "to support local brewers in marketing, advertising, quality control, and employee training" from 1972 to 1976, after which the program was discontinued (U.S. Department of Commerce 1979: vol. 2, pp. 99–100). In 1974, for example, of 1,720 firms operating under Fomento's auspices, 726 were local firms (Pantojas-García 1990: 114).

16. The reasons for the exit of the labor-intensive firms are numerous, some of which were touched on in the last chapter, but the federally mandated increase of the minimum wage in Puerto Rico combined with intense competition from newly industrializing countries, such as the East Asian economies, made operations located in Puerto Rico progressively less profitable. For example, over the 1965–1977 period, wages in the clothing industry in Puerto Rico rose by 6.8 percent, while worker productivity increased only 2.3 percent, thus increasing firm costs per worker (Alameda Lozada and González Martínez 2000: 8). There have been a number of excellent analyses on the impact of the minimum wage in Puerto Rico, among other labor issues; see, for example, Arbelo García, González Ortiz, and Pabón Meléndez 1991; and Rivera-Batiz and Santiago 1996.

17. The primary mechanisms for accelerating globalization have been the successive waves of tariff reductions among nations since the end of World War II resulting from the completion of a series of General Agreement on Tariffs and Trade (GATT) treaties and now institutionalized in the structure and operation of the World Trade Organization (WTO). This process has been complemented by the expansion of regional trade groupings (e.g., NAFTA, the European Union, Mercosur, and the Association of Southeast Asian Nations [ASEAN]). The impact of both of these thrusts has been to "open" economies to both trade and investment flows on a vast and ever-widening scale. As a consequence, nominal tariffs on most goods and the ease of movement of financial and productive capital have rendered national political boundaries of less and less importance for corporations around the world. Competition for markets has truly become worldwide. Of course, all of this has been made possible by dramatic changes in technology that have made the transport of goods ever cheaper and more rapid and by advances in communications technology that have made it easy for far-flung components of corporations to communicate with one another rapidly and cheaply. All of these changes increasingly have made the connection between the specific location of production facilities and the size of local markets less and less important, at least for most products.

18. Nontraded goods are commodities and services that are not traded between nations, regions, cities, and so on, due to either their immobility (e.g., housing, restaurant food) or the high cost of transportation relative to the value of the product (e.g., ready-mix cement) or other characteristics that restrain unfettered exchange and tend to equalize prices between markets. Price equalization does not occur necessarily with nontraded goods in different markets.

19. A consideration of the possibilities for import substitution has gained even more immediate currency given the phasing out of federal tax exemption begun in 1996, a change to be discussed in detail in Chapter 5. The end of federal tax exemption for profits earned in Puerto Rico for promoted firms eliminated a fundamental incentive to U.S. nonlocal capital offered by the Operation Bootstrap, industrialization-by-invitation strategy from the late 1940s onward. The local versus nonlocal mix of production and employment generation of each sector thus becomes of the utmost significance for economic expansion in the future.

20. In the manufacturing sector, the largest number of local firms in the early 1990s was in the food sector (105), followed by printing (61), wood and wood products (56), furniture (50), and clothing and textiles (43). The largest number of locally owned enterprises was concentrated in the agricultural sector and in retail and wholesale firms and other services (Aponte 1999: 366).

21. Pantojas-García (2000: 232–233) argues for a different perspective that theorizes economies like Puerto Rico as links, and subordinated links, within this "transnational economy." The view presented here is that, while there of course is an "international economy," there is also considerable space for autonomous national economic policymaking within each economy, even for small

economies like Puerto Rico. There is a danger in imagining that small economies cannot shape their own destinies—they can to a degree—and in reifying the international economy as if it existed independently of national economies and national policies. That even small economies, even those that seem to be "subordinated" economies, are able to shape their own destinies within the internationalized economy is supported by Meléndez's econometric work (1994) on the sources of growth and crisis in Puerto Rico. Policies do matter.

22. The following data concerns "committed" promotions, investments, and job creation at the time of signing an agreement with Fomento to be eligible for fiscal incentives. Commitments were not always fulfilled.

23. Gross domestic product measures all the income (which is identically equal to the value of new final production) created within the borders of Puerto Rico. Gross national product measures all of the income actually received by residents of Puerto Rico, regardless of the source of that income—that is, regardless as to whether such income was created in Puerto Rico or elsewhere. A substantial part of Puerto Rico's GDP belongs to and is received by U.S. residents as profits and dividends of the U.S. subsidiaries operating in Puerto Rico. These flows are sufficiently large so that, despite income flows from the United States to the island from federal transfer payments, Puerto Rico's GDP substantially exceeds its GNP. It is Puerto Rico's GNP and not its GDP, however, that is available for domestic spending by households and government and potentially for investment, and it is thus GNP and not GDP that is the relevant measure for analyzing the contribution of a sector to the economy's overall welfare—that is, to the living standard of the economy's residents. Among the 132 countries in the Penn World Tables data set ranked by GNP as a percentage of GDP, Puerto Rico was ranked 131st.

24. This is actually a net outflow, since, for example, there was an inflow of income from the rest of the world, primarily from the U.S. federal government, amounting to $882.5 million in 2000, while the total outflow of income payments to nonresidents of Puerto Rico amounted to $20,485.7 million (Junta de Planificación 2002: A-10). Thus the value shown in Table 3.3 for the GDP/GNP gap is a lower bound estimate.

25. Such profits are part of the Puerto Rico's GDP but not its GNP. On the other hand, they are primarily part of U.S. GNP though not U.S. GDP.

26. The U.S. Government Accounting Office (1997: app. 2, 30) commented on the change in the share of Puerto Rico's income received by nonlocal residents as follows: "The share of property income grew from 45.5 percent of domestic net income in 1982 to 54.6 percent in 1996, and the share of nonresidents in total property income grew from 67.6 percent to 73.6 percent. The result of these trends is that the share of domestic net income earned by Puerto Rican residents from both property and employee compensation declined from 69.3 percent to 59.8 percent between 1982 and 1996, although residents' income grew in absolute terms from $16.3 billion to $23.8 billion."

This shift of income from labor to capital can also be seen in the sources of growth per worker in the manufacturing sector. Over the 1950–1965 period,

48 percent of growth could be attributed to labor and 52 percent to capital. By the 1981–1992 period, only 14 percent of the increase in output per worker was contributed by labor, while 86 percent was due to capital's contribution (Alameda Lozada and González Martínez 2000: 12).

27. Backward linkages result when the operation of one industry contributes to the creation of supplying ("downstream") industries that can provide inputs to the production of the original firm or stimulates spending in such downstream industries. Forward linkages result when the production of one industry stimulates the income and production of "upstream" industries that utilize the original firm's output as inputs for further production, including transportation.

28. An income (output) multiplier indicates how much total income (or output) will change due to a unit change in the specified independent variable. Ruíz measured the impact of an additional $1 of federal transfers to Puerto Rico on each sector. Thus the average income multiplier of 1.49 means that for each additional $1 of federal transfers (or, in general, for Δx additional, where Δx is some numerical value of additional income), total income (value of output) will increase by an estimated $1.49 (or, in the general case, by $1.49 \times \$\Delta x$).

29. An interesting study would be how, since the middle to late 1990s, the entrance of multinational home-building warehouses like Home Depot have affected these particular multipliers. Have local *ferreterías* been adversely impacted? Or have local inputs like cement, plastics, paint, and so on expanded to supply the new warehouses with locally produced goods? The potential net effect of the expansion of nonlocal investment in these sectors where the possibility of local supply already exists is not at all obvious.

30. Looking first at forward linkages, in 1988 the total sales of pharmaceutical firms operating in Puerto Rico amounted to $3,371.8 million, of which $2,538.6 million (75.3 percent) represented exports to the United States, $629.9 million (18.7 percent) represented exports to Europe, while only $206.4 million, or 6.1 percent of total sales, reached the local market via wholesalers or as input sales to other producers. The latter value, that is, the $206.4 million, is the measure of forward linkages of the pharmaceutical industry in the economy. Considering backward linkages, local input purchases equaled $444.4 million, or 13.2 percent of total sales (Negrón Díaz and García López 1992: 151).

31. ISI does not need to be undertaken for all imports or even for 100 percent of all imports of a certain category. The question is whether, in the case of smaller economies, selective and partial ISI is possible and, if so, in which industries. "Economies of scale" refers to the relation between the level of production of a plant/firm and the cost per unit of production—that is, of the average total cost of production, or ATC. In an abstract sense, the "optimum" level of production for a production facility is that at which ATC is at a minimum— that is, at the bottom of the U-shaped ATC curve, where MC = ATC. Before that optimum level of output is reached, ATC is falling with greater levels of production, so unit costs fall as total production rises, hence the term "economies of scale" of production.

32. The cost of shipping is greater than it might otherwise be due to the application of the Jones Act, which requires that all goods shipped to and from Puerto Rico be carried on U.S. merchant marine–operated ships. This federally mandated requirement thus acts as a partial "tariff" on imported goods.

33. For each good, the change in coefficient of total input demand = the change in the coefficient of local input demand + the change in the coefficient of import demand.

34. It will be remembered that some of these industries are precisely those that, in the first stage of incipient intermediate ISI, the Puerto Rican government had tried, and failed, to promote local industrialization (see Chapter 2).

35. Imports of beer from the United States grew from about 5 percent of total sales in Puerto Rico in 1960 to nearly 75 percent in 1977 as the local beer industry faltered and failed to grow with demand. Total consumption more than doubled over the same time period, so the possibilities for import substitution were and remain quite robust for this industry. Local beers do have to compete with foreign brands such as Coors, Budweiser, and Heineken with substantial "goodwill" attached to their names. Local beers must find their niches, and good marketing, advertising, and pricing are fundamental to facing the strong external competition. Further, this industry has good export substitution possibilities in the United States and elsewhere (U.S. Department of Commerce 1979: vol. 2, pp. 98–100).

36. In 1967, the ratio of private-sector service-job creation to manufacturing employment was only 2.2 to 1, not the 4 to 1 ratio that now prevails, thus providing another measure of the declining importance of the manufacturing sector to total employment generation over time (Castañer and Ruíz Mercado 1997: 28).

4

Accounting for Economic Growth

One fascinating if controversial area of research in economic development and the macroeconomics of growth since the 1980s has been in the field of endogenous growth theory. As a result, there has been a renewed interest in identifying those factors most important in affecting a nation's level of income as well as its pace of economic growth. Fundamentally, all economic growth theories are constructed to "explain" the sources of economic progress by measuring the contributions made by what are believed to be the basic *independent* variables—such as physical capital, the labor force, trade, and political freedom—thought most likely to contribute to economic progress over time. In such exercises, the growth rate of income per capita is typically chosen as the *dependent* variable.

Until endogenous growth theory, most empirically applied economic growth analyses were one or another variant of the neoclassical, Solow growth model. At its most simple level, the Solow model assumes that the two key independent inputs to economic growth within the choice of economies are the size of the labor force and the total physical capital stock (Solow 1994, 2000). Given that the quantity of labor is somewhat less amenable to manipulation, at least in the short term, Solow-type growth models tend to focus on a country's stock of physical productive capital, the rate of investment, and the rate of savings as being the fundamental determinants of the level of economic development as well as being key to explaining different growth rates and levels of income per capita among countries.[1]

In neoclassical models, and following Solow's lead, technology, which obviously has had a significant impact on the level of world economic progress over the past two centuries, is presumed to be "autonomous"—that is, to be an exogenous force affecting all economies in roughly the same fashion regardless of their size, particular characteristics, history, or current level of development.

Typically, not all of a country's economic growth is fully accounted for by changes in the independent inputs in the regression equation used to estimate the effects of the independent variables on the rate of growth of income per capita. Some part of economic growth typically remains unexplained by the included independent variables. This unexplained portion, which contributes to economic growth—the value of which may be negative, zero, or positive—but which was unaccounted for by the independent variables, was long referred to as the "Solow residual." In modern economic parlance, this portion of economic growth that cannot be explained statistically by changes in the measured inputs to production now is called total factor productivity (TFP).

TFP, like the Solow residual, is to a great degree little more than a "measure of our ignorance" about what contributes to economic growth, unlike the measured inputs. TFP captures all those unmeasured inputs that have been left out of the regression analysis but that do affect economic growth by impacting positively or negatively the level of efficiency of the measured inputs in the production process. These unmeasured inputs can conceivably range from the legal system to the efficacy of the economy's infrastructure to the synergistic and positive external effects resulting from having an educated work force to the role of government in the economy, attitudes toward work, technological learning, and really the entire gamut of intangibles that can be imagined that might affect, directly or indirectly, total output through avenues other than the effects of the measured exogenous variables included explicitly in the analysis.

Calling this residual "total factor productivity" certainly sounds more scientific, but the fact is that precisely what is affecting output beyond the measured inputs is not at all clear. All one knows is that there is some effect that impacts the productivity of the inputs in production arising from an omitted variable or variables that somehow affect income and output growth. If TFP is positive over some period of time for an economy, this suggests that, whatever the source of such growth, this economy has been doing the "right" things, especially if

TFP accounts for a significant share of total economic growth. On the other hand, if the TFP for an economy is zero or negative over long periods, this is an indication of some fundamental underlying institutional, political, economic, or human resource failings that require attention if efficiency is to be improved. A zero or negative TFP value indicates that the economy's resources are performing at a suboptimal level compared to what is possible. Such an economy is operating inside its production possibilities frontier and is limiting the potential welfare of its citizens.

Endogenous Growth Theory

In endogenous growth theory, the level of technological sophistication and the usefulness of the ever-expanding pool of technological knowledge available at the world level are presumed to be country-specific and unique, requiring each country to acquire technological competence, hence the idea of endogenous growth.[2] In this view, technology is not exogenous and freely available to all economies as if it were some kind of a pure public good as it seems to be in the Solow, neoclassical growth theories. Via an ongoing array of government and private decisions on research expenditures, training, and other related decisions, countries must consciously work and invest in learning how to best incorporate the ever-expanding knowledge component of production to that country's own particular circumstances. Without such investments, no economy can become technologically proficient and more efficient in utilizing the always-evolving world pool of information in each country-specific situation. In effect, economies must "learn to learn," and they must continually invest in obtaining and maintaining such a critical capacity if the economy is not to fall further and further inside its production possibilities frontier and further behind other economies that do make such investments in technological autonomy and technological acquisition.

One of the key factors to the success of such endogenous learning is not the size of a country's labor force but its quality and skill levels, as these help to determine to what extent the world pool of knowledge can be appropriated and utilized in production to meet the needs of that specific economy. Not surprisingly, then, one of the fundamental independent variables found by endogenous growth theories to affect an economy's level of income and the rate of economic growth over time has been the education level of the economy's population. A more educated population tends to be better prepared to incorporate and elaborate upon the vast reservoir of knowledge that has been created at the world level, knowledge that must be appropriated and endogenized by each individual economy if it is to increase its level of efficiency and utilize its scarce resources more effectively. Countries with higher average levels of education among their work forces thus are more likely, everything else the same, to have a higher level of per capita income than are nations with a lower average level of education. Economies with a better-educated labor force are more likely to be able to do technology and to increase the effectiveness with which that economy's inputs are applied to the production process in a multitude of efficiency-enhancing ways, and often these effects are picked up in a higher value of TFP.

One contentious assumption of endogenous growth theories—which at the same time makes their predictions, policy insights, and analyses so interesting—has been the claim that the law of eventually diminishing returns does not necessarily apply to key reproducible inputs to production, in particular to education, to research and development expenditures, and to technological capital. The law of eventually diminishing returns has been a fundamental law of economic analysis at least since the classical economists, such as Adam Smith and David Ricardo. The implication of the law of diminishing returns is that at any point in time and with given available resources, inputs, and technology, there is some maximum level of income per capita that an economy can potentially produce.[3]

Endogenous growth theory posits that this is not necessarily true and that it is possible for an economy with the appropriate mix of complementary inputs to exhibit constant or even increasing returns, an assumption that implies that there is not necessarily a maximum level of output per capita to be obtained from any given set of inputs. The maximum income level per person can continue to grow over time even without any new inputs or new technology being added to production. How is this possible?[4]

This is the consequence of some inputs to production—particularly human capital—having what might be called "special properties." In fact, the special property of human capital is none other than the ability of human beings to build upon what they already have learned—that is, to utilize their current level of knowledge to improve the way they work, to impart information to coworkers, to learn from coworkers, to adapt and adopt ideas, to learn by doing, and generally, in a wide variety of ways, to augment their productivity in a dynamic way in the act of working—all without any additional investment being required.

The result of the special properties of human capital input is that income per person can rise even without any addition to society's total inputs, without any additional investment, or without a change in technology, at least as total inputs and technology are traditionally understood. In effect, the higher the existing level of human capital in an economy, the greater the possibilities for even more human capital and knowledge to be created through the actions of human beings in the process of working and doing. Human capital breeds more human capital, even without any further investment involved, so that output can increase even further as the human capital input expands on its own, thus leading to higher levels of income and faster economic growth.

If nothing else, endogenous growth theory has spurred a renewed interest in the causes of economic growth and has put a healthy focus on a wider array of independent variables that might have an impact on either the rate of economic growth or the level of income per capita. Human capital is one of these independent variables, but others—such as income and wealth inequality and political and social variables—have forced economists and policymakers to pay more attention to what might be called "institutional" variables, or social capital, as important contributors to economic progress.

Growth accounting not only permits a deeper look into the *proximate* causes of economic growth—these are the increases in the inputs to production and other fairly easily identifiable contributors to economic expansion—but also forces us to examine and think about what have been called the *ultimate* causes of growth. These ultimate causes include the entire array of an economy's institutions and its social, political, and economic structures, broadly defined, that create an environment that is either propitious or inhibiting for economic growth (Hofman 2000: 1–5). Some of the effects of the ultimate causes of economic growth surely are what are being captured in the TFP measure in growth accounting studies. More research that focuses on these ultimate causes is beginning to help clarify at least part of the unexplained TFP by explicitly including nontraditional variables such as political freedom and institutions in the growth analysis. This work is providing further valuable insight into the growth process in all its richness as not just economic inputs, but also political and social variables critical to progress, are integrated into the analysis (Hall and Jones 1999).

Sources of Growth in Puerto Rico

While many economists have published excellent econometric studies
focusing on particular aspects of the Puerto Rican economy or have
projected macroeconomic growth rates under, for example, alternative
political status scenarios, William Baumol and Edward Wolff (1996)
provided the first published growth accounting interpretation of Puerto
Rico's modern economic transformation. Utilizing a standard methodology that is perhaps best described as a modified Solow framework
with endogenous growth undertones, they estimate the coefficients (the
b_is) for five independent variables from a large sample of countries
using the following growth equation and then apply these results to the
Puerto Rican case (Baumol and Wolff 1996: 874):

$$\ln(RGDP_1 / RGDP_0) / T = b_0 + b_1 RGDPUS_0 + b_2 INVRATE + b_3 ENROLL + b_4 TRADE + b_5 POPGRTH + \varepsilon$$

The left-hand side of the regression equation shows the dependent
variable, $\ln(RGDP_1 / RGDP_0) / T$, which is the annual growth rate of
real gross domestic product per capita, $RGDP_0$, starting from year 0
until T years later when the real gross domestic product value, $RGDP_1$,
is reached for each country in the sample. The right-hand side of the
regression equation includes the independent variables that are
believed to be key in affecting economic growth rates.

The first of these independent variables, $RGDPUS_0$, is the ratio of
each country's real GDP per capita in 1950 (or 1960, depending on the
specific time period analyzed) to U.S. real GDP per capita in 1950 (or
1960).[5] This is a standard dependent variable in both Solow-type and
endogenous growth regressions included to capture the effects of what
has been called "unconditional income convergence." The thinking
behind including this variable is that the smaller this ratio for any particular economy (that is, the lower the income of a country relative to
U.S. income), the faster will be the per capita income growth of that
economy compared to countries where that ratio is higher—that is,
where initial income of a country is greater relative to U.S. income. It
is expected that investments will flow from higher-income nations with
lower profit rates due to diminishing returns to their large stocks of
physical capital, to lower-income nations with higher profit rates on
capital due to their relatively low stocks of physical capital. By speeding up growth rates in the poorer nations via expanded flows of invest-

ment, this will increase the level of income in poor nations at a faster rate than in higher-income nations and will thus tend to close the gap in income per person between rich and poor nations as poorer nations catch up to richer economies.

Since this variable enters the regression equation as a natural log, for countries that had a per capita GDP less than U.S. per capita GDP in 1950, the variable itself will have a negative value.[6] Thus the value of the coefficient on this first variable, b_1, would be expected to be negative ($b_1 < 0$), meaning that there is a positive expected effect on economic growth—the negative value of the coefficient multiplied by the negative value of the variable—for countries that had a real GDP per capita in 1950 (or 1960) lower than U.S. GDP per capita in that year. Incomes of poorer countries are expected to rise faster than those of richer economies, thus contributing to income convergence over time, everything else being the same—that is, regardless of other contributing factors to economic growth.

The second independent variable, INVRATE, on the right-hand side of the regression equation is a measure of average investment as a percentage of GDP over the period 1950–1990 (or the average over any subperiod). Since economic theory normally would expect that a larger share of GDP used for productive capital investment above replacement investments for depreciation would tend to contribute to a higher growth rate of GDP per capita, the value of the coefficient b_2 would be expected to be positive.

The third independent variable in Baumol and Wolff's growth accounting regression is ENROLL, which measures the ratio of the number of students in primary, secondary, and tertiary education to the total number of those of primary, secondary, and tertiary age. From the robust results of the human capital literature, higher average levels of education would be expected to contribute to higher GDP per capita by increasing productivity, learning by doing, and the whole range of factors discussed above that endow workers with the augmented capacity to add to the efficiency of the production process. Thus the value of the b_3 coefficient also would be expected to be positive.

The fourth independent variable in the regression is a measure of trade that captures the effects of the degree of openness to the world economy of each nation in the sample and the impact this might be expected to have on economic growth. The capacity to trade on world markets reflects upon the efficiency of the production processes of a nation, as was discussed in Chapter 2. For a country's exports to be price- and quality-competitive internationally, that economy must have attained a level of internal productive efficiency that permits its goods and services to meet foreign competition head-on. This "trade openness" variable, then, partly captures the effects of greater endogenous technological efficiency in a country as well as the more direct impact of trade per se as an "engine of growth" on income per person either via technology transmission through imports or via the boost given to production by exporting. The value of the b_4 coefficient thus would be expected to be positive on the assumption that more trade and greater openness to trade positively affect economic growth both through income and output multiplier effects as well as by enforcing a greater degree of competitiveness and productive efficiency.

Lastly, Baumol and Wolff include population growth as an independent variable as is common in many growth accounting studies. This variable is expected to have a negative impact on per capita economic growth ($b_5 < 0$) as larger population growth rates require faster total GDP growth rates if income per capita is to increase. This is a purely mathematical proposition.

The b_i coefficients for this equation were estimated from a sample group of sixty-two countries.[7] Baumol and Wolff (1996: 874) report the following estimated coefficients for one of their regressions covering the 1950–1990 period:[8]

$$\ln(RGDP_{1990} / RGDP_{1950}) / 40 = -0.029 - .011RGDPUS_{50} + 0.080INVRATE + 0.039ENROLL + 0.013TRADE - 0.47POPGRTH$$

All the coefficients have the expected values, though the trade coefficient is not statistically significant. The coefficient values can be interpreted in the following way. For example, a 1 percentage point increase in the rate of investment (let us say an increase in investment from 20 to 21 percent of GDP) would be expected to increase the annual growth rate of GDP per capita for a country by 0.08 percent, and a 10 percentage point increase in the investment ratio would increase the rate of growth of income per person by 0.8 percent per year. Likewise, a 10 percentage point increase in educational enrollment rates would be expected to raise income per person by 0.39 percent per year on average.

On the other hand, a 1 percentage point decrease in population growth would be expected to raise the rate of per capita income growth by 0.47 percent per year, though the overall impact of any population growth rate greater than zero always will be negative since, all else being constant, any population growth will tend to reduce the rate of growth of income per person for any achieved growth of total income. The coefficients thus provide a measure of the expected impact of a 1 percentage point change in any of the independent inputs to the growth of income per capita, recognizing that these values are an average expected effect for any given country's actual independent variable values, since the coefficients were estimated from a sixty-two-country sample.

Baumol and Wolff (1996: 878) then applied these coefficient values to see how well the actual independent variable values predict Puerto Rico's growth of GDP per person since 1950 using the sample coefficients as weights of the effectiveness of the inputs. A summary of their analysis is shown in Table 4.1, which also disaggregates the sources of economic growth by decades. Part I of the table shows the

Table 4.1   Sources of Economic Growth, 1950–1990

	% Change RGDP (1)	$RGDPUS_0$ (2)	INVRATE (3)	ENROLL (4)	TRADE (5)	POPGRTH (6)	TFP[a] (7)
Part I Actual Values of Variables (average over indicated period)							
1950–1990	4.17	−1.45	23.3	72.0	55.0	1.24	
1950–1960	5.28	−1.45	23.0	55.5	54.0	1.27	
1960–1970	6.41	−1.06	29.9	68.3	50.8	1.23	
1970–1980	1.51	−0.80	25.1	79.7	56.9	1.65	
1980–1990	3.47	−0.82	15.2	84.4	58.4	0.82	
Part II Contribution of Independent Variables to RGDP (b_i × actual variable value)							
1950–1990		0.0160	1.8640	2.8080	0.7150	−0.5828	−0.6210
1950–1960		0.0160	1.8400	2.1645	0.7020	−0.5969	0.1835
1960–1970		0.0117	2.3920	2.6637	0.6604	−0.5781	0.2893
1970–1980		0.0088	2.0080	3.1083	0.7397	−0.7755	−3.5500
1980–1990		0.0090	1.2160	3.2916	0.7592	−0.3854	−1.3910

Source: Baumol and Wolff 1996: 878, tab. 5, recalculated.
Notes: % Change RGDP = % change in real GDP
$RGDPUS_0$ = log value of ratio of Puerto Rico's real GDP to U.S. real GDP
INVRATE = average investment as a % of GDP
ENROLL = ratio of number of students in primary, secondary, and tertiary education to the total number of those of primary, secondary, and tertiary school age
TRADE = merchandise imports as a % of GDP
POPGRTH = population growth rate
TFP = total factor productivity
a. Total factor productivity growth for each time period = actual growth rate from column 1 in part I minus the sum of columns 2–6 in part II for each time period minus the constant term. This is a somewhat expanded definition of TFP, being the residual of under- or overpredicted growth rather than the part of growth unaccounted for by the changes in the capital, human capital, and labor inputs.

actual values of the variables over time. The first column shows Puerto Rico's percentage change in real GDP per person over time, which is the dependent variable, the growth of which is to be predicted. The next columns provide the actual values of the independent variables that are presumed to be sources of economic growth in Puerto Rico: the natural log value of the ratio of Puerto Rico's real GDP per person to real GDP per capita in the United States at the beginning of the relevant period (column 2), investment as a percentage of GDP over the indicated period (column 3), the average school enrollment rate (column 4), trade openness (column 5), and the average annual growth rate of population (column 6).

Part II of Table 4.1 shows how much economic growth would be expected to be generated by each of the actual individual independent variable magnitudes of Part I using the estimated b_is derived from the total sample of countries.[9] Thus, for example, over the entire 1950–1990 period, Puerto Rico's actual level of education and the collective human capital accumulation that this implies (the column 4 variable) would have been expected to generate an annual increase in real GDP per person of 2.81 percent. Given that average real income per person growth over the 1950–1990 period equaled 4.17 percent per year, about two-thirds of this income growth would be predicted to have been added by Puerto Rico's human capital stock over the entire period.

The second most important contributor to GDP growth was physical capital investment, which was expected to add 1.86 percent to the annual growth of GDP per person over the entire period. The expected contribution of trade and openness to the international economy to Puerto Rico's growth was quite small (and again not statistically significant), adding little more than the negative contribution expected from population growth. This result, though not necessarily conclusive, is suggestive. Given the emphasis often assigned to "trade as an engine of growth" by some economists, the actual contribution of trade to growth, while positive, was extremely modest, even for an economy like Puerto Rico, where the sum of total trade (that is, of the value of exports plus imports) exceeds the total GDP value by a significant amount. This lends credence to the conclusions of endogenous growth theory, which posits the major source of economic growth to come from inside an economy via greater efficiency deriving from the specific human capital accumulation undertaken and the technological learning that more education tends to foster, combined with sufficient and appropriate physical capital investment.

Over the entire 1950–1990 period, the amount of actual annual economic growth left unexplained by the included variables (which is the value in column 1 minus the sum of the values in columns 2–6 in Part II of the table plus the constant term of the regression equation) equaled –0.62 percent per year (column 7). In other words, the expected contribution to economic growth of the actual values of Puerto Rico's included variables (the sum of columns 2–6), valued at the sample estimated b_is, actually *overpredicted* Puerto Rico's average growth rate (column 1) over the entire modern period. If the value in column 7 is cautiously interpreted as total factor productivity,[10] then since the beginning of Operation Bootstrap the productive efficiency of the inputs available for production was less than would be predicted in terms of their contribution to total output and income.

Looked at in another way, the level of annual economic growth actually obtained from Puerto Rico's inputs available for production was lower by 0.62 percent per year over the 1950–1990 period than would have been expected based upon the average growth anticipated from those inputs for all the countries in the sample from which the regression equation was estimated. Puerto Rico's inputs were, for some reasons, less productive on average than were such inputs for the sample of countries. The "proximate" causes of growth, as captured by the contributions of the independent variables included in the regression equation, did not accurately predict Puerto Rico's actual growth rate of GDP per person, which was lower than would have been projected from Puerto Rico's inputs.[11]

It is interesting and revealing not just to look at the entire 1950–1990 period of industrialization and change, but also to consider the subperiods that coincided with the distinct phasing of industrialization reviewed in Chapter 2. Over the 1950–1960 and 1960–1970 subperiods, which coincide roughly with the first period of labor-intensive industrialization based on U.S. investments, the most important proximate contributors to economic growth were human capital accumulation and physical capital investment (columns 3 and 4), with the former contributing a bit more than 40 percent to the growth rate of GDP and physical capital accumulation being responsible for between 35 and 37 percent of actual output growth.

Further, over these two subperiods at the beginning of the industrialization process, there was a respectable increase in TFP, which added to the growth rate of total GDP over two decades to the annual growth of GDP per capita beyond what would have been expected from Puerto

Rico's inputs. This indicates that Puerto Rico's inputs to production "overproduced" compared to what would have been expected from the increase in the quantity of the inputs alone based on the average productivity of such inputs for the sample.

The precise source of this additional "unexplained" growth is not clarified, but what the positive residual or TFP values indicate over the 1950–1970 period is that Puerto Rico's economic growth was greater than would have occurred with *extensive growth* alone. Some additional growth in income per person per year was obtained from something other than the observed increases in the physical capital, human capital, trade, and population inputs. That is, there was some *intensive growth* occurring along with the extensive growth from adding more inputs to production, indicating increases in the efficiency in which Puerto Rico used its inputs, or the positive impact of other proximate causes on the efficiency of production. It could be argued, then, that there were some "fundamental" changes taking place in the economy and society, changes with a positive impact on productivity that made Puerto Rico's specific inputs more productive than anticipated, resulting in greater output growth than expected.

In the post-1970 period, however, the story is quite different but not unexpected from what is already known about the history of the industrialization process. The 1970s was a decade of slower growth of GDP per capita. Compared to the 1960s, income growth during the 1970s fell to less than a quarter of the annual growth in the previous decade. From the level of human capital and physical investment available, the economic growth rate would have been expected to be above 5 percent (2.01 percent from investment in column 3 plus 3.11 percent from human capital in column 4), not the 1.5 percent actually registered. As a consequence, the very large negative value for TFP (−3.55 percent) in the 1970–1980 period reflects the underperformance of Puerto Rico's inputs compared to what was predicted, resulting in the suboptimal growth from the actual inputs that a negative TFP value implies. The growth rate of GDP per capita recovered in the 1980s, but the underperformance of the economy given the inputs available remained, as reflected in the smaller but still negative TFP value over that period as well.

It is noteworthy that the investment rate dropped from 25 percent of GDP to 15 percent over the 1980s, contributing significantly to the decrease in the overall economic growth rate. With less new investment and new capital, the greatest share of Puerto Rico's predicted growth in that decade can be attributed to its human capital resources. The improvement in TFP in the 1980s, though it remained negative, may have been linked to changes in the federal tax laws and to the "high-finance" strategy's success in creating positive transformations and expanding local linkages and local spending. Perhaps, too, there were other "fundamental" forces that might be identified as having contributed to the improved effectiveness of the use of human and physical capital in production compared to the previous decade, though Puerto Rico's inputs to production continued to underperform compared to what would have been expected.[12]

Other Evidence on Technological Change and TFP

University of Puerto Rico economists José I. Alameda Lozado and Alfredo González Martínez (2000: 14–15, 23, tab. 9) have measured total factor productivity using a somewhat different model but with results that are broadly consistent with those obtained by Baumol and Wolff.[13] For example, they find that over the first period of industrialization, 1947–1965, TFP was strongly positive (as it was over the 1950–1970 period for Baumol and Wolff) and just as strongly negative over the 1966–1976 period of capital-intensive industrialization (as it was in the 1970–1980 Baumol and Wolff periodization). Alameda and González found TFP to be mildly positive over the 1977–1992 high-finance period of development, while Baumol and Wolff's findings (from Table 4.1) suggest that TFP growth was negative over the 1980–1990 period.[14] Total factor productivity is estimated by Alameda and González to have added 1.2 percent per year to economic growth over the entire modern period of development compared to the –0.62 percent estimated from the Baumol and Wolff study (though the latter study ends in 1990).[15]

Overall, Alameda and González's findings broadly tend to support the results of the Baumol and Wolff study on the direction of change of total factor productivity, even though the studies are based on different data sets and methodologies. Both studies find that the underlying "ultimate" factors affecting the direction of the economy had a positive effect on increasing the effectiveness of Puerto Rico's increasing human and capital resources during the early decades of Operation Bootstrap, at least as these are reflected in positive TFP values. This period also mirrors the early period of U.S. investment under the Operation Bootstrap promotion program and the positive effects of nonlocal investment expected from such investment when made at relatively low levels, as the discussion and empirical evidence in Chapter 3 explored. However, as more nonlocal capital flowed into the economy and as the industrialization strategy transitioned toward the capital-intensive petroleum and drug and pharmaceutical industries, total factor productivity turned negative as the adverse effects of an overdependence on nonlocal financing and investment became more dominant, providing further empirical support for the discussions and analyses in the previous chapters concerning the adverse trade-off of nonlocal versus local capital that Hirschman had predicted.

Alameda and González (2000: 20–23) found Puerto Rico's human capital to be the only statistically significant input to production over the entire 1948–1999 period. Physical capital was not found to have an independent effect on economic growth, a result that is quite consistent with what has been found in other endogenous growth models. That physical capital is not found to have a statistically significant independent contribution to economic growth does not imply that physical capital investment is unimportant. Obviously, human capital needs physical capital with which to work, and physical capital contributes to overall productivity. It is just that, by itself, and without the proper human capital to make use of it, physical capital does not add to output growth independently of the human capital input.

Other Growth Accounting Exercises for Puerto Rico

In a Harvard doctoral dissertation, Fernando Lefort (1997: 5, 19) argued that Puerto Rico's economy has grown at a rate that is more than 2 percent per year less than would be expected given the initial characteristics of that economy. Puerto Rico performed below the predicted growth rate implied by its initial level of per capita income, even after controlling for a standard set of control variables. Puerto Rico is the only economy in the sample (of Latin American and Caribbean countries) showing such a serious underperformance (Lefort 1997: 10). Though Lefort does not focus on the issue of total factor productivity directly, he does conclude that the bulk of Puerto Rico's growth can be explained by extensive growth factors—that is, the measured inputs and the initial conditions (Lefort 1997: 34).

The World Bank Endogenous Growth Model and Puerto Rico

The World Bank (1993) calculated the coefficients for an endogenous growth model from a comprehensive study of 113 nations in an effort to try to clarify how and why some East Asian nations had been able to grow so quickly. In this section, Puerto Rico's expected growth rate since the 1960s, using the World Bank coefficients applied to the actual values of the independent variables for Puerto Rico, will be compared with the achieved economic growth rate to determine how well the Puerto Rican economy performed relative to the World Bank's predictions. As in the previous sections, if it is found that the predicted growth rate exceeds the actual growth rate, this will suggest that some barriers to economic growth were operating that prevented the economy from reaching the expected level of economic growth from the given inputs based on their average productivity in other economies. If, on the other hand, the predicted growth rate is below the actual growth rate, this will suggest that the Puerto Rican economy's growth has been more robust than expected from the available inputs, and this would provide some evidence to validate the development path the Puerto Rican state followed.

The World Bank study covered only the 1960–1985 period, so it is not as complete as the growth accounting studies applied specifically to Puerto Rico discussed above. The results of one of the regression equations utilized by the World Bank (1993: 48–52, 60–61) was as follows:

$$GDPG = -0.0070 - 0.0430RDGP_{60} + 0.0264PED_{60} + 0.0262SED_{60} + 0.0578INV + 0.1015POP$$

The definitions of the variables are similar to those in the Baumol and Wolff regression above. GDPG is the average rate of real per capita income growth over the 1960–1985 period as measured by real gross domestic product. This is the dependent variable, the growth of which is to be explained. The independent variables used to try to explain the growth of output are $RGDP_{60}$, which measures each country's per capita GDP in 1960 as a ratio of the shortfall compared to U.S. GDP; PED_{60}, the primary school enrollment rate in 1960; SED_{60}, which is the secondary school enrollment rate in 1960; INV, investment as an average share of GDP over the 1960–1985 period; and POP, which is the rate of growth of the population over the period, which acts as a proxy for the growth of the labor force. The first term on the right-hand side of the equation is the intercept, or constant term, while the number before each of the independent variables is the estimated coefficient value for that variable.

Table 4.2 shows the actual values of the dependent and independent variables for Puerto Rico and the expected contribution of each of the independent variables to economic growth. These were found by multiplying the World Bank's estimated coefficient of each variable by its actual value. Given the values for Puerto Rico's independent variables, the expected annual growth rate, shown in the last row of Table 4.2, would have been 4.32 percent, compared to the actual annual growth rate of 3.4 percent over the 1960–1985 period. Given the expected impact of Puerto Rico's inputs to economic growth, the economy underperformed by about 0.9 percent per year over this quarter decade, growing on average at the rate of 3.4 percent per year compared to the expected 4.3 percent.

Table 4.2   World Bank Model and Puerto Rico's GDP Growth, 1960–1985

Variable	Value	Contribution to GDP
GDPG	3.40%	—
$RGDP_{60}$	28.80	−1.24%
PED_{60}	99.00[a]	2.61
SED_{60}	56.00[a]	1.47
INV	23.40	1.35
POP	1.39	0.14
Predicted GDPG	—	4.32

Sources: Calculated from the Penn World Tables, Alan Heston and Robert Summers data set, mark 5.6, available at http://datacentre.chass.utoronto.ca/pwt; and Baumol and Wolff 1996: 875 for the PED and SED values. The "Contribution to GDP" values are determined by multiplying the coefficient of each variable by its actual value. Predicted GDPG is the sum of the values in the last column plus the intercept value (−0.0070).

Notes: GDPG = growth rate of real per capita GDP
$RGDP_{60}$ = ratio of Puerto Rico per capita GDP in 1960 to U.S. per capita GDP in 1960
PED_{60} = primary school enrollment rate in 1960
SED_{60} = secondary school enrollment rate in 1960
INV = investment as a % of GDP
POP = population growth rate
a. 1965.

If the difference between Puerto Rico's predicted economic growth rate and its actual growth rate is interpreted as total factor productivity, there was negative TFP over the transition period from 1960 as the economy began to shift toward more capital-intensive production in the middle of that decade through the ill-fated period of petroleum processing and on through the early years of the high-finance strategy in the mid-1980s.[16] Per capita income would have been approximately 25 percent larger at the predicted growth rate compared to the actual growth rate in 1985. This represents substantial foregone income per capita from growing approximately 0.9 percent per year slower than if Puerto Rico's inputs to production had been as efficient as those in the World Bank study.

Conclusion

In this chapter, the results of various growth accounting studies have been considered. This empirical research tends to conform with the analysis in Chapters 1–3 on the impact, trajectory, and consequences of Puerto Rico's Operation Bootstrap industrialization strategy and subsequent strategy switches, particularly a greater emphasis on services and finance conditioned by changes in the federal tax laws. The lack of continued progress toward income convergence between Puerto Rico and the United States finds a basis in the tendency for total factor productivity to trend negatively over time, especially after 1970. What this means, of course, is that Puerto Rico's inputs have produced less output per person than would have been expected given the actual levels of human and physical capital that have been available.

The sources of this reduced efficiency are not typically specified, though Lefort (1997) is an exception in that he provides empirical evidence that the growth shortfall from expectations is a consequence of the commonwealth political status, discussed in more detail in the following chapter. What the specific "ultimate" causes may be that result in Puerto Rico's inputs underperforming remains a subject to be investigated further, but it is difficult to argue against the existence of fundamental structural weaknesses in the historical growth process given the compelling evidence on the time path of Puerto Rico's economic development since the late 1940s. Growth rates have been lower than would be expected given Puerto Rico's inputs to production.

Notes

1. More sophisticated Solow-type, neoclassical growth accounting models may have several "inputs," or independent variables that are presumed to contribute to economic growth. Inputs can be things other than the usual land, labor, and capital inputs common to many economic models, including political and social variables, which help to make these models richer in interpretation than those limited to more standard economic variables.

2. Some basic sources for understanding the endogenous growth framework are Barro 1991; Lucas 1988; Plosser 1993; Romer 1994; and Solow 1994. For an overall summary, see Cypher and Dietz 1997: chap. 8.

3. This is because as more of any input is added to production, output increases, but at a decreasing rate, so that eventually some maximum level of output per input is attained.

4. The jettisoning of the assumption of diminishing returns (which is distinct from whether an individual producer has increasing or decreasing returns *to scale*) is, for neoclassical economists, even those sympathetic to the efforts of the endogenous growth literature, the Achilles heel of this approach. See Solow 2000.

5. Baumol and Wolff actually use a five-year average of relative income for this variable, not just the 1950 or 1960 ratio.

6. For any x < y, ln(x / y) < 0; for any x > y, ln(x / y) > 0. Thus for any country with a GDP per capita in 1950 (x) less than U.S. per capita income in 1960 (y), the value of the dependent variable in the regression equation will be negative.

7. Baumol and Wolff (1996: 874) actually estimate six different regressions using two different time periods, 1950–1990 and 1960–1990 with different sample sizes, and three distinct definitions for the trade variable.

8. The b_is shown in the text are from their second regression for the 1950–1990 period; these values are used by Baumol and Wolff later in their article to account for Puerto Rico's growth.

9. The values shown in Part II of Table 4.1 are different from those published in Baumol and Wolff's tab. 5 (1996: 878) for the contributions of the "catch-up" variable shown in column 2, and hence the "residual," or TFP, values shown here in column 7. Baumol and Wolff appear to have overestimated, or misreported, the catch-up effect, which changes the values for their residual estimates.

10. This definition expands the usual concept of TFP, which looks at the contribution to economic growth beyond that explained by increases in the "factors of production" somewhat traditionally defined: physical capital, the labor force, and human capital (improvements in the quality of the labor force). Here the other factors of production included in the regression are trade and population growth; thus calling the unexplained part of growth TFP is not precisely correct. On the other hand, given the low, and mostly offsetting, values of the trade and population growth values, this may not be too far from the

truth. What is lacking from the Baumol and Wolff equation is the contribution, if any, of labor force size, separate from the human capital (ENROLL) variable, which would allow a calculation of TFP in the usual fashion as the residual of nonextensive growth. Still, the residual here called TFP is measuring that amount of growth not explained by the included variables, giving it something closer to the usual meaning of TFP, and perhaps this broader interpretation is more valuable for policymaking, since it reduces the unexplained portion of TFP by explicitly recognizing other contributions to output growth (here, trade openness, for example) that in more traditional models are mixed into the TFP residual.

11. How significant was this –0.62 percent annual loss to income per person? If the residual had been zero—that is, if Puerto Rico's GDP per capita had grown at the same rate as had been predicted given the magnitude of its independent variables (i.e., at 4.79 percent per year over the forty-year period, rather than at 4.17 percent), then GDP per capita would have been more than 25 percent higher in 1990 than it actually was.

12. There are a number of problems with the Baumol and Wolff (1996) analysis, besides the calculation errors and other lapses. Most troubling is that the income measure used in the growth accounting exercise and other analyses is GDP rather than GNP. Since the beginning of industrialization in Puerto Rico, the gap between GDP and GNP has been growing, as was discussed in detail in the previous chapter around the data presented in Table 3.3. A number of the conclusions reached by Baumol and Wolff, for example on the convergence of worker productivity between the United States and Puerto Rico or of income convergence based on looking at GDP and not GNP, while correct statistically, lead the authors, both of whom are eminently qualified and highly respected economists, to reach questionable conclusions, revealed most glaringly in the overstated final paragraph of their paper, which points to Puerto Rico's style of development and industrialization as an alternative model— alternative, say, to an "East Asian" strategy—that poorer nations interested in speeding economic progress might emulate (1996: 893).

The importance of the GDP/GNP gap and the impact of the federal tax laws in biasing measured GDP upward, resulting in Puerto Rico having the highest level of "apparent" productivity among 127 countries in their sample, is commented on by Robert Hall and C. Jones (1999) in their study of the sources of growth. They note that the productivity value in Puerto Rico certainly is substantially overstated because of the artificial boost given to the GDP value by Section 936 prior to 1996, the implications of which Baumol and Wolff do not fully appreciate in drawing the conclusions in their analysis.

13. Alameda and González (2000) estimate a modified production function using time-series data for Puerto Rico only, rather than for a sample of countries over time. They also directly estimate TFP rather than estimating it as the residual of a growth accounting methodology.

14. Remember, too, that what here is called TFP in the Baumol and Wolff example is not quite correct, since the labor input as separate from the human

capital input is not used in their estimation. That may partly explain some of the differences between the TFP values found in these two studies. While estimating the order of magnitude of TFP is important, to some degree having an idea about the direction of change of TFP is extremely important and revealing too, and the negative values during recent decades are indicative of the weaknesses of the direction the economy was taking.

15. Alameda and González (2000: 26, tab. 11) find the following TFP values when using a production function with four inputs: 1947–1965, 6.9 percent; 1966–1976, –0.9 percent; 1977–1992, 1.07 percent; and 1993–1999, –0.7 percent. The TFP values for the same time periods using a production function with only two inputs are 5.6 percent, –3.0 percent, 0.6 percent, and –1.4 percent, with the overall TFP value for the 1947–1999 period being 1.0 percent.

16. This may be a slight overestimate, since the schooling variables are for 1965, rather than for 1960. If the actual values of PED and SED each had been, for example, 10 percentage points lower, the predicted annual rate of growth of GDPG would have been 3.79 percent and the negative value of TFP would be in the neighborhood of –0.3 percent.

5

The End of
Operation Bootstrap

This chapter examines the challenges to Operation Bootstrap and issues of poverty and income distribution. While these may seem to be quite disparate topics, they are intimately intertwined themes that unmistakably demonstrate the links between politics, economics, and social issues.

The U.S. government's decision in 1996 to eliminate federal tax exemption on U.S. corporate profits earned in U.S. territories and repatriated to the United States undercut one of the essential girders of Puerto Rico's Operation Bootstrap strategy for stimulating industrialization and the financial- and service-sector expansion that has been the hallmark of the economy since the late 1970s. The elimination of federal tax exemption was a change that statehood supporters had lobbied long and hard to achieve, but that others, for the most part commonwealth defenders, had struggled equally vigorously to maintain.

The efficacy of Operation Bootstrap, certainly from the viewpoint of many politicians in Washington, had come to be closely linked to the cost to the federal government of lost tax revenues from U.S. corporations operating in Puerto Rico. Additionally, there was the rising level of federal transfer payments for food assistance, housing, and other means-tested programs that the slowdown in economic growth since the 1970s had necessitated. Significantly, it has been precisely these flows of transfer payments that have been most responsible for the reductions in the incidence of poverty and for the positive trends observed in Puerto Rico's distribution of income over time, as will be seen below.

A Short History of Tax Exemption in Puerto Rico

From its inception in the late 1940s, the central premise of Operation Bootstrap was to attract U.S. firms to locate subsidiary manufacturing plants in Puerto Rico, as the discussion in Chapter 2 on the evolution of Puerto Rico's development phases showed. This fact makes the name of the program somewhat ironic, if not suspect. It was not Puerto Ricans "pulling themselves up by their own bootstraps," as the name seemed to imply. Nor did the U.S.-dominated manufacturing sector generate a transfer of knowledge that empowered a domestic class of entrepreneurs in manufacturing who could contribute to a locally dominated process of growth and development. Instead, U.S. investments and entrepreneurs became substitutes for local financing and local capitalists, not complements that stimulated the expansion of local factors of production.

Local Dimensions of Tax Exemption

Federal corporate tax exemption in Puerto Rico had been part of U.S. tax law since the passage of the Foraker Act in 1900 (retained in the Jones Act of 1917), which legislated the legal relations between the United States and Puerto Rico. Under Section 931 of the U.S. Internal Revenue Code, U.S. corporations were permitted to exclude their profits from any U.S. tax liability on so-called possessions income, as long as these profits were not repatriated to the United States.

Until 1947, however, Puerto Rico's own income tax on corporations had nullified any significant overall tax advantage for U.S. corporations that might have considered locating in Puerto Rico. The elimination of the Puerto Rican corporate tax and the extension of exemption from other fees and taxes in the first Industrial Incentives Act (IIA) in May 1947 tipped the balance of incentives in Puerto Rico's favor (Ross 1969: 44–45, 98–100; Stead 1958: 55). With this local tax exemption legislation, Puerto Rico inaugurated its Operation Bootstrap strategy of attracting mainland U.S. firms to the island so as to win "the battle for production," as one of the early slogans of the economic development program put it. By adding exemption from Puerto Rican income taxes, property taxes, building permits, and other fees on top of federal income tax relief, qualifying U.S. corporations locating subsidiary operations in Puerto Rico were able to substantially boost their profitability compared to mainland operations and other foreign locations. The payoff to U.S. subsidiaries for locating in Puerto Rico was evident in the "bottom line." Edwin Meléndez (1994: 238) found profit rates in Puerto Rico that averaged two to three times the rates in the United States over the period 1951–1984.

Puerto Rico amended its local industrial tax exemption a number of times (1948, 1954, 1963, 1978, and 1987; see Dietz 1986: 209–210, 250–252, 302 for details) to encourage the deconcentration of industrial locations, for example, and to correct other shortcomings in the local tax legislation as they appeared and were recognized. It was the 1978 Industrial Incentive Act, however, that introduced the first "radical" change to the local tax rules. The regime of full tax exemption from local taxes and other fees that had prevailed since the beginning of Operation Bootstrap came to an end. Instead, a sliding exemption scale for property and corporate income taxes was introduced by a pro-statehood administration interested in creating a tax regime closer to that prevailing in the United States.[1] A 90 percent exemption was available for the first 5 years of tax immunity; 75 percent for years 6–10; and, for enterprises with longer exemption periods, 65 percent for years 11–15, 55 percent for years 16–20, and 50 percent for years 20–25 of the exemption.

Another innovation of the 1978 law, and one far more fundamental, was the eligibility of export-oriented service firms—in distribution, consulting, accounting, banking, computers, and the like—for 50 percent exemption (later raised to 75 percent) from all taxes and fees over the entire period of their qualifying exemption. Previous local tax exemption laws had been aimed exclusively at manufacturing firms (see Department of the Treasury 1983: 30–31 for details and effective local tax rates). This shift toward promoting export-service industries marked an important change in Puerto Rico's efforts toward encouraging knowledge-intensive firms, a shift in priorities that helped to transform the economic structure after the 1980s and one that fit with changes in U.S. tax law taking place at the same time.

It is no coincidence that complete tax exemption was curtailed by a prostatehood PNP administration ensconced in the governor's mansion. Besides the need for expanding the local tax base to provide funding for services and infrastructure essential to economic expansion and social development and to reduce the need for debt financing by the commonwealth government, easing the transition to an environment in which U.S. corporations in Puerto Rico paid taxes was part and parcel of the strategy of positioning the economy for statehood. Though this may not have been the primary motivation for the change in the tax law, in retrospect it certainly was better to know which firms might be so tax-elastic in their location decision that they would leave Puerto Rico if they were to be taxed rather than to face that uncertainty when Puerto Rico became a state and federal taxes became obligatory.

In 1987, but now under a procommonwealth PPD administration, a new Tax Incentive Act became law. This would be the first incentive law to omit "industrial" from its title, reflecting the importance that service and financial firms had obtained in Fomento's promotion efforts to stimulate economic growth. Further, and backtracking somewhat from the sliding exemption scale introduced by the 1978 tax incentive law but falling short of returning to complete local tax exemption, the 1987 Tax Incentive Act provided for a uniform exclusion of 90 percent of profits from local taxes for all qualifying industrial and service firms over their entire exemption period.

The PNP's experiment with partial taxation had demonstrated that promoted firms were not so tax-sensitive as to flee en masse if they were required to shoulder some of the local tax burden. Given the drain that these enterprises imposed on the local infrastructure for electricity, water, roads, and other services, there could be little argument that not only was there a compelling equity argument against reintroducing complete tax exemption, but there also was no evidence that the introduction of a low marginal tax rate had acted as a significant disincentive for nonlocal investors. Even the PPD, which had introduced and championed full tax exemption as the foundation of Operation Bootstrap in the 1940s, could not ignore the evidence.

Federal Dimensions of Tax Exemption

For some time, it had been evident that there were problems with the Section 931 federal tax exemption law as it applied to U.S. subsidiaries in Puerto Rico, some of which were discussed in Chapter 2. In brief, Section 931 encouraged "ghost liquidations" of U.S. subsidiaries in Puerto Rico when their local tax exemption period ended so that profits could be repatriated to the parent company in the United States without being liable for any federal corporate income tax.[2] Most of these liquidations were on paper and were nothing more than legal fictions. To end this wasteful and dubious practice, the possessions tax law was redefined in 1976 by replacing Section 931 of the federal Internal Revenue Code with Section 936 (though Section 931 continued to be applicable to individuals until 1986).

Under Section 936, U.S. possessions corporations could remit to their parent corporation qualifying profits on a current basis effectively free of the U.S. corporate income tax. A tax credit equal to the federal taxes due on returned earnings replaced the "income exemption" rule of Section 931. Repatriated profits on Section 936 operations thus *were* subjected to federal income taxes. However, an offsetting tax credit (the "possessions tax credit") for the same amount was subtracted from the total federal tax liability of such corporations, making the result equivalent to a full exemption from the federal corporate income tax on eligible repatriated earnings. The motivation behind the passage of Section 936, as for previous federal tax holidays, was stated explicitly as being "to assist the US possessions in obtaining employment-producing investment by US corporations" (Department of the Treasury 1983: 14). This quid pro quo would turn out to be critical over the future history of Section 936.

Firms qualified for the offsetting tax credit if over the three-year period preceding the close of a taxable year 80 percent or more of their income was derived from sources within Puerto Rico and 50 percent or more (later increased to 75 percent) of that income was derived from the "active conduct of a trade or business" within the U.S. possession. Section 936 made "passive" or investment income eligible for the possessions tax credit treatment, effectively making such income free of the federal corporate income tax as well, as long as the 80–50 (later 80–75) income test on the source of all income and the share from trade or production activities was met and the passive income was earned *and* reinvested within Puerto Rico.

Though under Section 936 possessions corporations could repatriate qualifying earnings at any time during the life of their exemption period free of any federal corporate tax liability, Puerto Rico imposed a 10 percent "tollgate" tax on any such repatriated earnings. The tollgate tax burden could be substantially reduced by depositing any profits planned for repatriation in qualifying accounts in financial institutions in Puerto Rico for a specified period of time prior to their remittance to the parent corporation. This provision had the effect, as was seen in Chapter 2, of stimulating the local financial and service sectors and, later, providing funds that would be used for expanding investments in Puerto Rico and throughout the Caribbean. Section 936 and the tollgate tax, with its requirement that profits be deposited in Puerto Rico, had been crafted in part to expand the local financial markets by eliminating the practice of U.S. subsidiaries of holding their profits in offshore banks and other institutions outside U.S. jurisdiction.

Section 936 was amended by the 1982 Tax Equity and Fiscal Responsibility Act (TEFRA) and the 1986 Tax Reform Act in an attempt to close loopholes and reduce unnecessary losses of federal revenue. Congress changed the tax treatment of income derived from so-called intangible assets such as trademarks, patents, and trade names, and from passive investments. Specifically, the 1982 legislation in Section 936(h) required possessions corporations to allocate to their U.S. parent some of the income realized in Puerto Rico from intangible assets that had been transferred at no cost to the possessions corporation. Prior to this change, U.S. companies had been assigning all the income derived from the production and sale of patented and copyrighted goods to their possessions corporation, while all the costs of creating such intangibles accrued to the parent in the United States, thus providing a double tax saving (Department of the Treasury 1983: 20–23).

The 1986 tax law revisions further altered the allocation procedures for income earned from intangibles to ensure that a greater portion of income from the transfer of intangible assets was accrued as income of the U.S. parent corporation. Such income then would be subject to the federal income tax without an offsetting tax credit. The 1986 tax change did, however, expand the eligible activities in which so-called qualified possessions source investment income (QPSII), or passive income, could be invested and still qualify for federal tax exemption. QPSII exemption could now be gained on possessions corporation deposits at the Puerto Rican Government Development Bank and in other financial institutions in Puerto Rico used to make loans in qualified Caribbean Basin Initiative (CBI) countries as part of the CBI program of the Reagan administration.

In the first serious challenge to federal tax exemption for possessions corporations, Senator David Pryor (D–Ark.) introduced legislation into the 103rd U.S. Congress in February 1993. Pryor at one time had called Section 936 "the mother of all tax shelters" (Isaac 1993). Senate Bill S-356 was not designed to totally eliminate tax exemption for possessions corporations. Rather, it was intended to replace the existing 100 percent tax credit with a maximum $8,000 per employee wage credit calculated as 40 percent of qualifying wages up to $20,000 to be applied as a dollar-for-dollar offset on federal taxes owed.

The purpose of this proposed legislation was twofold. First, it was targeted toward rewarding firms with larger wage bills as a share of their total costs. Since the purpose of 936 tax exemption was to stimulate and presumably reward employment creation, basing tax exemption on a firm's wage bill was more in the spirit of achieving that goal than the existing legislation, which subsidized overall firm costs and rewarded high profits only.

Second, substituting a wage credit provision for the 936 tax credit was expected to generate up to $3 billion in new federal tax revenues due to the difference in exempt income under the two schemes, since not all of the taxes on distributed profits of possessions corporations to their parents would be offset. Of this total gain in tax revenues, approximately $1 billion per year was expected to come from the drug and pharmaceutical companies.

President Clinton included a proposal similar to Pryor's bill in his budget package for 1993, though the wage credit he substituted was a more generous 65 percent of a company's wage payroll, thus reducing the potential revenue gains to the U.S. Treasury from ending full 936 exemption.

Though the U.S. Internal Revenue Code is equally applicable in all U.S. possessions, the reality is that more than 90 percent of all 936 corporations have been located in Puerto Rico, and nearly half of the 936 tax benefits have been received by just one U.S. industry alone, the drug and pharmaceutical companies, whose operations are concentrated on the north coast. The cost of creating each job in this relatively capital-intensive industry in terms of foregone revenue to the U.S. Treasury was estimated at more than $70,000 in the late 1980s, well more than twice the average $26,471 paid in wages to workers employed in such jobs. "Companies accounting for 12.6 percent of Section 936–related employment received 63.5 percent of the loophole's benefits, according to the April 1993 testimony of Samuel Sessions, Deputy Assistant Secretary of the US Treasury" on the proposed tax law changes (Isaac 1993).

The 1993 Omnibus Budget Reconciliation Act (Public Law 103-66), as finally passed and signed into law, took a middle position on amending Section 936, being neither fully a wage credit exemption nor a 100 percent tax credit. Qualifying firms were required to "elect" to operate under either the "percentage limitation" or the "economic activity limitation" option in determining their federal tax credit on any repatriated earnings.

Under the percentage limitation, typically chosen by firms with relatively small wage bills, the possessions tax credit first was to be calculated in the usual manner. However, the actual tax credit that could be applied to reducing the federal tax burden on "active" income (importantly, passive income remained free of any restrictions) was to be 60 percent of the full tax credit in 1994, 55 percent in 1995, 50 percent in 1996, 45 percent in 1997, and 40 percent in 1998 and all subsequent years. No more could possessions corporations electing to operate under the percentage limitation repatriate earnings to their parent corporation totally free of any federal tax liability.

For firms electing the "economic activity limitation" for determining the size of their federal tax credit, they could take 60 percent of full wage costs up to a maximum wage equal to 85 percent of wages subject to social security taxes as a credit against taxes on repatriated earnings, as well as a further credit for capital depreciation and for a part of any taxes paid to the commonwealth government (U.S. Government Accounting Office 1997: app. 1).

The 1993 amendments to Section 936 continued to provide tax rewards for both labor-intensive producers and capital-intensive possessions corporations. There was a little something for everyone, though the tax benefits of possessions corporations were clearly under attack and corporate tax savings were reduced by this legislation. Firms with relatively high wage bills or high levels of depreciation typically chose the economic activity limitation option, finding that any taxes paid were quite small. In 1995, three-quarters of possessions corporations (264 of the 353) elected the economic activity exemption option. These firms, however, received but slightly more than 30 percent of all possessions tax credits.

The high-technology, capital-intensive producers, such as the pharmaceutical firms, which chose the percentage limitation method for determining their tax credit, claimed nearly 70 percent of all possessions tax credits in 1995, with the drug companies capturing nearly three-fourths of those. They also earned more than 77 percent of all taxable possessions income. The changes in the tax law impacted this group substantially, as applicable tax credits declined by 40 percent from the maximum in the first year and more in subsequent years (Miller 1999: 170–171).

Despite the best efforts of the procommonwealth forces to shield it from attack, the Section 936 tax loophole could not escape the intense scrutiny of a U.S. Congress increasingly intolerant of tax avoidance abuses. Part of the impetus for the concern shown in Washington about Section 936 came from the success of the lobbying efforts of the prostatehood PNP party, which long had worked to end any special exemption for Puerto Rico, at least partly to ease the path to permanent union with the United States by standardizing tax treatment for U.S. corporations located in Puerto Rico with that in the fifty states of the union. It will be remembered that it was in support of just such parity that during the prostatehood administration of Governor Carlos Romero Barceló (1976–1984) Fomento had scaled back its complete local tax exemption program.

On top of this pressure, fiscal crises in the United States in the 1980s and 1990s brought tax exemptions, loopholes, and "corporate welfare" of all sorts under greater examination, and Section 936 of the U.S. Internal Revenue Code was no exception to this resolute reconsideration. With federal budget deficits yawning larger under President Ronald Reagan as economic growth slowed in the 1980s, the U.S. Congress was desperate to hold the line on spending and, if not exactly keen to increase taxes, to somehow find the means to increase revenue receipts, including cutting expensive and inefficient tax dodges that could boost tax revenue inflows without the need to actually pass new taxes.

Though the estimated losses in revenues from tax exemption on the repatriated profits of 936 corporations in Puerto Rico was not a very large amount—about a quarter of a percent—relative to total federal tax receipts, there was understandable concern that the cost of the exemption, compared to its supposed benefits—which were job and income gains in Puerto Rico—could no longer be justified.[3]

The End of Section 936

The full cost to the U.S. Treasury of the Section 936 tax exemption program, even as modified in 1993, went beyond the direct costs in lost tax revenues per job created. The failure to stimulate significant "employment producing investment by US corporations" in Puerto Rico as had been intended by the Congress meant that U.S. tax dollars needed to be directed as transfer payments that, as U.S. citizens, Puerto Ricans were entitled when their income fell below federal guidelines. Federal transfer payments grew rapidly beginning in the 1970s when the food stamp program was extended to Puerto Rico, contributing significantly to both total income and personal income.

In 1975, transfers to individuals from the federal government
equaled 16.1 percent of GNP, 21.6 percent in 1980, 22.3 percent in
1985, 21.2 percent in 1990, 20.5 percent in 1995, and 19.0 percent in
2000. Looking at federal transfers as a share of personal income, transfers contributed 15.1 percent of personal income in 1975, 21.7 percent
in 1980, 22.7 percent in 1985, 21.2 percent in 1990, 20.7 percent in
1995, and 20.4 percent in 2000 (Junta de Planificación 1989: A-1, A-
15, A-19; 1999: A-1, A-16, A-22; 2002: A-1, A-22).

Further, a small number of companies in the drug industry disproportionately reaped the federal tax benefits. This inequity had prompted
the effort by Senator Pryor and others in the U.S. Congress and then by
President Clinton to find a more efficacious means for the United States
to assist Puerto Rico in building a more viable and expanding economic
base as represented by the changes made to Section 936 in 1993. By
creating a mechanism by which federal tax exemption depended more
on the wage bill of corporations, an effort was being made to target tax
exemption toward obtaining a larger effect on. employment. Those
firms with more employees and paying more in wages up to the legislated limit were rewarded by the revised tax law's attempt to shift the
fulcrum of federal tax-saving gains away from capital-intensive operations, as in the drug and pharmaceutical industry, toward more labor-
intensive operations in textiles and even computer assembly operations
and other enterprises, including services of all types.

The battle over tax incentives did not end with the 1993 changes to
Section 936, though that had been the hope of the procommonwealth
PDP and Fomento, which long had championed federal tax exemption
as central to the development program. The gap between the perceived
level of corporate welfare accruing to 936 corporations and the small
benefits to Puerto Rico continued to chafe lawmakers in Washington,
despite intense lobbying efforts from the 936 corporations themselves
and the commonwealth government's efforts to deflect attention away
from Section 936. Also part of the equation was long-standing concern
about the adverse effect of federal tax exemption on U.S. employment
and federal expenditures on the mainland caused by "runaway" U.S.
firms.[4]

The end to Section 936 came when President Clinton signed the
Small Business Job Protection Act of 1996 (H.R. 3448, Public Law
104-188). This was made effective as of October 13, 1995, though the
legislation permitted a ten-year transition period for companies operating under this section of the tax code at the time of the change in the

law.[5] No new exemptions could be extended after the passage of the bill, and federal tax exemption for U.S. corporations operating under Section 936 expires completely at the end of 2005. In the interim period, 936 corporations with prior exemptions can choose, temporarily, to operate under Internal Revenue Code Section 30A, which is set to expire along with Section 936. Section 30A allows companies to claim 60 percent of wages and capital investment as allowances against their federal tax liability on repatriated profits during the 936 phase-out.

Firms, both new and existing, also have the option of incorporating themselves as "controlled foreign corporations" (CFCs). As CFCs, they are able to receive the tax benefits provided by Section 901 of the U.S. Internal Revenue Code available to all U.S. corporations operating abroad, since the IRS views Puerto Rico as a *foreign* country for federal corporate tax purposes. As a CFC, a U.S. company can claim a foreign tax credit on taxes paid in Puerto Rico against any income tax liability in the United States when profits are repatriated to the United States. Until repatriation, the company can retain the difference between what would be paid under the U.S. tax rate and the Puerto Rican income tax paid.[6]

Table 5.1 provides summary information related to the "possessions tax credit" since 1976, when Section 936 replaced Section 931 of the Internal Revenue Code. The data is for all possessions corporations claiming the possessions tax credit. For some years when that information was available, the number of possessions corporations in Puerto Rico is noted separately. The overwhelming majority of possessions corporations are located in Puerto Rico, however, particularly those firms claiming the possessions tax credit, so the data primarily represent Puerto Rican operations.[7]

The 936 possessions tax credit grew from about $700 million in 1976 to its maximum of $4,587 million in 1993. By 1999 the possessions tax credit had fallen to a level not seen since the late 1970s, reflecting the changes in the tax law that had made more of the income of the remaining 936 claimants subject to federal taxes. The lower possessions tax credit was also the result of an increasing number of 936 corporations choosing to take advantage of other tax-status options available to them with the end of Section 936 in sight, such as reconstituting themselves as CFCs. The number of claimants of the possessions tax credit has declined since 1995, reflecting the impact of the changes in federal tax law on corporate decisions about how to organ-

Table 5.1   Tax and Income Measures for Possessions Corporations, 1976–1999

	Possessions Corporations Claiming Credit (Puerto Rico)	Possessions Tax Credit (millions of $)	U.S. Income Tax Collected After All Credits (millions of $)
1976	384	700.0	—
1977	519	800.0	—
1978	598	1,200.0	—
1979	597	1,400.0	—
1980	589	1,572.3	25.3
	(575)		
1981	565	1,900.0	—
1982	544	2,100.0	—
1983	553	1,996.2	31.7
1984	536	1,978.6	—
1985	510	2,450.6	—
1986	520	2,907.3	—
1987	452	2,784.9	30.2
	(428)		
1988	458	2,138.0	—
1989	434	2,820.3	—
1990	400	3,194.5	—
1991	400	3,472.3	—
1992	414	3,748.6	—
1993	395	4,587.7	31.2
1994	390	3,792.9	560.1
1995	345	3,082.2	1,453.2
	(336)		
1996	335	3,059.3	1,833.5
1997	303	2,722.2	3,421.8
1998	260	2,393.3	2,603.3
1999	217	1,485.3	2,152.6

Sources: Bradford 1991; Contos and Legel 2000; U.S. Department of the Treasury 1983: 122; Internal Revenue Service, various years; Nutter 1997; Nutter 1998–1999; Szeflinski 1983; unpublished statistics of income corporations data for tax years 1993–1999 provided by the Internal Revenue Service.

Note: Numbers in parentheses are numbers of Puerto Rican possessions corporations.

ize their operations for tax advantages, and in some cases, about continuing to operate in Puerto Rico at all.

From 1976 to 1999, the possessions tax credit claimed by possessions corporations totaled $58,286.5 million.[8] This represents the extreme upper boundary of the costs to the U.S. Treasury of the tax credit and likely exceeds it by 20–30 percent in total since in the absence of this particular credit, there were available other tax-saving options that would have reduced tax revenues. Given that total federal corporate income tax receipts from 1976 to 1999 totaled $2,339.7 billion, even the full possessions tax credit was the equivalent to only about 2.5 percent of actual federal corporate tax receipts and a much smaller share (0.25 percent) of total federal tax receipts. Over the same period, the aggregate federal deficit grew by $3,146.3 billion, so although the possibility of an additional (maximum) $58.3 billion in corporate tax revenues was not inconsequential, it would not have mattered significantly either, and actual revenues would have been lower than this amount as corporations utilized other tax-saving mechanisms open to them under alternative corporate structuring arrangements (Council of Economic Advisers 2001: 413, tab. B-78).

After the 1993 change to Section 936, federal tax collections on possessions income increased dramatically from around $30 million per year to $3.4 billion, reached in 1997. By 1998 and for subsequent years, the allowable possessions tax credit was only 40 percent of the full tax credit offset. If one of the intentions of the changes in federal tax laws vis-à-vis the possessions corporations since 1993 had been to increase the federal tax contribution of U.S. firms with possessions subsidiaries, this effort was successful, though after 1997 federal tax receipts on 936 corporations began to steadily decline as companies reorganized and searched for alternative tax-saving strategies.

In reality, the cost of the possessions tax credit in terms of foregone federal tax revenues was extremely small relative not only to federal corporate tax revenues but especially to total federal tax revenues. Did the possessions tax credit serve the overall purpose for which it was intended, however? The stated rationale of the 936 tax credit was to create employment in Puerto Rico, especially in manufacturing. Table 5.2 examines the evolution of employment in various key sectors of the economy. Over the period 1976–1994, before the beginning of the phase-out of Section 936, total employment grew by 49 percent, for a net gain of 333,000 jobs. Manufacturing employment growth was responsible for 40,000 of these posts, or just 12 percent of the employment gain. On the other hand, the services sector accounted for 39 percent of the total employment growth over the period 1976–1994, with increased employment of 130,000. Another twenty percent of the employment growth was in retail trade, with 67,000 additional jobs.[9]

The peak of employment in terms of the total number of jobs in manufacturing was reached in 1995, when manufacturing accounted

**Table 5.2   Evolution of Employment in Key Sectors, 1976–2000
(thousands of jobs)**

	Total	% Change	Manufacturing	% Change
1976	678	—	126	—
1977	691	1.92	135	7.14
1978	722	4.49	145	7.41
1979	735	1.80	146	0.69
1980	753	2.45	143	−2.05
1981	759	0.80	141	−1.40
1982	719	−5.27	134	−4.96
1983	703	−2.23	131	−2.24
1984	743	5.69	142	8.40
1985	758	2.02	138	−2.82
1986	777	2.51	140	1.45
1987	834	7.34	152	8.57
1988	873	4.68	157	3.29
1989	948	8.59	165	5.10
1990	963	1.58	168	1.82
1991	977	1.45	164	−2.38
1992	977	0.00	164	0.00
1993	999	2.25	168	2.44
1994	1,011	1.20	166	−1.19
1995	1,051	3.96	172	3.61
1996	1,092	3.90	167	−2.91
1997	1,128	3.30	162	−2.99
1998	1,137	0.80	161	−0.62
1999	1,147	0.88	159	−1.24
2000	1,159	1.05	159	0.00
1976–1994, % change	49.12		31.75	
1994–2000, % change	14.64		−4.22	
Net employment gain, 1976–1994	333		40	
Share of net employment gain, %	—		12.01	

Sources: Junta de Planificación 1990, 1999, 2002.
Note: Components do not sum to total because of omitted sectors.

for 16.4 percent of total employment. The relative contribution of the manufacturing sector to total employment had reached its pinnacle of 20 percent in 1978. After that the share of total employment accounted for by jobs in manufacturing followed a steady downward trend. From 1995 to 2000, the period of dramatic change in federal treatment of possessions corporation income, the manufacturing sector lost 13,000

Table 5.2   (continued)

	Retail Trade	% Change	Services	% Change
1976	113	—	114	—
1977	118	4.42	119	4.39
1978	120	1.69	128	7.56
1979	121	0.83	130	1.56
1980	121	0.00	135	3.85
1981	124	2.48	137	1.48
1982	123	−0.81	132	−3.65
1983	118	−4.07	132	0.00
1984	126	6.78	140	6.06
1985	128	1.59	151	7.86
1986	130	1.56	157	3.97
1987	139	6.92	167	6.37
1988	149	7.19	182	8.98
1989	159	6.71	201	10.44
1990	161	1.26	206	2.49
1991	170	5.59	221	7.28
1992	170	0.00	224	1.36
1993	180	5.88	234	4.46
1994	180	0.00	244	4.27
1995	188	4.44	249	2.05
1996	193	2.66	270	8.43
1997	200	3.63	285	5.56
1998	210	5.00	297	4.21
1999	204	−2.86	306	3.03
2000	212	3.92	307	0.33
1976–1994, % change		59.29		114.04
1994–2000, % change		17.78		25.82
Net employment gain, 1976–1994		67		130
Share of net employment gain, %		20.12		39.04

jobs, a decrease of more than 4 percent. By 2000, manufacturing employment accounted for less than 14 percent of total employment.

Those who would argue that the loss of Section 936 has been a disaster for the Puerto Rican economy are perhaps looking at the absolute decline in employment in manufacturing since 1995 as evidence of the impact of the change in federal tax treatment on U.S. subsidiaries in

Puerto Rico. It is worth noting, however, that there previously *had been* absolute decreases in manufacturing employment prior to the ending of Section 936, in 1980–1983, 1985, 1991, and 1994.

Further, the trend in the relative contribution of manufacturing to total employment had been decisively downward since 1978, just two years after the implementation of Section 936. As total employment grew over time, it was almost inevitable that such a relative downward trend would sooner or later result in an absolute decrease in employment in manufacturing. Manufacturing's declining importance in the economy predates the ending of Section 936 by two decades at least, and though the ending of 936 might have contributed marginally to less employment in manufacturing, the tendency for a smaller role for manufacturing already was evident long before.

Assuming unrealistically that *every* job in manufacturing was due to some degree to the stimulative effect of the Section 936 legislation and that the actual cost in foregone federal tax revenue was equal to 70 percent of the possessions tax credit, the average cost of creating each manufacturing job in terms of foregone federal tax revenues rose from $3,684 in 1976 to $19,115 in 1993 and began to decline thereafter, equaling $6,539 in 1999 as the possessions credit claims continued to decease after the end of 936.[10] This calculation is the least-cost measure of per job creation in terms of foregone federal tax revenues, since it assumes that every job in manufacturing existed because of the federal tax-forgiveness stimulus. Given that local firms also create employment and do not receive the federal tax credit, these figures actually understate the cost for each job created.

The IRS periodically made estimates of the tax benefits per worker to possessions corporations (data for this and the following paragraphs come from Miller 1999: tab. 3, p. 184). For all possessions corporations in Puerto Rico, the tax benefits per worker in 1995 were estimated to be $18,736. Alternatively, this can be viewed as the maximum cost to the U.S. Treasury in foregone tax revenues per job created in the possessions corporations. Any indirect employment effects, which are quite low due to the paucity of backward and forward linkages of possessions corporations in Puerto Rico, would reduce somewhat the foregone revenues per job created. Gross compensation per worker in possessions corporations equaled $23,835 in 1995, so income per worker exceeded the cost of creating each job, a positive benefit/cost ratio from the perspective of employment creation. Tax benefits per worker on average were 78.6 percent of income per worker in possessions corporations in 1995 compared to the 1.5 ratio that had existed prior to the change in the Section 936 tax laws.

The most controversial possessions corporation sector has been the drug industry. In 1995 the tax benefits per worker totaled $56,040 while gross worker compensation equaled $39,404, a negative benefit/cost ratio from the viewpoint of job creation, though obviously not from the viewpoint of the possessions corporations. Tax benefits per worker to possessions corporations equaled 142 percent of income paid to each worker in the drug sector.[11] Possessions corporations producing pharmaceutical products employed 21,113 workers. Compare this with the apparel and textile industry, which employed 16,222 workers at a much lower foregone federal tax cost per worker of $2,393. Of course, gross compensation per worker in this sector was significantly lower, too, at $12,307, reflecting the more labor-intensive nature of production in this sector and the presumably lower skill and human capital requirements for workers.

Nevertheless, there were possessions corporations intermediate to these two examples that created relatively high levels of employment within manufacturing at a relatively low cost in foregone federal tax revenues per job. For example, the electrical and electronic equipment industry created 19,531 jobs paying an average of $21,572 at a foregone federal tax cost of $10,036 per worker. This suggests that properly targeted tax incentives might be able to promote remunerative *and* abundant employment at a relatively low cost in foregone tax revenues if these benefits are provided selectively.

In an aggregate sense, the possessions tax credit cost the U.S. Treasury relatively little as a percentage of actual total tax receipts. However, until 1993, foregone tax revenues per job created in possessions corporations exceeded the average wage paid. With the changes in the possessions tax law in 1993 and the phase-out of Section 936 beginning in 1995, federal tax receipts from possessions corporations increased significantly, thus reducing average foregone tax receipts per job created to a value below the average compensation per worker.

The Impact of Eliminating Section 936

The debate over "how to develop" in Puerto Rico was forced into a mode of "rethinking" in the 1990s. With the end of federal tax exemption for U.S. corporations in Puerto Rico, one significant prop of the

"three-legged," fifty-year period of federal support to the development
strategy came to an end—the three legs being federal tax exemption,
federal transfer payments, and unrestricted migration.[12] Amid this
uncertainty, Puerto Rican policymakers found themselves in a position
of being forced by federal policy changes to "look locally" at how to
continue to promote future economic progress absent one of the central
incentive components of the Operation Bootstrap strategy and one that
many long had thought essential to economic success.

While the full impact of ending Section 936 will not be apparent
until the exemption actually expires at the end of 2005, the dire predictions of higher unemployment and a massive outflow of nonlocal capital have failed to materialize, at least in the short term. As Table 5.3
shows, in 1995 and 1996 the unemployment rate averaged 13.8 percent.
By 2000, unemployment had fallen to 11.0 percent and in 2001 to 10.5
percent, the lowest rate since 1973 and the lowest on record. The labor
force participation rate, however, fell steadily after reaching its peak in
1998 of 48.1 percent. In 2000 it was 46.2 percent, and in 2001 labor
force participation was 45.4 percent. Some of the decline in unemployment was thus the result of fewer labor force participants looking for
employment and not of an economy operating more effectively.

The number of employed rose by 10.3 percent (108,000 workers)
over the entire 1995–2000 period, outpacing the 6.9 percent expansion
of the labor force. This occurred at the same time that total manufacturing employment was declining from its peak in 1995 of 172,000 to
159,000 positions in 2000 (Table 5.2). Significantly, this substantial
growth in total employment happened over the entire initial period of
the phase-out of the Section 936 federal tax credits. Where did the
expansion of employment over the period 1995–2000 come from if the
manufacturing sector was losing employment?

Table 5.3   Impact on Employment and Unemployment of Ending
            936 Tax Exemption, 1995–2001

	1995	1996	1997	1998	1999	2000	2001
Labor force total[a]	1,219	1,268	1,298	1,317	1,310	1,303	1,293
Employed[a]	1,051	1,092	1,128	1,137	1,147	1,159	1,158
Unemployed[a]	168	175	170	179	163	143	135
Participation rate	45.9	47.2	48.0	48.1	47.1	46.2	45.4
Unemployment rate	13.8	13.8	13.1	13.6	12.5	11.0	10.5

Source: Junta de Planificación 2002: A-37.
Note: a. Thousands.

Growth in employment to replace lost manufacturing jobs was most apparent from 1995 to 2000 in construction (28,000), government (17,000), trade (28,000), and services (58,000), precisely the sectors in which expansion might be expected to occur given the high-finance, high-technology thrust of economic policy since the late 1970s and especially since the early 1980s. These also are sectors where local ownership is more prominent. The primary product sector of agriculture, forestry, and fishing continued its pattern of declining employment, losing 10,000 jobs over the same period. Employment also declined slightly in the transportation, communications, and the public utilities sectors (Junta de Planificación 2002: A-37, A-38).

There thus do seem to have been some minor adverse employment effects in manufacturing after 1995 and the ending of Section 936 tax credits. Total employment has continued to rise, however, as other sectors of the economy have increased their contributions, resulting in a net gain in total employment over the 1995–2000 period.

Importantly, investment does not seem to have been negatively affected by the end of Section 936. Gross domestic investment in machinery and equipment attributable to private firms rose from $3.1 billion in 1995 to $4.8 billion in 2000, a 55 percent increase. While it is the case that total manufacturing output as a share of GDP fell from 41.9 percent of GDP in 1995 to 38.3 percent in 2000, other sectors, especially services, grew faster, taking up the slack. GDP grew at the annual rate of 7.2 percent from 1992 to 1995, 7.4 percent from 1995 to 2000, and 6.7 percent from 2000 to 2001, based on preliminary data, hardly indicative of an economy on the ropes.

In fact, looking at every conceivable economic indicator, one strains to find any negative effects due the end of Section 936 beyond the decline in manufacturing employment and the smaller share of manufacturing in total GDP. This employment decrease, however, may simply reflect an underlying tendency that would have occurred anyway due to the capital-intensive character of much of that sector at this juncture. Commonwealth revenues increased steadily from both individual and corporate tax sources, though obviously tollgate tax collections from 936 companies decreased. Manufacturing exports rose dramatically from 1995 to 2000 by more than 61.9 percent, led by a surging 134.1 percent increase in exports in the drug and pharmaceutical industry, the 936 sector that might have been expected to be most negatively impacted by the change in federal tax exemption (Junta de Planificación 2002: A-3, 10, 26, 30). Such numbers do not hint at an economy forced into a precipitous crisis by the end of federal tax exemption, as some had conjectured would happen.

Perhaps these results following the end of federal tax exemption are less surprising than they might seem. It will be recalled that federal tax exemption for U.S. corporations operating in U.S. territories had been part of U.S. tax law since 1921, but no massive inflow of U.S. firms had materialized until Puerto Rico introduced its own local tax exemption law in the late 1940s. U.S. firms operating in foreign countries had long known how to reduce their federal tax liability if they wished to do so. What attracted them to Puerto Rico depended significantly on the local tax environment they encountered as a key component in their overall global profit calculation. Only after Puerto Rico had enacted its first Industrial Incentive Act in 1947 did some U.S. firms find it worthwhile to relocate subsidiary operations to produce for export to the United States and other markets.

It was thus not the existence of federal tax exemption or low wages or even a disciplined labor market that mattered most to the industrial promotion program since those conditions long had existed. Rather it was *local* tax exemption that turned out to be essential to Operation Bootstrap's success in promoting U.S. firms to make the decision to relocate their production facilities. Given the other federal tax relief options that remain viable for U.S. firms in Puerto Rico even with the elimination of Section 936, it is not particularly surprising that no doomsday outcome materialized as long as Puerto Rico continued to offer special treatment to investors, even if this was not complete exemption from all taxes. Years of PPD opposition to ending the special federal tax exemption for Puerto Rico based on the PPD's predictions of imminent collapse of the manufacturing sector simply have not materialized.

Another sector of the economy that was expected to suffer from the termination of Section 936 was banking and finance. The 936 legislation, besides permitting tax-free profit remittance to the United States on the operation of qualifying manufacturing operations, also had exempted any tax on profits on funds awkwardly termed "qualified possession source investment income" deposited in the local financial system, as discussed above. There can be little doubt that, as it was designed to do, the QPSII provision had increased short-term deposits in local financial institutions after 1976. Lenders were restricted in the use of these funds; they could not be used for consumer loans, for example. Rather, QPSII deposits were created to fund loans in manufacturing in Puerto Rico, and later for specific investments in the Caribbean as part of President Reagan's Caribbean Basin Initiative.

The volume of deposits from QPSII was not insignificant, reaching more than $20 billion at one point for all financial institutions. While 936 corporate tax exemption was subject to the ten-year phase-out discussed above, the QPSII exemption was eliminated immediately for all firms, and it did result in the withdrawal of some $4 billion from the local financial sector. Two banks—Chase Manhattan Bank and Royal Bank—disappeared as independent entities, but most financial institutions survived the end of QPSII and may even have been strengthened.

That U.S. firms have not left en masse with the ending of Section 936 has been welcome news. Nonetheless, to try to recapture the pace of economic growth characteristic of the first twenty years of Operation Bootstrap will require new initiatives, some of which will be examined in the next chapter, if Puerto Rico's income gap with the United States is to be closed over the future and if a more stable future economy is to be built.

Puerto Rico's Response to the End of Section 936 Tax Exemption

A new local Tax Incentives Act (TIA) became effective on January 1, 1998 (Act no. 135 of December 2, 1997), replacing the 1987 TIA for all new qualifying corporations.[13] The 1998 TIA eliminated the tollgate tax on dividends corporations remit to their parent company in the United States, as well as the 5 percent annual tollgate tax prepayment on profits that had been required by the 1987 TIA. The new law put in place a fixed income tax on "active-conduct industrial development income (IDI) for qualifying corporations, be they industrial or service industries engaged, directly or indirectly, in serving markets outside of Puerto Rico." The top tax rate is now 7 percent, down from 9 percent in the 1987 TIA legislation, and may be as low as 2 percent and no more than 4 percent for labor-intensive industries such as textiles.

The new legislation provides generous "superdeductions" of up to 200 percent of the cost for training and research and development. Physical capital investments, including expenditures for used machinery, are also quite liberal. The 1998 TIA continues to grant 90 percent exemption (100 percent during the first year of operation) from property taxes and 60 percent exemption from municipal taxes after a short period of complete exemption, making the effective tax rate on property 2.5 percent or less (Griggs 1998).

The incentives being offered by Puerto Rico are available to any qualifying corporation, including U.S. and all foreign firms and local firms. They are without doubt some of the most generous local incentives ever offered in the hopes of retaining U.S. investments and encouraging new investment by sweetening the pot prior to the end of Section 936. U.S. firms in Puerto Rico operating under the 936 phaseout may find that operating under the 1998 TIA as CFCs and forgoing the repatriation of profits to their parent may offer substantial benefits that compensate for the eventual loss of Section 936 exemption. Given that there has been no significant flight of possessions corporations suggests that this substitution of incentives has been successful to some degree.

The 1998 TIA also makes it clear that Puerto Rico now sees itself as being in competition with other countries for U.S. firms thinking of relocating and no longer fears concerns about runaway companies. The 1987 TIA had included a provision to deny incentive status to any new operation that adversely affected employment in the United States, but the 1998 legislation included no such protection against U.S. job losses. The new legislation does not deny the extension of incentives to relocating activities or expansions by U.S. subsidiaries, even when these clearly result in plant closures and job losses in the United States (Griggs 1998).

This local initiative, and others examined in the next chapter, show the adaptability of the Puerto Rican economy to external change, although this took place under some level of duress with the ending of Section 936 federal tax exemption.[14] However, it does clearly suggest that economic policymaking always had more freedom in shaping the local economy than was reflected in Operation Bootstrap's overreliance on U.S. investment and on U.S. firms for the dynamic of the economy. Now, with one prop of the three-legged federal support to the Puerto Rican model of development removed (the other two legs, unrestricted migration and federal transfer payments, continue to be important), it is perhaps becoming clearer to an increasing number of observers that the economy can stand on its own more than had been supposed in the not too distant past, when the end of Section 936 often was equated with potential apocalypse for the economy. Other sectors of the economy have stepped up their activity and incomes have continued to grow, though labor force participation continues to be a worry.

The Role of Federal Transfer Payments

One of the other essential legs of federal support to the Puerto Rican economy has been federal transfer payments. Federal transfers to individuals began to expand rapidly when the federal food stamp program was extended to Puerto Rico in the 1970s, first as coupons, then as checks, and beginning in 2000, as debit cards (see Dietz 1986: 298–300 for a brief consideration of the early years of the program; also see Weisskoff 1985).

Total federal transfers, shown in Table 5.4, have contributed substantially to total income in Puerto Rico, averaging slightly more than 20 percent of personal income, depending on the year, since the late 1970s. Transfers to individuals comprise the largest component of total federal transfers and can be divided into two categories: "earned" and "means-tested."[15] Examples of earned transfers are veterans' benefits,

Table 5.4 Federal Transfers to Puerto Rico, 1970–2000 (millions of $)

	Total Transfers (% of total GNP)	To Individuals	Nutritional Assistance[a] (% of all individual transfers)
1970	303.3 (6.5)	282.4	—
1975	1,184.3 (16.5)	1,153.5	388.4 (33.7)
1980	2,537.5 (22.9)	2,476.5	812.1 (32.8)
1985	3,352.4 (22.3)	3,287.8	780.4 (23.7)
1990	4,648.5 (21.5)	4,576.9	880.1 (19.2)
1995	5,911.6 (20.8)	5,837.7	1062.6 (18.2)
1996	6,518.5 (21.5)	6,419.4	1,071.3 (16.7)
1997	7,076.5 (21.9)	6,942.8	1,087.2 (15.7)
1998	7,364.0 (21.7)	7,175.3	1,109.3 (15.5)
1999	8,057.2 (21.0)	7,866.2	1,087.6 (13.8)
2000	7,968.1 (19.2)	7,870.4	1193.4 (15.2)

Source: Junta de Planificación, various years.
Note: a. Until 1982, value of food stamps.

social security and Medicare benefits, supplemental medical insurance, and federal retirement pensions. In 1995, earned benefits equaled $4,137.7 million, or roughly 71 percent of all transfers from the federal government to individuals in Puerto Rico. These federal transfers are obligations of the federal government to individuals in Puerto Rico due to service to the country or as a result of employment in the past. These are not welfare payments but earned income rights.

Means-tested transfers, however, depend on the income status of the recipient. These flows of funds are affected by the trajectory of economic growth in Puerto Rico (see U.S. Department of Commerce 1979: vol. 1, chap. 4 for a discussion of these issues). The largest single means-tested transfer program to individuals since 1975 has been for "nutritional assistance" (originally food stamps), though this item as a share of all individual transfers has decreased over the years as earned transfers have grown more rapidly than means-tested transfers.[16] In 1999, nutritional assistance declined not only relatively but also absolutely, the first such downturn in nearly two decades, though funding rose again in 2000. Other means-tested transfers besides food assistance are for student scholarships; housing; Women, Infants, and Children (WIC); school breakfast and lunch programs; unemployment compensation; and other such expenditures. Only about 29 percent of all federal transfers to individuals in Puerto Rico were means-tested in 1995, and nutritional assistance dominated such programs, accounting for $3 out of every $5 of such transfers in that year.

The U.S. Department of Agriculture's food stamp program was extended to Puerto Rico in 1971, though funding did not begin until 1975. Beginning in 1983, Puerto Rico was shifted to the nutritional assistance program, which provides a block grant to the commonwealth government for distribution and determination of eligibility by the commonwealth's Department of the Family. When Puerto Rico was moved to the block grant program, funding dropped by more than 13 percent as part of a federal cost-saving effort, though this subsidy began to increase again in 1985. Funding for the program in 1983 was set at a level that was less than would have been the case for a state operating under the food stamp program given the level of potential eligibility and the extent of poverty in Puerto Rico. This unequal treatment of U.S. citizens in Puerto Rico when determining food stamp/nutritional assistance benefits, as for some other federal programs, has been one of the criticisms of the prostatehood forces of the commonwealth status arrangement (see U.S. Department of Commerce 1979: Vol. 1, chap. 3 for a comprehensive early review of these differences in the areas of Aid for Families with Dependent Children (AFDC), Medicaid, education, anticyclical spending, and other programs).

Puerto Rico has had more recipients of nutritional assistance/food stamps annually than most U.S. states. In 1977, only New York had more. By 1981, Puerto Rico had more beneficiaries than all U.S. states and eligible U.S. territories except New York and California. Since 1989, Puerto Rico has ranked fourth in terms of the number of beneficiaries, after California, New York, and Texas. Given Puerto Rico's small population relative to that of these three states, this is an indication of the much higher incidence of poverty in Puerto Rico than in other parts of the United States. It is also a reflection of the limited income convergence that has occurred over the last half century even though Puerto Rico's poverty line is lower than on the mainland.

What has been the importance of federal transfer payments to Puerto Rico's development?

Poverty and Income Distribution: Unmasking the Puerto Rican Model

Critics in Washington of the U.S. role in Puerto Rico have targeted their dissatisfaction primarily on the expensive and wasteful use of federal tax dollars in failing to stimulate employment in Puerto Rico. On the other hand, opponents in Puerto Rico of the existing relation have been more likely to be most concerned about the relation of dependency, or even subservience, engendered by the weight of U.S. economic and political forces in the local economy.

Political criticisms from the Puerto Rican side have been focused on the status issue, reviewed in the next chapter. On the economic side, the preoccupation has been with the dominance of the manufacturing sector by subsidiaries of U.S. firms that, from this critical perspective, have created an economic structure unable to sustain economic growth and improve living standards on its own, thus creating a situation of extreme dependence on the United States that requires ongoing federal assistance.

A detailed examination of trends in poverty and income distribution tends to lend support to both of these viewpoints. In a fascinating study, University of Puerto Rico economist Orlando Sotomayor (1998) has made excellent use of U.S. census data on Puerto Rican income to interpret poverty and income distribution trends. While poverty and income distribution may be interrelated, they nonetheless are separable empirical issues. Poverty is concerned, typically, with some level of absolute deprivation, though there are poverty measures sensitive to more relativist definitions. For example, defining a poverty line as one-half of median income is a relativist definition, as opposed to an absolute income or consumption standard below which those with lower incomes are determined to be living in poverty. Income distribution, however, is by its nature completely relative—that is, it compares how the given income in an economy is shared among all income recipients without asking whether any particular share is "adequate" or not.

Poverty Trends

Using the headcount index measure and a poverty line in Puerto Rico derived from the official U.S. poverty line, which differs by family size, age, and other relevant characteristics, the percentage of Puerto Rico's families living in poverty fell from 62.8 percent in 1970, to 56.4 percent in 1980, and to perhaps as low as 49.3 percent in 1990 (Sotomayor 1998: 50; also see Sotomayor 1996 for a slightly different methodology).[17] These numbers would seem to support those who have lauded the economic successes of the Puerto Rican style of growth. There are, however, other factors associated with the decrease in poverty that raise questions about this interpretation.

Not surprisingly, families with no working members or those suffering unemployment were much more likely to be poor than were other families receiving regular incomes. However, it is startling to learn that the share of the population whose head of household was either out of the labor force or unemployed rose from 40 percent in 1970 to 50 percent in 1980 to 53 percent in 1990, even as overall poverty decreased according to the headcount measure. These same families made up 52 percent, 64 percent, and 67 percent of all poor families in their respective years (Sotomayor 1998: 25–29).

Over the period 1970–1990, Operation Bootstrap qua economic strategy left more than half of all heads of household outside the workplace, either as unemployed workers or, more commonly, completely outside the labor force, where they are not counted as unemployed. Perhaps these figures should not be so surprising given what is known about Puerto Rico's historically high unemployment rates and low labor force participation, but it is nonetheless disconcerting to find a growing share of heads of households not working at a time when the economy was ostensibly becoming "more developed" by some measures, such as the growth in manufacturing as a share of GDP. This trend for household heads to be nonworking raises the question as to just *how* poverty levels were able to fall.

Not even accumulating educational capital provided foolproof escape from the poverty rolls. Whereas in the United States only 6 percent of families whose heads of household had a high school education were living in poverty in 1980 and only 3 percent of families whose head had a college education were poor, in Puerto Rico 48 percent of families whose head was a high school graduate and 26 percent of families headed by a college graduate fell below the poverty line (Sotomayor 1998: 32).[18] This suggests a very high level of wasted human resources and foregone output and income within the local economy, and this squandering of human talent surely must be ranked as one of the real tragedies of the Operation Bootstrap period—and this neglects the large losses in human capital due to migration.[19]

The headcount measure of poverty is subject to some well-known limitations. For example, it counts every family below the poverty line as being poor without regard to how close or how far family income is from the poverty line. Obviously, if 75 percent of the poor are within 10 percent of the poverty line, that is poverty of a different and less severe magnitude than if 75 percent of the families are at or below 50 percent of the poverty standard. The headcount measure counts each family below the poverty line as if they suffered the same degree of poverty, when in fact that is unlikely to be the case.

Under the headcount measure, poverty in Puerto Rico fell by 4.8 percent from 1970 to 1980 and by an additional 4.2 percent from 1980 to 1990. However, under alternative definitions that distinguish income recipients by their income position relative to the poverty line, the reduction of poverty was even more dramatic. Utilizing the poverty measure most sensitive to income changes at the lower end of the income scale, which assigns more importance to raising the incomes of the poorest of the poor, poverty fell by nearly 20 percent over the 1970s and by an additional 22 percent over the 1980s. This is the minimum change in poverty calculated; under different assumptions on price changes in Puerto Rico relative to the United States, the actual change in poverty may have been even greater (Sotomayor 1998: 38, 50). This substantial reduction in poverty levels occurred as the incomes of the poorest of the poor families grew most rapidly, bringing their incomes closer to and above the poverty line.

What Accounts for the Decrease in Poverty Levels?

In assessing the success of the strategy of development, it is important to determine *why* poverty decreased over these two decades and how that was possible with low labor force participation and high unemployment. Was the observed reduction in poverty as measured by either a headcount or some other index the result of a better-functioning economy stimulated by the Operation Bootstrap strategy of development and the structural changes at work?

The simple and painful answer is no. Poverty levels actually decreased the most among households headed by individuals who were outside the labor force, a group who grew in size over the 1970s as former workers left the labor force as employment opportunities shrank. Unemployment levels rose over the 1970s and real earned income fell sharply for all education groups except those with zero to four years of schooling. In fact, the largest absolute declines in real earned income actually occurred among families headed by a college graduate (Sotomayor 1998: 26).

How, then, could fewer families have been in poverty over time if the economy was underperforming? According to Sotomayor's analysis, poverty fell over the 1970s solely because of a growth in income transfers of social security payments and welfare payments that flowed from the federal government to Puerto Rico. Absent such transfers, poverty would have risen from 1970 to 1980 by 1.1 percent by the headcount index (it fell by 4.8 percent when the transfers are counted) and would have jumped by a full 15.1 percent using the more sensitive Foster, Greer, and Thorbecke (FGT) index (whereas poverty fell by 19.8 percent when transfer payments are considered) (Sotomayor 1998: 59–63; 2000). The improvements observed in reducing poverty were not the consequence of the improved functioning of the economy or due to Operation Bootstrap. In fact, just the opposite was true. Poverty decreased because of the growth of federal transfer payments to individuals that compensated for the structural failures of the development program and industrial phasing to reduce the incidence of poverty.[20]

Over the 1980s, the same conclusion holds that without federal transfers there would have been increases in the prevalence of poverty, except for the headcount index, which would have fallen by 0.3 percent without transfers. With transfers, it was the very poor who gained the most. It also becomes clearer in the 1980s that even those families who did succeed in remaining out of poverty did so by virtue of having multiple income earners, not because individual incomes within families were rising rapidly. Single-income-earning families were four to five times more likely to be in poverty than were multiple-income-earning families (Sotomayor 1998: 67–71).

Federal transfers of income not only helped to directly reduce poverty, but also contributed to employment growth by virtue of the multiplier effects of increased spending within the local economy on production and services that such spending induced. Economist Angel Ruíz estimated that every million dollars of transfer payments contributed to the creation of twenty-six jobs and that the total amount of employment created by transfer payments from the federal government to Puerto Rico was "greater than those created by tourism, agriculture, most manufacturing industries and most service sectors, except the Commonwealth Government" (Ruíz 1994: 66).

Over the period 1970–1990, poverty in Puerto Rico declined and, particularly among the very poor, the conditions of daily life were undoubtedly improved significantly. However, this improvement did not result from superior economic conditions coming from a stimulus to the economy provided by the outward-oriented Operation Bootstrap strategy of promoting U.S. subsidiaries in the manufacturing sector and the particular phasing of industrialization followed by Fomento. Instead, poverty fell in spite of local economic conditions and the existing economic model, which on their own would have generated higher levels of poverty.[21] The decline in poverty as measured by the distinct indices Sotomayor used came almost exclusively from federal transfer payments to recipients whose labor-market activity alone, or lack thereof, could not provide sufficient family income to raise them above the poverty line.

The evolution of Puerto Rico's poverty thus tends to confirm the fears of those Washington policymakers who believed that U.S.–Puerto Rico relations, especially the tax incentives imbedded in Section 936, were too expensive given the employment and income gains that the federally subsidized Operation Bootstrap program was able to generate. Employment and income growth in manufacturing and other sectors were insufficient to reduce poverty despite the generous local and federal fiscal incentives to qualifying businesses. The increases in

poverty that would have resulted without the federal transfers reflect
the underperformance of the local economy under the Operation Bootstrap strategy and the industrialization it fostered. This bolsters the perspective of critics of the development strategy as one that failed to provide sufficient employment or high enough incomes to significantly
improve broadly based living standards without federal assistance to
prop up and mask a failing economic strategy.

Income Distribution

Turning now to Puerto Rico's income distribution, Sotomayor (1998:
96, 100) calculates income shares by "equivalent income," as shown in
Table 5.5.[22] Decreasing income inequality over time as measured by
the Gini coefficient in the last row of the table has been confirmed elsewhere in the literature (see, for example, Andic 1964; Mann 1985; and
Mann and Ocasio 1975).[23] This tendency toward greater equality also
can be seen by the gains in the relative share of income obtained by the
bottom 60 percent of income recipients and the decline in the share of
total income going to the richest income quintile, though the richest 10
percent of income earners increased their share over the 1980–1990
period (Sotomayor 1996: 52). The increase in the income share of the
poorest 20 percent and the reduction in the share of the richest 20 percent can be seen in the first and penultimate rows of Table 5.5.

The critical questions are: What are the sources of this reduced
income inequality? Did income inequality fall as a result of a better-
performing economy or was this too the result of federal transfers, as it
was for poverty reduction?

The largest relative gains in income were received by households
headed by those over age fifty-six and by households with no income

Table 5.5   Income Distribution, 1970–1990

Families	1970	1980	1990
Poorest 20%	0.946	1.770	2.640
Second 20%	6.050	7.650	7.830
Third 20%	12.550	13.690	13.560
Fourth 20%	22.790	23.150	22.640
Richest 20%	57.660	53.730	53.330
Gini coefficient	0.560	0.510	0.499

Source: Sotomayor 1998: 96, 100.

earners. How is it possible that families with older members and those with no source of earned income had the largest income gains? Again, federal income transfers in large part answer this question. The other major source of more equal family incomes came not from higher wages per worker within families but from families having a larger number of income earners per family. This multiple-income-earner effect, combined with federal transfers, explains the overwhelming bulk of the observed decline in income inequality.[24]

Once again, as for the decrease in poverty, income inequality was reduced not as a consequence of improved economic conditions and the phasing of industrialization but rather primarily from federal transfer payments, especially funds for food stamps and nutritional assistance, which raised the income of the poorest of the economy's income recipients. Families with lower-middle incomes increased their share of the economy's total income over time primarily by increasing the number of family members in the labor force rather than from higher wages per job. Sotomayor's research on the origins of reduced poverty levels and less inequality shows that the Operation Bootstrap qua development strategy was unable to reduce poverty or substantially to improve living conditions per worker. Federal transfer payments, not the U.S.-dominated manufacturing sector, have been the motor force for progress in the standard of living.

Notes

1. Full exemption over the qualifying period for license and other municipal fees was not affected.

2. Under Section 931, this was the only condition under which profits earned in Puerto Rico could be remitted to the U.S. parent without any federal tax liability.

3. In 1993, 455 of the total 474 active registered possessions corporations operated in Puerto Rico (U.S. Government Accounting Office 1997: 7). The last publicly available revenue estimate that the Joint Committee of Congress made of the revenue effect of an immediate repeal of the possessions tax credit was in February 1993. At that time, it was estimated that the repeal of the 936 tax credit would increase federal tax revenues by $4.1 billion in 1996. This was an overestimation, however, since it assumed that all corporations would remain in operation in Puerto Rico and that there were no other options available for reducing their tax burden. There were, as Table 5.1 shows. The Joint Committee on Taxation and the Treasury Department also made a number of so-called tax expenditure estimates that measured the cost of lost revenues

from Section 936. For example, one Joint Committee estimate indicated that foregone tax revenues would total $3.4 billion in 1996, growing to $4.4 billion by 2000. The Treasury Department estimated the tax revenues sacrificed in Puerto Rico as $2.8 billion in 1996, rising to $3.4 billion by 2000.

4. One estimate had put direct and indirect job losses in the United States over the period 1985–1993 due to the operations of Section 936 corporations at more than 80,000 positions, the result of so-called runaway U.S. corporations taking advantage of the preferential tax treatment in Puerto Rico relative to what could be offered by U.S. states. The research on these job losses identified "50 cases—involving 23,664 jobs at a total of 59 plants—of layoffs and major plant closings in which work was transferred to US possessions. California was the state hardest hit with 4,295 job losses at 10 locations, followed by Pennsylvania (3,660 jobs), New Jersey (3,450 jobs) and Maine (2,515 jobs)" and "an additional 56,342 mainland workers [who] lost their jobs due to a ripple effect." The resulting unemployment was estimated to "have cost local, state and federal governments between $71 and $94.7 million in the form of fewer taxes collected, reduced business taxes and increased social benefits for workers, including unemployment compensation, welfare and food stamps."

For example, the American Home Products plant in Elkhart, Indiana, transferred in November 1991 some 500 jobs directly to Guayama, Puerto Rico. The savings to the parent corporation of this move, according its own 1991 annual report, was "$105.6 million in taxes—or $75,000 per Puerto Rican employee" (Isaac 1993).

5. This applied to U.S. corporations actively conducting a trade or business in Puerto Rico on October 13, 1995 (called "existing credit claimants" or simply ECCs) and to corporations that acquired all of the assets of an ECC's trade or business. These companies were to continue to receive certain tax benefits during the ten-year transition period, though with some new restrictions. New operations established after October 13, 1995, however, would not be entitled to any benefits under the phased-out Section 936. The specific tax benefits to ECCs during the phase-out period depended on whether they were operating under Section 936 as wage credit ECCs or income credit ECCs (Aviles 1996).

6. There is an ongoing effort to reintroduce federal tax credits at a 90 percent level for controlled foreign corporations by adding Section 956 to the U.S. Internal Revenue Code. This proposal was introduced into the House of Representatives on July 18, 2001, in the 107th Congress, first session, as H.R. 2550, Economic Revitalization Tax Act of 2001. The bill had not been reported out of committee at the time of this writing.

7. In 1995, more than 95 percent of possessions corporations claiming the possessions tax credit were located in Puerto Rico. They claimed more than 99 percent of the total possessions tax credits (Miller 1999: 168). There are more possessions corporations than entities claiming the possessions tax credit, as some firms are inactive or earned no profits. For example, in 1997 there were

367 possessions corporations in total, but only 306 claimed the possessions tax credit.

8. This offset federal taxes of an equivalent aggregate amount. However, in the absence of the possessions tax credit, not all of that foregone tax revenue would have been received by the IRS. This is because possessions corporations paid taxes to the Puerto Rican government (for example, the tollgate tax) that were not eligible to be claimed as foreign tax credits by possessions tax credit claimants. In the absence of the possessions tax credit, these and other taxes presumably would be claimed by U.S. corporations in Puerto Rico as a foreign tax credit. Other tax-saving efforts also might have been utilized. Thus the possessions tax credit overstates the full federal tax loss attributable to the 936 legislation.

9. Agriculture; mining; construction; wholesale trade; finance, insurance, and real estate; transportation; communications; other public service; and government are not shown.

10. Unrealistically since manufacturing employment in 1950 at the start of the industrialization process already numbered 55,000.

11. The sector with the worst benefit/cost ratio was scientific instruments, with tax benefits per worker of $58,946 and compensation per worker of $35,842, meaning $1.65 in tax savings per $1 in worker compensation. However, there were only 9 firms in this sector employing 1,268 workers compared to the much larger number of workers employed in the 47 drug enterprises. Thus the total cost in foregone tax revenues was greatest in the possessions drug corporations.

12. For a more detailed look at the "three-legged" strategy, see Dietz 2001.

13. Firms operating under the 1987 TIA can continue to do so until the end of their exemption period. Many of the former 936 corporations and those choosing to operate under Internal Revenue Code Section 30A have done just that, while those corporations that have reorganized as "controlled foreign corporations" operate under the 1998 TIA.

14. Other examples of targeted incentives that have been introduced and that the industrial development agency refers to as "new laws for economic development" can be viewed at www.pridco.com/1.2_laws.html.

15. The transfer values in the Table 5.4 are "gross" transfers. There is also a flow of funds going in the other direction from individuals and firms in Puerto Rico to the federal government. In 1995, for example, transfers by individuals to the federal government amounted to $1,051.7 million, with collections for social security of $888.4 million being the largest component. Typically, but not always, recipients of federal transfers will be different than those making payments collected by the federal government.

16. From 1975 to 2000, all federal transfers to Puerto Rico and transfers to individuals grew by an average 8.3 percent per year. Nutritional assistance grew more slowly, by about 5.7 percent per year.

17. The headcount measure of poverty calculates the percentage of the total population or families who fall below some specified minimum level of income—that is, it counts everyone whose income falls below the specified income line as poor. This income standard, once determined, is adjusted over time for price changes to determine the percentage of the population or families falling below the poverty line in subsequent years.

Sotomayor calculates the level of poverty using both U.S. price trends and Puerto Rican prices to adjust the poverty threshold level of income over time. The percentages shown in the text are based on using prices in Puerto Rico. This results in a lower poverty line than using U.S. prices, so the extent of poverty is less using this price adjustment. Using changes in U.S. prices to calculate the poverty line, the percentages of families in poverty would be: 1970, 62.8 percent; 1980, 59.8 percent; and 1990, 57.3 percent (Sotomayor 1998: 24–25).

In a recent working paper, Sotomayor (2002: tab. 1) estimates the extent of poverty in terms of number of individuals, rather than by number of families. From 1970 census data, 66.2 percent of individuals were in poverty by the headcount measure; in 1980, 62.3 percent; and in 1990, 58.2 percent. In 1953, using another data source, 88.3 percent of Puerto Ricans were below the poverty line! Puerto Rico's extent of poverty in, say 1980, was more like that found in low-income countries in Latin America, such as Honduras, with 64 percent of the population living in poverty, than the level of poverty observed in countries with average incomes closer to Puerto Rico's, such as Argentina, which had a headcount poverty rate equal to about 8 percent of the total population (Sotomayor 1998: 24).

18. In fact, over the 1970s, the incidence of poverty among all education groups, except those with zero to four years of education, worsened. Among college graduates poverty increased by 37 percent during the 1970s (Sotomayor 1998: 53).

19. In simple economic terms, this underutilization of available human capital meant that the Puerto Rican economy was operating inside its production possibilities frontier. This also suggests why in certain periods Puerto Rico's total factor productivity, as examined in Chapter 4, was negative. The apparent level of resources available for use in production, especially human capital, was not fully employed, with large numbers of educated workers with the potential to contribute to total output being outside the labor force.

20. Sotomayor (2002: 18–19) writes: "During the mature stage of growth both inequality and poverty fell unambiguously due largely to the rapidly increasing size of the welfare state. . . . [S]elf-reliant poverty showed no significant improvement during this latter stage of growth," meaning that even if "all working age individuals worked to capacity," families were not going to be able to escape poverty by their own efforts.

21. If easy migration to the United States had not been available as the third leg of the Puerto Rican strategy, poverty levels would have been higher too.

22. "Equivalent income" adjusts household income for the number of family members, recognizing that each additional member of the family adds less to household expenses than the previous member. In other words, measuring household income in equivalent income units takes into account the economies of scale inherent in family size (Sotomayor 1998: 78–79).

23. The Gini coefficient can theoretically range between 0 (perfect equality) and 1 (perfect inequality). Thus a falling Gini coefficient is consistent with a reduction in income inequality. Other indexes of income distribution used by Sotomayor (the Theil and the mean logarithmic deviation [MLD]) also demonstrate reduced inequality over this period (Sotomayor 1998: 100).

24. Sotomayor (2002: 10) points out that from 1970 to 2000, federal transfers and an equalizing tendency among female incomes offset the tendency toward greater inequality of male incomes alone. Looking at wage income only for the period 1970–1980, inequality increased as the Gini coefficient for wage income rose from 0.630 to 0.667. In 1989, the wage distribution Gini coefficient had decreased slightly to 0.665 (Sotomayor 1996: 56–58).

6

The "New"
Economy

The previous chapters have focused on the weaknesses of Puerto Rico's particular path of economic growth and industrial phasing qua development strategy since the 1950s. None of that criticism can negate the obvious improvements in the standard of living of the great majority of Puerto Ricans since the 1950s, as was reviewed in Chapter 1. The economy became more "modern" in the sense of shifting workers from agriculture to industrial and service employment and production. Certainly the particular and mostly sui generis Operation Bootstrap model of development contributed to some degree to this higher level of social and economic welfare, though for those at the bottom of the income pyramid federal transfers have been the essential component of the story of poverty reduction, as we saw in the previous chapter.

However, it has been precisely the point of the previous analysis to argue that the development experience has been suboptimal and full of missed opportunities, at least some of which were within Puerto Rico's grasp. The colonial relation with the United States, the recent history of which is reviewed in this chapter, has had extremely mixed effects. Given the narrow vision of a long line of decisionmakers in Puerto Rico about the impossibility of local entrepreneurs being able to form the base of a modern industrial and service economy, the opportunity provided by federal tax exemption as a means to attract U.S. corporations to locate in Puerto Rico complemented by local tax and other fiscal incentives resulted in an economic structure that has been unnecessarily dependent on nonlocal capital and knowledge, as Chapter 3 emphasized.

In terms of employment generation, the development strategy can be judged to have been a failure.[1] Unemployment has never been below 10 percent and labor force participation rates have been low by any reasonable standard. Further, to an important degree, it has been labor migration to the United States and not economic expansion in Puerto Rico that has been integral to achieving unemployment rates that, in virtually any other modern economy, would be unacceptable and that would certainly have been viewed as an indicator of failure in the development strategy requiring some sort of fundamental change. This was not the case in Puerto Rico because it was precisely the same "special" relation that Puerto Rico has had with the United States that made the nonlocal capital focus of the development strategy possible that also, when this strategy severely underperformed over the four decades of its existence, provided the resources to mask its systemic failures and to postpone unreasonably the need for change.

In part, then, the development strategy's failings were disguised by the migration safety valve that Puerto Ricans, as U.S. citizens, could freely exercise. Just as profoundly, federal transfer payments boosted personal incomes and were instrumental in both significantly reducing poverty levels and in creating greater income inequality. Without those two legs of the development strategy to ameliorate the costs of inadequate employment and income generation that resulted from the third leg—tax exemption—Operation Bootstrap would have been forced to reinvent itself or face the inexorable social pressures that would surely have festered and then boiled over into social discontent.

Without federal transfers and the increased local spending they stimulated, the multiplier effects of spin-off expenditures that supported local firms would have been absent, depressing local economic activity even more. Until this culture of dependency is ended by forging an economy that is internally dynamic and self-sustaining and where local producers begin to increase their roles, the gap between U.S. and Puerto Rican living standards will not be closed. Fortunately, since 1995 there does seem to be a movement in that direction as a result of the end of the Section 936 tax credits, which has forced the economy to look inward for its dynamic.

Unlike independent nations, Puerto Rico has no binding balance of payments account to force decisionmakers to confront needed strategy switches when the development program begins to falter and sputter and economic growth stalls. Unrestricted migration to the United States and the flow of federal funds in the other direction screened Operation

Bootstrap from the intense scrutiny it deserved and softened the social and economic disorder that simmered just below the surface. In an important sense, migration and federal transfers were equivalent to capital account inflows in independent countries.

Rising income levels compared to other nations in Latin America and elsewhere imparted a false sense of success to the development program's supporters. The real standard of accomplishment, however, should have been convergence to U.S. income levels and U.S. standards of employment, a norm of comparison that does not put Puerto Rico's experience in the best light, as Chapter 1 showed.

In 1996, when the United States eliminated federal tax credits for new firms locating in Puerto Rico and phased out exemption for existing firms, one of the legs of Operation Bootstrap was cut away, and it is difficult for a strategy designed to operate with three components to continue when one of its essential elements has been eliminated, especially when the other two legs acted essentially as crutches holding up the underperforming tax exemption leg of the strategy.

This chapter looks briefly to Puerto Rico's future and to the search for both a solution to the ever present status issue and the effort to forge a new economic strategy that the end of the 936-era demands.

The Status Battle

The seemingly perpetual search for a solution to Puerto Rico's status vis-à-vis the United States—a pursuit that was barely sidetracked by the approval in 1952 of a commonwealth that was supposed to resolve the matter—has sapped valuable resources, both human and financial, that could have been better utilized elsewhere in the economy and in the public sector. The boundaries of the possible in Puerto Rico are to some degree circumscribed by the parameters within which any economic development strategy ultimately must operate, and to an important extent, the precise nature of Puerto Rico's ultimate status situation—whether it is a territory of the United States, a state of the union, a freely associated "state," or an independent nation—defines these limits.

Status does matter, but it is not the only determinant of what happens in the economy and society. There are other external barriers that Puerto Rico must confront, such as the global market and its regulations on the possible, just as independent countries must deal with them. The colonial relation is an additional barrier that independent countries do not face, but it also has provided some benefits too, such as unrestricted access to the U.S. market. Still, the status issue has become such a distraction that it is in the interest of both Puerto Rico and the United States to resolve it, and the sooner the better.

From the time of Spanish colonialism and Puerto Rico's brief taste of autonomy in 1898, the issue of political status vis-à-vis first Spain and then the United States has seethed near the surface of day-to-day events, certainly among the political classes and intellectuals. The story of the impact of U.S. colonialism in Puerto Rico from the time power was transferred from Spain in 1898 after the Spanish-American-Cuban War has been well documented and need not be repeated here.[2]

The modern history of U.S.–Puerto Rican political relations began in the middle to late 1940s contemporaneous with the initiation of the Operation Bootstrap industrialization strategy. The beginning of this change can be marked in 1946, when President Harry Truman named Jesús T. Piñero to replace Rexford Guy Tugwell as governor. Piñero, who at the time was Puerto Rico's resident commissioner to the U.S. Congress in Washington and a member of Luis Muñoz Marín's dominant Popular Democratic Party, thus became the first Puerto Rican to be governor and the last presidential appointee.[3] Then in August 1947, President Truman signed into law a bill that had been passed by the U.S. Congress authorizing Puerto Rico's first elections for governor to be held in 1948.

Luis Muñoz Marín, the founder of the PPD and a political leader since the 1930s, easily won the governorship with more than 61 percent of the vote, thus becoming the island's first elected governor, a position he would hold until 1964. However, no one seriously believed that this administrative change as to who was governor had altered the dominion of the United States over Puerto Rico as spelled out in the Jones Act of 1917.[4]

Muñoz had been an outspoken independence supporter and a socialist as a young man, and he had influenced the PPD in its early days to include independence as a goal of the party and for Puerto Rico. As governor, however, his position moderated, and he became uncertain about the economic viability of independence, as was noted in Chapter 2. Muñoz had promised when he ran for governor that he never would impose his personal views on the public simply because he wielded power from the governor's mansion at La Fortaleza. Ultimately, Muñoz lent his support to a proposal that had been floated by former governor Tugwell for a "commonwealth, dominion—call it anything indicating a half-way relationship" that was somewhere between statehood and independence.[5]

With Muñoz Marín's embrace of this middle ground for Puerto Rico's relations with the United States, the way was paved for the creation of a dominionlike status, and in March 1952 Puerto Rican voters overwhelmingly approved a constitution for this new halfway arrangement.[6] On July 25, 1952, fifty-four years to the day after the United States had invaded the south coast of Puerto Rico at Guánica during the Spanish-American-Cuban War, the Commonwealth of Puerto Rico, or the Estado Libre Asociado, as the commonwealth is called in Spanish, was inaugurated.[7]

Commonwealth status did little to quell the dissatisfaction of increasing numbers of Puerto Ricans with the precise nature of their external political union.[8] That is perhaps due to the calculated "halfway" nature of such status as envisioned by both Tugwell and Muñoz, as neither independence nor statehood, and hence as a somewhat nebulous and malleable concept. The level of discontent with the commonwealth status can, at one level, be measured by the number and increasing frequency of plebiscites and referenda held since 1952 attempting to resolve or otherwise define the status issue and matters intimately related to status. These votes took place in 1967, 1991, 1993, 1994, and 1998.[9] At a deeper level, however, certainly in the highly politicized and somewhat closed universe of Puerto Rican politics and civil society, virtually every election at every level has come to be riddled with status overtones and undertones as political parties and candidates with opposing and conflicting status agendas vie for power and approbation for their preferred political position.

The 1998 Status Plebiscite

The December 1998 plebiscite is revealing of the deterioration of the political situation in terms of both Puerto Rico's relations with the United States and among the political parties in Puerto Rico jockeying for position and power, justifying a closer look at the process and its outcome.[10] The original hope of many in Puerto Rico had been that, finally, there would take place a definitive self-executing status vote at the end of 1998 that would put to rest the wasteful and constant internal bickering invoked year-in and year-out by the commonwealth status issue and uncertainty over Puerto Rico's final political future.

Enabling legislation in the form of the United States-Puerto Rico Political Status Act (H.R. 856), commonly referred to as the Young bill,[11] was introduced into the 105th session of the U.S. House of Representatives on February 27, 1997, and passed in amended form, albeit on the narrowest of margins, with a vote of 209 in favor and 208 against on March 4, 1998.[12] From there, the bill went to the U.S. Senate, where it failed to be brought to a floor vote and thus died, ending the hopes of those who supported a final resolution of the status issue that this bill would have mandated. The Young bill would have required "a referendum to be held by 31 December 1998 on Puerto Rico's political status for either: (1) retention of its present commonwealth status; (2) full self-government through separate sovereignty leading to independence or free association; or (3) full self-government through U.S. sovereignty leading to statehood."

If the outcome of a referendum had favored either free association or independence, the bill was to require "the President to develop and submit to the Congress for approval legislation for: (1) a transition plan of not more than ten years which leads to full self-government for Puerto Rico; and (2) a recommendation for the implementation of such self-government consistent with Puerto Rico's approval." On the other hand, a vote in favor of statehood would "(1) include proposals and incentives to increase the opportunities of the people of Puerto Rico to expand their English proficiency, including teaching in English in public schools, awarding fellowships and scholarships, and providing grants to organizations to promote English language skills; (2) promote the use of English by U.S. citizens in Puerto Rico; and (3) include the effective date of Puerto Rico's incorporation into the United States."

Last, "In the event of a vote in favor of Commonwealth, [the government of Puerto Rico was] to call a Special Convention to develop proposals for submission to the President and the Congress for changes in Federal policy on economic and social matters of concern to the Puerto Rican people."

The House bill required only a simple majority vote among Puerto Rican voters for the winning status to be certified to the president of the United States as an expression of the will of the Puerto Rican people. Importantly, the bill would have made the results of the election binding on the United States. However, and most interestingly and controversially, the bill would have authorized "further referenda, at least once every ten years, if the referendum conducted under this Act does not result in a majority vote for separate sovereignty or statehood."[13] In other words, even if the majority of voters had continued to support some form of commonwealth status, the bill would have required that plebiscites be held again and again—at least every ten years, but more frequent plebicites were possible too under the legislation—until there was a majority vote in favor of either statehood, independence, or free association.

Implicitly, this legislation took the position that the commonwealth status was an illegitimate permanent political choice, even if this was the "will" of the Puerto Rican people, a point of view in fact held by many, if not all, the proponents of both statehood and independence. That this anticommonwealth provision was included in the legislation is perhaps less surprising when it is realized that the Young bill had been drafted and shepherded through the U.S. Congress by statehood supporters. The stated purpose of the Young bill was "to encourage the development and implementation of procedures through which the permanent political status of the people of Puerto Rico can be determined," and commonwealth status did not fit that definition in terms of permanency, at least in this legislation, much to the dismay of commonwealth supporters.[14]

All political parties in Puerto Rico, even the procommonwealth PDP, now accept the proposition that the current political status vis-à-vis the United States is in need of fundamental change. No political party supports the existing political arrangements, and all agree that the present commonwealth status has what are typically referred to as "colonial vestiges." The New Progressive Party desires full and permanent association through statehood. The Independence Party (PIP, Partido Independentista Puertorriqueño) favors complete separation from the United States and independence, while the PDP wishes to create an arrangement that provides for augmented political and economic autonomy for the Puerto Rican government and people within a continuing commonwealth-type framework in permanent union with the United States.

Puerto Rico Goes Ahead with the Status Vote

The Puerto Rican government decided to hold a plebiscite on the planned date in December 1998 despite the fact that the Young bill, for which they had strongly lobbied and which would have made the results self-executing and binding on the United States, had not been approved by the U.S. Senate and was a dead issue in Washington. The plebiscite was to go forward with the full knowledge that, at best, the results would serve as little more than information to the U.S. Congress. The vote would have no legal standing or power to actually alter Puerto Rico's existing status and did not require, not that it could have been mandated, that the United States respond in any way regardless of the outcome of the vote. In effect, the Puerto Rican government chose to conduct yet another expensive poll of voters as to their status opinions, as if virtually every national vote for governor over the past thirty years were not evidence enough to reveal the almost even split of support between statehood and commonwealth among the voting public.

The prostatehood government controlled the plebiscite process, and they crafted the ballot in a way that they hoped would put the best possible light on the final results, with the goal of spotlighting support for statehood. As a result, the status options presented as choices did not include an "augmented" or improved commonwealth option for which the procommonwealth PPD had long lobbied and to which PPD loyals could lend support.[15] Instead, voters in Puerto Rico on December 13, 1998, were obliged to choose among the following ballot options (total votes, followed by the percentage of total votes for that category in parentheses): "territorial" commonwealth, 993 (0.1%); free association, 4,536 (0.3%); statehood, 728,157 (46.5%); independence, 39,838 (2.5%); none of the above, 787,900 votes (50.3%).[16]

What did the results of this voting indicate? First, and certainly to the surprise of very few longtime observers of the Puerto Rican political process, there had been virtually no change in the preferences of voters for the two major options in recent years—statehood and some form of commonwealth—if the votes cast in 1998 are interpreted properly. Commonwealth supporters had been encouraged by the procommonwealth PPD to vote the fifth-column choice, "none of the above," which explains the extraordinarily large numbers—more than half of all votes cast—choosing that alternative and the miniscule number of votes cast for the commonwealth alternative. The "territorial" commonwealth option in the first column of the ballot was considered to be colonial and nonaugmented and thus was completely unacceptable to the PPD and most commonwealth supporters, as the prostatehood PNP, which formulated the plebiscite process, had been well aware when the ballot was designed. In fact, that was their purpose in constructing the ballot in that way. The effort by the PNP to argue that the 46.5 percent vote in favor of statehood showed a plurality of support for that option fooled no one.

Remembering that the "none of the above" vote was primarily chosen by procommonwealth supporters, comparing the results of this nonbinding vote to past outcomes only served to confirm that commonwealth supporters continue to maintain a slight edge in numbers over prostatehood voters, at least among those who voted.[17] Statistically, however, there is an almost even split among voters between the commonwealth and statehood status choices, a bipolarity that has not changed over the last three decades, with only a small minority of voters favoring some form of independence, including the "free association" option. Those nonaligned voters, who move back and forth between voting for either the PPD or the PNP depending on the candidate or the specific issues, continue to be able to sway the outcome of local elections. The two major status options are in a virtual dead heat in overall political support.

What is the value of these increasingly more frequent votes on status?[18] And what, perhaps just as important, is their cost? The 1998 plebiscite cost in the neighborhood of $10 million according to the government, and that counts only direct costs. Excluded from this figure are funds expended in Puerto Rico and in the United States lobbying for a binding Washington-approved voting process. Just as significant were the indirect costs and the opportunity costs of the campaign leading up to the vote on Sunday, December 13. How much money and how much of the time of government officials, both high and low, was spent in winning votes for their preferred status choice to the detriment of important business that needed to be accomplished, responsibilities such as implementing innovative plans for future economic development as the era of Operation Bootstrap comes to an end; improving the deteriorating educational system; restoring outdated infrastructure in the areas of water, sewage treatment, electrical generation, and roadways; confronting the rising tide of crime afflicting urban areas; and the day-to-day, mundane but essential business of government that should not be mixed up with the question of status but constantly is?

The plebiscites and referenda have taken away energy, financing, and expertise from these and other pressing problems that need to be addressed regardless of Puerto Rico's ultimate status. These obstacles to well-being and further progress have received less attention than they deserve as a result of the status indecision. The heightened political drama surrounding the voting on status—including local elections for governor and for municipalities and other positions that serve to some degree as internal referenda—tends to displace attention away from these other issues begging to be resolved, real concerns that likely have a more immediate impact on the welfare and lives of the majority of the population.

This is not to imply that Puerto Rico's political status has no importance to the future or to the current standard of living; it obviously does, as the many studies on the impact of various status options have demonstrated.[19] Each possible status relation brings with it both measurable and immeasurable costs and benefits that are worthy of analysis and consideration.[20] It is just that there can be no denying that there is an unacceptable level of waste of public resources and human capital surrounding the political process that is exacerbated by the inability to resolve the status question in a definitive manner and that deflects attention away from concerns that need immediate attention.

There is little doubt that the status problem, coupled with the thorny issue of the role of the U.S. military's use of the island of Vieques for target practice, will not go away. There is also little debate anymore about the colonial nature of the U.S. relationship vis-à-vis Puerto Rico. For all parties concerned, putting to rest this divisive issue is perhaps not quite a positive-sum game, but more robust future economic and social progress demands a resolution of the status conundrum and never more so than with the end of the 936 era.[21] Part of the preparation of the road for transitioning to an altered political status, particularly if the choice is either statehood or independence, already has been paved by the ending of tax exemption, a change that, while not written in stone, has forced a reevaluation of Puerto Rico's entire development strategy and raised questions about the future.

Silver Linings

There is an old saying that "in every cloud, there is a silver lining," meaning that with adversity also comes opportunity. The end of the Operation Bootstrap era of federal tax subsidies provides the possibility for positive changes for the future if the right choices are made. While Puerto Rico's growth strategy has created an unusual pattern of path dependence in which nonlocal capital has dominated the local economy, there are some noteworthy aspects of the past development path that promise to ease the transition to next stage of transformation (also see Goldsmith and Vietorisz 1979).

First and foremost, Puerto Rico has a highly educated labor force. By international standards, the human capital base is quite extraordinary. Table 6.1 shows some evidence of Puerto Rico's level of educational attainment based upon U.S. census data, which show that nearly 30 percent of the population had at least some college education in 1990.

Going back to 1983, Puerto Rico already had a higher educational enrollment ratio—49 percent of those of college age were in some institution of higher learning—than did most countries, developed or less developed. For example, the average higher-education enrollment level for Latin American and Caribbean countries was about 15 percent. For a group of high-income economies, 31 percent of the college-age population was enrolled in some higher-education institute (in the United States, the ratio was 56 percent in 1983, one of the highest ratios in the world). By comparison, South Korea's higher-education enrollment ratio was 24 percent in 1983 (Baumol and Wolff 1996: 875). Clearly, the potential human capital base available is a strength of the economy and society that reflects both personal and social decisions made over the last generation.

From Chapter 4 and the discussions surrounding the issue of growth accounting, the importance of the appropriate human capital foundation to modern economic development is clear. It was precisely prior human capital accumulation that made possible the success of the East Asian economies in the 1990s (World Bank 1993). Puerto Rico's potential in this regard is impressive, allowing decisionmakers to take advantage of an existing a pool of talent rather than having to construct their human capital base, as is the case for many other economies. This does not mean that physical capital is unimportant to economic success in Puerto Rico. Rather, and as the examples of Germany's and Japan's

Table 6.1 Educational Attainment, 1950–1990

	1950	1960	1970	1980	1990
Less than high school	92.9%	85.0%	72.9%	59.5%	50.4%
High school graduate	3.6	7.5	15.0	21.3	21.0
Some college	1.7	4.0	6.0	8.9	14.3
College graduate	1.8	3.5	6.1	10.3	14.3

Source: Rivera-Batiz and Santiago 1996: 81.

rapid ascents after having their physical capital ravaged and destroyed during World War II suggest, physical capital can be added fairly easily as a complement to a substantial, existing human capital base. The reverse is not true.

Puerto Rico's human capital resources augur well for the future, being the fundamental input upon which any economy can build a solid future, though of course there are gaps that must be filled and improvements that can and must be made. Still, the successes of the East Asian economies, reviewed in Chapters 1 and 2, show what is possible if the human capital base is in place and the proper policies are implemented in an environment of private and public cooperation with the goal of expanding local productive capacity controlled by local owners.

Second, and somewhat ironically and certainly unintentionally, Section 936 had supported the expansion of Puerto Rico's service sector after its implementation in 1976, particularly the financial segment of that sector, as deposits of 936 corporations remained in the local economy in order to be eligible for reduced Puerto Rican tollgate tax rates. Modern economies are some combination of service and industrial sectors, with the former perhaps most significant in terms of employment and total output, but with the industrial sector nonetheless essential to the overall process. To use a metaphor, the industrial sector is to an economy as are the wheels and tires to an automobile. A car is not of much use without tires and wheels, and an economy rests on its industrial sector in much the same way.

Puerto Rico's service sector has expanded as banking and financial services, consulting, legal, accounting, marketing, insurance, film-making, tourism, retail sales, and a whole host of other service activities have grown and matured. It is not unrealistic or farfetched to imagine Puerto Rico as the "Singapore of the Caribbean," acting as a financial, consulting, and travel hub for the other smaller and still poorer economies of the region. It is a role to which Puerto Rico has paid lip service in the past, but there is a real possibility for success along these lines with the right outreach, the right incentives, and the correct attitude about what this role means. This represents an opportunity for both local capital and local human capital (except, to some degree, in air travel, where the comparative advantage resides with international investors) to increase their participation. Such possibilities also exist in many of the highly specific areas of consulting, accounting, insurance, marketing, and finance, for example, in which economies of scale do not exist, allowing small and medium-sized

Puerto Rican firms with specific Caribbean knowledge to be leaders in the region and to forge new comparative advantages vis-à-vis multinational investors. This already is taking place, and the prospects of further such developments are good news for the Puerto Rican economy and for those educated workers who do, or can, work in these sectors.

Third, new ways of looking at getting businesses started have been explored and motivated by the end of Section 936. This has been made all the more important by the reasonable expectation of a smaller inflow of external financial capital into the local market in future years. For many years, venture capital came from the local or federal government or from sources in the United States. Now, the Puerto Rican government and the private sector have initiated the Puerto Rico Private Equity Market Development Strategy to channel investments into promising local firms. Local investors have to be convinced that there are opportunities beyond the traditional grocery stores, fast food locations, and other more conservative investment locations of the past, when Puerto Ricans all too often filled niches rather than being cutting-edge innovators for the new economy.

At the same time, and as a consequence of failures of the development strategy reviewed in the previous chapters, Puerto Rico does not yet have a substantial core of entrepreneurs ready to step in and perform new roles on the wider scale needed in the new environment. The Puerto Rican Economic Development Bank has become an important financing alternative for small and medium-sized businesses and needs to be focused on recognizing and encouraging new entrepreneurs to expand this base over the future. The bank already has financed, as examples, a mango farm and a company dedicated to retreading truck tires, both of which are import substitution firms that could have been a larger part of the development strategy long ago, as Chapter 3 suggested. More recently, the bank has worked with a variety of small entrepreneurs with projects as diverse as funding an optometrist, a cybercafe, the production of soap, and the manufacture of children's mattresses. These are a mix of import substitution, service firms, and "new economy" enterprises that demonstrate the range of initiatives of which entrepreneurs are capable in the right environment and with the proper support.

The public and private universities can and must play an important and complementary role in creating entrepreneurs too. Training in modern financial, accounting, managerial, and information systems should be as important as the teaching of philosophy and history within the mission of the university systems. The opportunities to create dynamic programs in business and technology fields rich with interdisciplinary training is something that should be embraced and not seen as contrary to the goals of a university system.

The New Economic Development Model

Even prior to the end of Section 936 in 1996, the outlines of what came to be called the "new economic development model" were floated by the prostatehood government of Pedro Rosselló in the early 1990s (Consejo de Productividad Económica 1994). Unlike the procommonwealth Popular Democratic Party, which fought long and hard to retain federal tax exemption, the New Progressive Party was not only comfortable with the end of the special federal tax treatment of U.S. corporations in Puerto Rico, but also seemed to welcome the change.

A careful reading of the "new development model" monograph reveals a profound understanding of the structural weaknesses of the Operation Bootstrap path and a recognition of the substantial costs imposed upon the economy and society as a consequence of persisting with a strategy that had outlived its usefulness by the 1970s at least (also see Pantojas-Garcia 1999: 17–19 for a review of this and other executive level documents on forging a "new" economy). For example, the report laments the slowdown in economic growth rates over the decades, the persistently high unemployment rates, and the overextended emphasis on industrial promotions at the expense of other sectors of the economy due to an "obsolete model" of economic development (Consejo de Productividad Económica 1994: 5, 8; the page references in the following paragraphs are to this document).

Economic development is but a part, albeit an important part, of overall development in all its many faceted dimensions. The days when Puerto Rico could sell itself as a low-cost production location to U.S. firms are in the past, and the report does not lament this but recognizes that the goal of development is to improve the standard of living in the broadest sense for the largest numbers of persons possible. No longer being a low-cost production location is actually a good thing that must be recognized and built upon, since no country can hope for long-term development if low wage levels are the lure for producers. It is in further developing Puerto Rico's regional comparative advantage in its human capital and knowledge-intensive resources in ways that promise to significantly raise employment and per capita income that is at the heart of the new development model (pp. 6–7).

The document for a new economic model begins by elaborating a "vision" for the future (pp. 9–10). First is to achieve levels of income, poverty, and unemployment comparable to those prevailing in the United States—that is, to have an economy that converges to the United States in terms of the major economic variables. Given that the gap in income between the United States and Puerto Rico remained unchanged from the 1970s until the late 1990s, when it began to close, Puerto Rico will be required to grow much more rapidly than the United States for some period of time.

Second is to attain a diversified economy that is based on Puerto Rico's human capital resources, an economy that is competitive on the world stage and that has the appropriate infrastructure and a more efficient government. Third, the new economic model will be based on an agile private sector focused on the market, assisted by a supportive government with more targeted incentives to achieve its goals.

While the industrial sector will remain an important part of the economy, the new economic model will continue the trend begun after 1976 as part of the high-finance strategy in shifting the promotional balance away from an overreliance on manufacturing. Services and service exports, including tourism, will continue to receive more emphasis, as will the elaboration of agricultural products, from juices to milk to frozen chicken, as part of an effort to pursue targeted import substitution (p. 11).

The new economic model recognizes the need to support and expand the base of domestic entrepreneurs and to strengthen the local financial, capital, and equity markets to counteract the overreliance in the past on external capital and external firms (pp. 12–13, 15, 19). One of the objectives of the new order is to replace the culture of economic dependency, particularly on federal transfers, with a sustainable economy that promotes self-sufficiency and provides workers with the skills and productivity to have a decent standard of living based on their own productivity and effort, not handouts (pp. 17–18).

It is accepted, too, that to achieve these goals the local economy needs to be better integrated via backward and forward linkages (pp. 19–20) that increase the multiplier effects of any spending. Also recognized is the importance of technological acquisition by local entrepreneurs and workers and the capacity for Puerto Rico "to do" technology, a role in which it can act as a leader vis-à-vis other economies in the region (p. 37).

The document for a new economic development model is replete with specific proposals for attempting to reach the goals of greater self-sufficiency and a larger role for local firms and local finance, for a streamlined government, and for further expanding and improving the economy's human capital resources. The 1998 Tax Incentives Act discussed near the end of Chapter 5 is in the spirit of these proposals, encouraging service exports and rewarding firms doing research and development and investing in new technologies that help to bring them closer to the world production possibilities frontier. There is now a flat 7 percent corporate tax rate applied to all local and U.S. firms, with a 200 percent "superdeduction" for investments in research and development and job-training expenditures that are in the spirit of the new model.

Alternative Federal Assistance: Revenue Sharing

If the U.S. Congress and president seriously want to support a viable and sustained program of economic development as an alternative to either the "controlled foreign corporation" or the Section 30A provisions in the Internal Revenue Code or an entirely new federal tax exemption law for U.S. corporations in Puerto Rico in the post-936 age, a revenue reimbursement and revenue sharing program that returns a percentage of the increased federal tax revenues obtained from U.S. subsidiaries is such an alternative.

This money could be funneled to an appropriate agency of the Puerto Rican government—like its development bank—to be used exclusively for the expansion of locally owned business projects and for investments in badly needed infrastructure or other predetermined and earmarked purposes as part of a reorientation of the local economy that would strengthen its base. Such funding could be selective and should be targeted toward sectors of the economy showing the most promise for future growth and for contributing to local linkages. Any subsidies should be tied to well-defined performance criteria as was done by the East Asian economies (see Amsden 1989 for a discussion of the "rules, rewards, and referees" approach). For example, the achievement of a minimum level of local linkages after some specified period of time could be a condition for the continued receipt of subsidies, local tax exemption, low-cost loans, or whatever fiscal incentives that are being funded.

Such targeting and quid pro quo subsidization would be superior to any general tax exemption program that lacks a focus on creating employment, local linkages, or some other identifiable goal that can be monitored easily. Firms not meeting their targets should lose funding and access to other incentives. A carrot-and-stick approach in which firms that achieve previously agreed-upon targets that help to create a more integrated and linked local economic structure are rewarded, and those that do not are penalized by being excluded from such fiscal and financial benefits, would be an important step toward providing the right incentives for achieving broader economic goals. There is nothing about the current status relationship with the United States that would prevent such a targeted industrial- and service-sector program from being implemented right now.

If returning federal taxes seems an unusual suggestion, it should be remembered that there already is precedent for rebating to the Puerto Rican government federal tax revenues collected in the United States. Federal excise taxes paid in the United States on purchases of Puerto Rican rum have long been returned to the Puerto Rican treasury to be added to general commonwealth revenues. These funds amounted to more than $200 million annually in the 1990s.

For Puerto Rico, even $500 million returned for local development purposes would loom large in the economy. For the United States, such a sum is relatively small, equaling just 6.3 percent of total federal transfer payments to Puerto Rico in 2000 (Junta de Planificación 2002: A-22).[22] Further, such funds would be derived from new federal revenues on 936 corporations, and at the $500 million level, they would be equal to less than 25 percent of 936 tax revenues being collected. The opportunity cost of these funds, while obviously not zero, is quite low since these are new federal tax receipts. Once 936 was phased out, it still would be possible to earmark a portion of federal tax receipts collected from U.S. corporate operations in Puerto Rico for economic development purposes until such funding was no longer necessary.

Such funding also would add to the pool of total "savings" available to finance investments. One of the longtime concerns of many observers has been the relatively low rate of savings out of personal income, which, as was seen in Chapter 2, often has been negative. In traditional economic thinking, saving out of income is needed to allow for productive investment to take place. Nonetheless saving can come from government or from business or from abroad—that is, funds above and beyond the difference between income and consumption can come from sources other than households. Such a federal payback of tax revenues could be one such source of nonlocal savings that could contribute significantly to fixed investment and future economic growth. At the $500 million level suggested, such funding would be equivalent to about 10 percent of the 2000 level of investment in machinery and equipment (Junta de Planificación 2002: A-3).

One goal of federal assistance to Puerto Rico ought to be not only to expand employment but also to make such assistance from Washington less necessary over time by creating an economic structure that creates jobs and economic growth without special incentives. Over time, such employment-generating growth also would contribute to reducing the level of federal means-tested transfers, thus saving on future federal expenditures as well. The sharing with Puerto Rico of some of the new federal tax revenues collected on possessions corporations to be used to promote locally owned and locally controlled businesses and to promote more integrated and linked economic growth could prove to be a more productive investment in Puerto Rico's long-term expansion and progress than was the fifty years of indirect, blanket, and nontargeted support via federal tax exemptions.

Looking to the Future

The full effects of the end of Section 936 and Puerto Rico's new initiatives to diversify and restructure the economy will not be known for some time. In 2000, the PDP regained the governorship, as Sila Calderón became Puerto Rico's first woman to attain this post. To what extent any procommonwealth administration might try to recapture the past, including attempting to hold to the externally oriented economic strategy, is not certain. It may be too late to go back in time and restore federal tax exemption, though such an effort is on the table, as was noted in the previous chapter. Without that leg of the past economic model, Puerto Rico must continue to reinvent its economic strategy with a look to the future and build upon its most abundant resource, its human capital, but also with an eye toward generating and controlling more of the local economy's financial assets used for investment purposes.

There is no question that the perspectives as to what needs to be done as expressed in the "new economic development model" conform closely with what this book suggests is needed to foment lasting progress. These are lessons that the East Asian experiences and those of the United States and Western Europe before them amply illustrate. That the "new economic model" was promulgated by a prostatehood government does not make its proposals any more or any less valid as a guide for the future. An economy with added backward and forward linkages and with more local capital and more local entrepreneurs producing a larger proportion of total output will be an economy providing more jobs and a more secure future for its citizens. Such a vision is nonpartisan and is one that all who care about Puerto Rico should be working toward, regardless of their political position.

Notes

1. Again, as mentioned in the first chapter, success and failure are being judged in terms of overall social welfare and how the Puerto Rican population was affected by the style of development followed. Of course, certain actors in the economy benefited greatly from Puerto Rico's economic growth, especially some U.S. corporations, but the interest of this book is in social welfare broadly defined.

2. For example, see Bloomfield 1985; Carr 1984; Falk 1986; García-Passalacqua 1984; Heine and García-Passalacqua 1984; Meléndez 1998; Meléndez and Meléndez 1993: chaps. 1–4; Johnson 1980; and Trías Monge 1997. For a useful chronology of the issues related to status up to mid-1998, see Laney 1998.

3. Puerto Rico has a nonvoting resident commissioner sitting in the U.S. House of Representatives. The resident commissioner has the right to speak to issues in the U.S. Congress and to serve on committees but does not have a right to vote on the House floor. This position had been created by the Foraker Act (the first Organic Act for Puerto Rico, in 1900), with revisions in the role of the commissioner made in 1902 and 1904 (Luque de Sánchez 1980: 173–181).

4. The Jones Act (the second Organic Act) gave Puerto Rico the right to a bicameral, elected legislative body and, among other measures, conferred U.S. citizenship. The U.S. president and the U.S. Congress, however, retained absolute veto power over all legislation approved in Puerto Rico, as they had since the Foraker Act was passed in 1900. Except for the provisions for a local legislature and a few other minor administrative changes, all the rights of the United States in Puerto Rico—over tariffs, immigration, treaties, defense, shipping, and so on—remained intact. Puerto Rico's status as an unincorporated territory, as a "colony" in plain words, was spelled out in these acts (for a short summary of the issues, see Dietz 1986: 97–98).

5. Tugwell 1947: 491–492. Also see Dietz 1986: 233–235 for a fuller story of Muñoz's change of heart and mind on the issue of independence and the nature of Puerto Rico's relations with the United States.

6. U.S. Public Law 600 (1950) permitted Puerto Rico to write this constitution, which replaced the Jones Act as the governing document for Puerto Rico's local political and legal system. However, according to Public Law 600, this new constitution could not include either statehood or independence as options for Puerto Rico's status, and the new constitution had to be approved by the U.S. Congress. The Jones Act, which governed the relations between the United States and Puerto Rico, was replaced by the Federal Relations Law, which, in the words of a U.S. Senate report on Public Law 600, "would not change Puerto Rico's fundamental political, social and economic relationship to the United States" (Johnson 1980: 151).

The initial draft of the constitution for the Commonwealth of Puerto Rico was presented to Puerto Rican voters in March 1952 and was approved by 81.9 percent of those voting, though only 51.8 percent of registered voters went to the polls. After this approval had been given, the constitution was slightly modified by the U.S. Congress, with one section of the bill of rights eliminated. This modified constitution became the legal basis for the government of Puerto Rico (García Martínez 1978: 229–230; Bayrón Toro 1976: 215; the results of the 1952 vote by municipality and in total are available at www.eleccionespuertorico.org/archivo/proceso.constituyente/1952.html).

7. There was an international dimension to these maneuvers to codify Puerto Rico's status that cannot be ignored. At the insistence of the United States, which was interested in gaining access to Europe's colonial markets, the United Nations at the end of World War II had taken as one of its earliest acts the initiative for overseeing the process of decolonization around the world. The colonial status of Puerto Rico was thus something of an embarrassment to the United States, at least at the UN. Following upon the approval of the Commonwealth of Puerto Rico, the United States in 1953 notified the Secretary-General of the United Nations that the United States no longer would provide information regarding Puerto Rico as required by Article 73(e) of the UN Charter for non-self-governing territories. The U.S. position was that, based upon the majority acceptance by Puerto Rican voters of the commonwealth status in March 1952, Puerto Rico could no longer be considered a colony, and hence the United States was no longer subject to the UN's reporting requirement. The General Assembly of the United Nations accepted the U.S. explanation of Puerto Rico's new status and adopted Resolution 748 (VIII) by a vote of 22 to 18—with, significantly, 19 abstentions—recognizing the opinion of the United States. Thereafter, the United States was not obliged to report to the United Nations on the status of Puerto Rico.

However, the issue did not end with that narrow vote. In 1960, the UN General Assembly approved Resolution 1541 (XV), which made it clear that, under UN standards regarding the political status options available to the people of territories yet to achieve full self-government, the three acceptable political arrangements are limited to national independence, free association based on separate sovereignty, or full integration with another nation on the basis of equality. Given these options, Puerto Rico's commonwealth status would seem to be out of compliance.

Ironically, in an example of the right hand not knowing what the left hand is doing, even the U.S. Supreme Court would seem to agree with this interpretation of the US-Puerto Rican relation as colonial. In 1980, in the case of *Harris v. Rosario* (446 U.S. 651), the Court argued that the U.S. Congress continued to exercise authority over Puerto Rico under the Territorial Clause of Article IV (3)(2) of the U.S. Constitution. Whatever the intent of the U.S. Congress in permitting the establishment of the commonwealth status, this ruling argued that it did not alter Puerto Rico's fundamental standing as a territory of the United States.

To further illustrate the ambiguity and discontentment with the commonwealth status, and quoting from the Young bill introduced into the U.S. House of Representatives to frame the 1998 referendum process for deciding the status issue, "The Commonwealth remains an unincorporated territory and does not have the status of 'free association' with the United States as that status is defined under United States law or international practice."

8. For much of Puerto Rico's political history, the status issue was a preoccupation of, with some exceptions, members of the intellectual, economic, and political elites. The average Puerto Rican typically perceived political status as irrelevant to the daily struggle for survival and reproduction, to the extent the issue was considered at all. In recent years, the concern over status has become a more general preoccupation and one that has permeated political issues at all levels of government, affecting the efficiency and transparency of decisions and expenditures from the lowliest municipal agency to the top of the commonwealth government and everywhere in between.

9. Detailed election results on local elections of all types in Puerto Rico since 1932, including the plebiscite and referendum results, and other extremely valuable material can be accessed at www.eleccionespuertorico.org/home_en.html.

10. One might equally argue that the conflict over the U.S. military's use for target practice of the island municipality of Vieques off the east coast of Puerto Rico has been the sharpest point of conflict between the United States and Puerto Rico in recent memory. All political parties, despite their other differences, objected to the U.S. military's training missions and its obvious disregard for Puerto Rican rights. To many, the inability of Puerto Rico to control the use of its own territory in Vieques, especially following the death of a civilian caused by a wayward bomb during a practice mission, is concentrated evidence of the continuing colonial arrangement afflicting the island and of the helplessness of Puerto Rico vis-à-vis the United States.

11. The official title of the legislation was "An Act to Provide a Process Leading to Full Self-Government for Puerto Rico." The bill's principal sponsor was Representative Don Young, a Republican from Alaska, but the bill was

cosponsored by a long list of both Republican and Democratic members in the House.

12. Leading up to the introduction of this bill, in a joint letter dated January 17, 1997, cosigned by the prostatehood governor Pedro Rosselló and the presidents of the Popular Democratic Party and the Puerto Rican Independence Party, the two main opposition political parties, the United States was formally advised that "the People of Puerto Rico wish to be consulted as to their preference with regards to their ultimate political status." The letter continued that, "since Puerto Rico came under the sovereignty of the United States of America through the Treaty of Paris in 1898, the People of Puerto Rico have not been formally consulted by the United States of America as to their choice of their ultimate political status."

On January 23, 1997, the legislature of Puerto Rico adopted Concurrent Resolution 2, which called upon the U.S. Congress to establish a self-determination process that would permit the people of Puerto Rico to complete the decolonization process that had begun in 1952. For a chronology, reaching back to 1996, on the Young Bill and incisive commentary, see García-Passalacqua (1998).

13. All quoted material in the previous paragraphs comes from either the "Bill Summary and Status for the 105th Congress" or the version of the bill as passed by the U.S. House of Representatives. For the bill and supporting documents, see http://commdocs.house.gov/committees/resources/hii40445.000/hii40445_0.htm.

14. The following "finding" concerning the Young bill is instructive on the view of the prostatehood supporters of this bill: "Full self-government for Puerto Rico is attainable only through establishment of a political status which is based on either separate Puerto Rican sovereignty and nationality or full and equal United States nationality and citizenship through membership in the Union and under which Puerto Rico is no longer an unincorporated territory subject to the plenary authority of Congress arising from the Territorial Clause." This language would seem to be quite consistent with that of the UN resolutions discussed in note 7.

15. Again, this was the result of the fact that the plebiscite was organized by the prostatehood PNP, whose leader, Pedro Rosselló, was also governor of Puerto Rico at the time. The PNP's control over the process resulted in a ballot formulation of the commonwealth option that was unacceptable to PDP supporters because of the definition of the choice as "territorial"—that is, colonial. The legislature of Puerto Rico had approved Public Law 249, mandating the 1998 plebiscite.

16. Blank and voided ballots numbered 4,846 (0.3 percent). The voter turnout was 71.3 percent, as 1,566,270 of 2,197,824 registered voters cast their ballots. For a summary of the votes, see www.eleccionespuertorico.org/1998/summary.html. Also see http://resourcescommittee.house.gov/106cong/fullcomm/61203.htm for the official report on the results of the vote by the U.S. House of Representatives.

17. In the 1993 status plebiscite the commonwealth option received 826,326 votes (48.6 percent of the total), while 788,296 voters (46.3 percent) cast their ballots for statehood and 75,620 votes (4.4 percent) were recorded for independence. See www.eleccionespuertorico.org/1993/summary.html for the official results.

18. The prostatehood party has made it clear that it plans to hold votes on status when it can do so until Puerto Rico becomes a state of the union or chooses independence. The U.S. Congress is likely to be pressured in the future to come to some sort of closure on this issue, as was expected to happen when the Young bill was introduced into the U.S. House of Representatives in 1997. The issue of Vieques and the U.S. military's role in Puerto Rico has pushed the status issue more directly into the mainstream of discussion and public consciousness, involving the Clinton White House directly in talks with the major parties in June 2000, though nothing substantive came out of those meetings. In the November 2000 election for governor, which is indicative of the cleft in the electorate, the procommonwealth PPD candidate, Sila María Calderón, defeated the prostatehood PNP's Carlos Pesquera, providing perhaps another referendum on status, as the PPD replaced the PNP in the governor's residence once again.

19. See Maldonado 1974; Meléndez and Ruíz 1998.

20. As an example, an immeasurable benefit of independence might be the sense of freedom from domination experienced by independence supporters, though that gross benefit would need to be balanced by the equally intangible cost to others who prefer permanent association with the United States. Likewise, an intangible benefit of statehood would be a sense and reality of first-class, and not second-class, U.S. citizenship, though this change would also bring concrete monetary gains, benefits that are more easily quantified.

21. See Berman Santana (1999) for an overview of the status issue in Puerto Rico and other U.S. territories.

22. In 2000, $500 million would have been equal to about 5 percent of the commonwealth government's net recurrent revenues. Excise taxes returned to the Puerto Rican government totaled $245.7 million in 2000 (Junta de Planificación 2002: A31–A32).

References

Alameda Lozada, José I., and Alfredo González Martínez. 2000. *Cambio Tecnológico, Productividad y Crecimiento Económico en Puerto Rico.* Mayagüez: University of Puerto Rico, Department of Economics. Mimeo.

Alexander, Robert J. 1990. "Import Substitution in Latin America in Retrospect." In James L. Dietz and Dilmus D. James (eds.), *Progress Toward Development in Latin America: From Prebisch to Technological Autonomy.* Boulder: Lynne Rienner, pp. 15–28.

Amsden, Alice. 1989. *Asia's Next Giant: South Korea and Late Industrialization.* New York: Oxford University Press.

Andic, Fuat M. 1964. *Distribution of Family Incomes in Puerto Rico.* Río Piedras, Puerto Rico: Institute of Caribbean Studies.

Aponte, Maribel. 1999. "Política Industrial Estratégica, Producción y Empresas en Puerto Rico." In Francisco E. Martínez (ed.), *Futuro Económico de Puerto Rico.* San Juan: University of Puerto Rico Press, pp. 345–385.

Arbelo García, Milagros E., Víctor Javier González Ortiz, and Eric Pabón Meléndez. 1991. "Enfoque Interindustrial del Impact de los Nuevos Salaries Minimos Legales." *Ceteris Paribus* 1 (April): 47–76.

Aviles, Luis Aníbal. 1996. "Section 936 Repealed with Ten Year Phase-Out." *Puerto Rico Business Law Notes* (Summer).

Baer, Werner. 1959. "Puerto Rico: An Evaluation of a Successful Development Program." *Quarterly Journal of Economics* 73 (November): 645–672.

Banco Popular. 2000. "The Human Development Index and Puerto Rico." *Progreso Económico* (Second Quarter): 1–3.

Barro, Robert J. 1991. "Economic Growth in a Cross Section of Countries." *Quarterly Journal of Economics* 106 (May): 407–443.

Baumol, William J., and Edward N. Wolff. 1996. "Catching Up in the Postwar Period: Puerto Rico as the Fifth 'Tiger'?" *World Development* 24 (May): 869–885.

Baver, Sherrie L. 1993. *The Political Economy of Colonialism.* New York: Praeger.

———. 2000. "The Rise and Fall of Section 936: The Historical Context and Possible Consequences for Migration." *Centro Journal* 11 (Spring): 45–55.

Bayrón Toro, Fernando. 1976. *Elecciones y Partidos Políticos en Puerto Rico, 1809–1976.* Mayagüez: Isla.

Berman Santana, Déborah. 1999. "No Somos Únicos: The Status Issue from Manila to San Juan." *Centro Journal* 11 (Fall): 127–140.

Birdsall, Nancy, Carol Graham, and Richard H. Sabot (eds.). 1998. *Beyond Trade-Offs: Market Reforms and Equitable Growth in Latin America.* Washington, D.C.: Brookings Institution and Inter-American Development Bank.

Bloomfield, Richard J. (ed.). 1985. *Puerto Rico: The Search for a National Policy.* Boulder: Westview Press.

Bonilla, Frank and Ricardo Campos. 1981. "A Wealth of Poor: Puerto Ricans in the New International Order." *Daedalus* 110 (Spring): 133–176.

Bradford, John J. 1991. "U.S. Possessions Corporation Returns, 1987." *SOI Bulletin* 11 (Summer): 51–60.

Carr, Raymond. 1984. *Puerto Rico: A Colonial Experiment.* New York: New York University Press.

Carroll, David J. 1993. "The Puerto Rican Model of Development: Foreign Capital Dependence and the Limits of Autonomous Development." Ph.D. thesis, University of South Carolina.

Castañer, Juan A., and Angel L. Ruíz Mercado. 1997. *The Importance of Trade to an Export-Led Economy in the Present Context of Free Trade Agreements in the Western Hemisphere: A Quantitative Analysis for the Puerto Rican Economy.* Río Piedras: University of Puerto Rico, Department of Economics.

Centro de Estudios Puertorriqueños (History Task Force). 1979. *Labor Migration Under Capitalism: The Puerto Rican Experience.* New York: Monthly Review Press.

Clark, Victor S., et al. 1930. *Porto Rico and Its Problems.* Washington, D.C.: Brookings Institution.

Colón, Leandro A. 1994. "Industrial Policy and Technological Capacity in Puerto Rico." *Ceteris Paribus* 4 (April): 27–54.

Colón, Leandro A., and Francisco E. Martínez. 1999. "Los Flujos Financieros en Puerto Rico: Una Vision Panorámica." In Francisco E. Martínez (ed.), *Futuro Económico de Puerto Rico.* San Juan: University of Puerto Rico Press, pp. 287–313.

Comité Interagencial de la Estrategia de Puerto Rico. 1976. *El Desarrollo Económico de Puerto Rico (Informe Echenique).* Río Piedras, Puerto Rico: Editorial Universitaria.

Consejo de Productividad Económica. 1994. *Nuevo Modelo de Desarrollo Económico.* San Juan: Office of the Governor, February.

"Consolidation and Deregulation Fortify the Banking Industry." *Washington Times*, September 29, 1999.

Contos, George, and Ellen Legel. 2000. "Corporation Income Tax Returns, 1997." *SOI Bulletin* (Summer): 101–121.

Council of Economic Advisors. 2001. *Economic Report of the President.* Washington, D.C.: GPO.

Curet Cuevas, Eliézer. 1976. *El Desarrollo Económico de Puerto Rico, 1940–1976.* Hato Rey, Puerto Rico: Management Aid Center.

———. 1986. *Puerto Rico: Development by Integration to the US.* Río Piedras, Puerto Rico: Editorial Cultural.

Cypher, James, and James Dietz. 1997. *The Process of Economic Development.* London: Routledge.

De Jesús Toro, Rafael. 1982. *Historia Económica de Puerto Rico.* Cincinnati, Ohio: Southwestern Publishing.

Del Valle, Jaime. 1999. "Políticas Tecnológicas en Puerto Rico: Pasado, Presente y Futuro." In Francisco E. Martínez (ed.), *Futuro Económico de Puerto Rico.* San Juan: University of Puerto Rico Press, pp. 61–81.

Department of the Treasury. 1983. *The Operation and Effect of the Possessions Corporation System of Taxation.* Washington, D.C.: GPO.

Dietz, James L. 1986. *Economic History of Puerto Rico.* Princeton, N.J.: Princeton University Press.

———. 1989. *Historia Económica de Puerto Rico.* Río Piedras, Puerto Rico: Ediciones Huracán.

———. 1990. "Technological Autonomy, Linkages, and Development." In James L. Dietz and Dilmus D. James (eds.), *Progress Toward Development in Latin America.* Boulder: Lynne Rienner, pp. 177–199.

———. 2001. "Puerto Rico: The 'Three-Legged' Economy." *Integration and Trade* 5 (September–December): 247–273.

Duany, Jorge. 1999. "La Población y la Migración en Puerto Rico de Cara al Siglo XXI." In Francisco E. Martínez (ed.), *Futuro Ecónomico de Puerto Rico.* San Juan: University of Puerto Rico Press.

Durand, Rafael. 1980. "Progreso, Problemas y Perspectivas del Desarrollo Industrial de Puerto Rico." In Gerardo Navas Dávila, *Cambio y Desarrollo en Puerto Rico: La Transformación Ideológica del Partido Popular Democrático.* Río Piedras: University of Puerto Rico, pp. 171–198.

Economic Development Administration (EDA). 1986. *Import Substitution: Prospects and Policies for Puerto Rico in the 1980's and Beyond.* San Juan: EDA. Mimeo.

Falk, Pamela S. (ed.). 1986. *The Political Status of Puerto Rico.* Lexington, Mass.: Lexington Books.

García Martínez, Alfonso L. 1978. *Puerto Rico: Leyes Fundamentales.* Río Piedras: Editorial Edil.

García Passalacqua, Juan M. 1984. *Puerto Rico: Freedom and Equality at Issue.* New York: Praeger.

————. 1998. "The Puerto Rico Question Revisited." *Current History* (February): 82–86.

Gerschenkron, Alexander. 1962. *Economic Backwardness in Historical Perspective.* Cambridge: Harvard University Press.

Goldsmith, William W., and Thomas Vietorisz. 1979. "Operation Bootstrap, Industrial Autonomy, and a Parallel Economy for Puerto Rico." *International Regional Science Review* 4 (Fall): 1–22.

Griggs, Robert S. 1998. "Puerto Rico Enacts New Tax Incentives Law to Counteract Section 936 Phase-Down." *Journal of International Taxation* 9 (February).

Grilli, I., and H. Yang. 1988. "Primary Commodity Prices, Manufactured Goods Prices, and the Terms of Trade of Developing Countries: What the Long Run Shows." *World Bank Economic Review* 2 (January): 1–47.

Hall, Robert E., and C. Jones. 1999. "Why Do Some Countries Produce So Much More Output Per Worker Than Others?" *Quarterly Journal of Economics* 114 (February): 83–116.

Hartzok, Jeff. 1988. "U.S. Possessions Corporation Returns, 1983." *SOI Bulletin* 7 (Spring): 55–64.

Heine, Jorge, and Juan M. García-Passalacqua (eds.). 1984. *The Puerto Rican Question.* New York: Foreign Policy Association.

Hexner, J. Tomas, and Glenn Jenkins. 1998. "Puerto Rico: The Economic and Fiscal Dimensions." *Puerto Rico Herald* available at www.puertorico-herald.org/issues/vol2n03/hexner-jenkins.shtml

Hirschman, Albert O. 1971. "How to Divest in Latin America, and Why." In Albert O. Hirschman, *A Bias for Hope.* New Haven, Conn.: Yale University Press, pp. 225–252.

Hofman, André. 2000. *The Economic Development of Latin America in the Twentieth Century.* Cheltenham, UK: Edward Elgar.

Internal Revenue Service. 1987. *Statistics of Income-1984. Corporation Income Tax Returns.* Washington, D.C.: GPO.

————. 1989. *Statistics of Income-1986. Corporation Income Tax Returns.* Washington, D.C.: GPO.

————. 1991. *Statistics of Income-1988. Corporation Income Tax Returns.* Washington, D.C.: GPO.

————. 1993. *Statistics of Income-1990. Corporation Income Tax Returns.* Washington, D.C.: GPO.

————. 1994. *Statistics of Income-1991. Corporation Income Tax Returns.* Washington, D.C.: GPO.

————. 1995. *Statistics of Income-1992. Corporation Income Tax Returns.* Washington, D.C.: GPO.

————. 1997. "1994, Corporation Income Tax Returns." Available at www.irs.gov/taxstats/display/0,,i1%3D40%26genericId%3D16841,00.html

————. 1999. "1996, Corporation Income Tax Returns." Available at www.irs.gov/taxstats/display/0,,i1%3D40%26genericId%3D16841,00.html

———. 2000. "1997, Corporation Income Tax Returns." Available at www.irs. gov/taxstats/display/0,,i1%3D40&genericId%3D16902,00.html
———. 2001. "1998, Corporation Income Tax Returns." Available at www.irs. gov/taxstats/display/0,,i1%3D40&genericId%3D16902,00.html
Irizarry Mora, Edwin. 1989. "Wealth Distribution in the Puerto Rican Model of Development." Ph.D. diss., University of Sussex, UK.
———. 2001. *Economía de Puerto Rico*. Mexico: Thompson Learning.
Isaac, Katherine. 1993. "Losing Jobs to 936." *Multinational Monitor* 15 (July/August) available at http://multinationalmonitor.org/hyper/issues/1993/08/mm0893_01.html.
Johnson, Roberta A. 1980. *Puerto Rico: Commonwealth or Colony?* New York: Praeger.
Junta de Planificación. 1977. *Informe Económico al Gobernador 1976*. San Juan: Junta de Planificación.
———. 1981. *Informe Económico al Gobernador 1980*. San Juan: Junta de Planificación.
———. 1986. *Informe Económico al Gobernador 1985*. San Juan: Junta de Planificación.
———. 1987. *Informe Económico al Gobernador 1986*. San Juan: Junta de Planificación.
———. 1988. *Informe Económico al Gobernador 1987*. San Juan: Junta de Planificación.
———. 1989. *Informe Económico al Gobernador 1988*. San Juan: Junta de Planificación.
———. 1990. *Informe Económico al Gobernador 1989*. San Juan: Junta de Planificación.
———. 1994. *Socioeconomic Statistics of Puerto Rico*. San Juan: Junta de Planificación.
———. 1999. *Informe Económico al Gobernador 1998: Apéndice Estadístico*. San Juan: Office of the Governor, February.
———. 2001. *Informe Económico al Gobernador 2000*. San Juan: Junta de Planificación.
———. 2002. *Informe Económico a al Gobernadora 2001*. San Juan: Junta de Planificación.
———. 2002a. *Selected Statistics on Puerto Rico's External Trade*. San Juan: Planning Board.
Laney, Garrine P. 1998. *Puerto Rico: A Chronology of Political Status History*. Washington, D.C.: Congressional Research Service.
Lara, Juan A., and José J. Villamil. 1999. "El Contexto Económico Actual." In Francisco E. Martínez (ed.), *Futuro Económico de Puerto Rico*. San Juan: University of Puerto Rico Press, pp. 27–59.
Lefort, Fernando. 1997. "Puerto Rico: Divergence Not Convergence." *Puerto Rico Herald* 2 (June) available at www.puertorico-herald.org/issues/vol2n03/lefort.shtml.

Lucas, Robert E. 1988. "On the Mechanics of Economic Development." *Journal of Monetary Economics* 22 (July): 3–42.

Luque de Sánchez, María Dolores. 1980. *La Ocupación Norteamericana y la Ley Foraker: La Opinion Pública Puertorriqueña, 1898–1904*. Río Piedras, Puerto Rico: Editorial Universitaria.

Maldonado, A. W. 1997. *Teodoro Moscoso and Puerto Rico's Operation Bootstrap*. Gainesville: University of Florida Press.

Maldonado, Rita. 1974. "The Economic Costs and Benefits of Puerto Rico's Political Alternatives." *Southern Economic Journal* 41 (October): 267–282.

Mann, Arthur J. 1985. "Economic Development, Income Distribution, and Real Income Levels in Puerto Rico, 1963–1977." *Economic Development and Cultural Change* 33 (April): 485–502.

Mann, Arthur J., and W. C. Ocasio. 1975. "La Distribución del Ingreso en Puerto Rico: Una Nueva Dimensión." *Revista de Ciencias Sociales* 19 (March): 3–23.

Marqués Velasco, René. 1994. "Nuevas Realidades, Nuevo Modelo Económico." *Ceteris Paribus* 4 (April): 1–25.

Martínez, Francisco E. (ed.). 1999. *Futuro Económico de Puerto Rico*. San Juan: University of Puerto Rico Press.

Meléndez, Edgardo. 1998. *Partidos, Política Pública y Status en Puerto Rico*. San Juan: Ediciones Nueva Aurora.

———. 2000. *Puerto Rican Government and Politics: A Comprehensive Bibliography*. Boulder: Lynne Rienner.

Meléndez, Edwin. 1994. "Accumulation and Crisis in a Small and Open Economy: The Postwar Social Structure of Accumulation in Puerto Rico." In David M. Kotz, Terrence McDonough, and Michael Reich (eds.), *Social Structures of Accumulation: The Political Economy of Growth and Crisis*. Cambridge: Cambridge University Press, pp. 233–252.

Meléndez, Edwin, and Edgardo Meléndez (eds.). 1993. *Colonial Dilemma: Critical Perspectives on Contemporary Puerto Rico*. Boston: South End Press.

Meléndez, Edwin, and Angel L. Ruíz. 1998. *Economic Effects of the Political Options for Puerto Rico*. San Germán, P.R.: Centro de Publicaciones, Interamerican University.

Miller, Randy. 1999. "U.S. Possessions Corporations, 1995." *SOI Bulletin* (Summer): 168–184.

Moscoso, Teodoro. 1954. "Un discurso antes la convención de orientación de Puerto Rico," quoted in Blanca Slivestrini and Maria Dolores Luque de Sánchez, Historia de Puerto Rico: Trajectoria de un pueblo. San Juan: Editorial Cultural Panamericana, 1988.

———. 1980. "Orígen y Desarrollo de la 'Operación Manos a la Obra.'" In Gerardo Navas Dávila, *Cambio y Desarrollo en Puerto Rico: La Transformación Ideológica del Partido Popular Democrático*. Río Piedras: University of Puerto Rico, pp. 161–169.

Navas Dávila, Gerardo. *Cambio y Desarrollo en Puerto Rico: La Transformación Ideológica del Partido Popular Democrático*. Río Piedras: University of Puerto Rico.

Negrón Díaz, Santos, and José G. García López. 1992. "Sintesis del Estudio del Compartamiento, Impact Económico y Perspectivas de Industrias Manufactureras Seleccionadas." *Ceteris Paribus* 2 (April): 149–160.

Nutter, Sarah E. 1997. "U.S. Possessions Corporations, 1993." *SOI Bulletin* 17 (Fall): 144–157.

———. 1998/99. "Statistics of Income: Studies of International Income and Taxes." *SOI Bulletin* (Winter): 151–177.

Pantojas-García, Emilio. 1984. *La Crisis del Model Desarrollista y la Reestructuración Capitalista en Puerto Rico*. Cuaderno de Investigación y Análisis 9. San Juan: CEREP.

———. 1990. *Development Strategies as Ideology*. Boulder: Lynne Rienner.

———. 1999. "Los Estudios Económicos sobre Puerto Rico: Una Evaluación Crítica." In Francisco E. Martínez (ed.), *Futuro Económico de Puerto Rico*. San Juan: University of Puerto Rico Press, pp. 11–24.

———. 2000. "End-of-the-Century Studies of Puerto Rico's Economy, Politics, and Culture: What Lies Ahead?" *Latin American Research Review* 35, no. 2: 227–240.

Perloff, Harvey. 1950. *Puerto Rico's Economic Future: A Study in Planned Development*. Chicago: University of Chicago Press.

Plosser, Charles I. 1993. "The Search for Growth." In Federal Reserve Bank of Kansas City, *Policies for Long-Run Economic Growth*. Kansas City: Federal Reserve Bank, pp. 57–86.

Puerto Rico Planning Board. 1951. *Economic Development of Puerto Rico: 1940–1950; 1951–1960*. San Juan: Government Service Office.

Ranis, Gustav. 1981. "Challenges and Opportunities Posed by Asia's Superexporters: Implications for Manufactured Exports from Latin America." *Quarterly Review of Economics and Business* 21 (Summer): 204–226.

Rivera Figueroa, Manuel. 1988. "Structural Change and Unemployment in Puerto Rico, 1963–1977: An Input-Output Analysis." M.A. thesis in economics, University of Puerto Rico, Río Piedras.

Rivera-Batiz, Francisco L., and Carlos E. Santiago. 1996. *Island Paradox: Puerto Rico in the 1990s*. New York: Russell Sage.

Romer, Paul M. 1994. "The Origins of Endogenous Growth." *Journal of Economic Perspectives* 8 (Winter): 3–22.

Ross, David. 1969. *The Long Up-Hill Path: A Historical Study of Puerto Rico's Program of Economic Development*. San Juan: Edil.

Ruíz, Angel L. 1994. "The Impact of Transfer Payments (Federal and Others) to Individuals and to Government on the Puerto Rican Economy." *Ceteris Paribus* 4 (April): 55–72.

Santana Rabell, Leonardo. 1984. *Planificación y Política Durante la Administración de Luis Muñoz Marín*. Santurce: Análisis (Revista de Planificación).

Solimano, Andres, Eduardo Aninat, and Nancy Birdsall (eds.). 2000. *Distributive Justice and Economic Development: The Case of Chile and Developing Countries.* Ann Arbor: University of Michigan Press.

Solow, Robert M. 1994. "Perspectives on Economic Growth." *Journal of Economic Perspectives* 8 (Winter): 45–54.

———. 2000. *Growth Theory: An Exposition—Intermezzo.* New York: Oxford University Press.

Sotomayor, Orlando J. 1996. "Poverty and Income Inequality in Puerto Rico: 1969–1989: Trends and Sources." *Review of Income and Wealth* 42 (March): 49–61.

———. 1998. *Poverty and Income Inequality in Puerto Rico, 1970–1990.* Río Piedras, Puerto Rico: Centro de Investigaciones Sociales.

———. 2000. "Análisis Comparado de las Estructuras de Salaries de Puerto Rico y los Estados Unidos." *Revista de Ciencias Sociales* 9 (June): 106–133.

———. 2002. *Rapid Growth, Poverty, and Income Distribution: The Case of Puerto Rico.* Department of Economics Working Paper. Mayagüez: University of Puerto Rico.

Stead, William H. 1958. *Fomento: The Economic Development of Puerto Rico.* Washington, D.C.: National Planning Association.

Stewart, John R. Jr., and Saúl Chico Pamias. 1990. "Puerto Rico's Economic Development Strategy and Structural Change." *Journal of the Flagstaff Institute* 14 (March).

Suárez, Sandra. 2001. "Political and Economic Motivations for Labor Control: A Comparison of Ireland, Puerto Rico, and Singapore." *Studies in Comparative International Development* 36 (Summer): 54–81.

Szeflinski, Kenneth. 1983. "U.S. Possessions Corporation Tax Credit, 1980." *SOI Bulletin* 2 (Spring): 41–45.

Tata, Robert J. 1980. *Structural Changes in Puerto Rico's Economy, 1947–1976.* Latin American Series no. 9. Athens: Ohio University, Center for International Studies.

Trías Monge, José. 1997. *Puerto Rico: The Trials of the Oldest Colony in the World.* New Haven: Yale University Press.

Tugwell, Rexford Guy. 1947. *The Stricken Land.* Garden City, New York: Doubleday.

U.S. Bureau of the Census. 1999. *Statistical Abstract of the United States: 1999.* Washington, D.C.: U.S. Government Printing Office.

———. 2001. *Statistical Abstract of the United States: 2001.* Washington, D.C.: U.S. Government Printing Office.

U.S. Department of Commerce. 1979. *Economic Study of Puerto Rico.* 2 vols. Washington, D.C.: U.S. Government Printing Office.

U.S. Department of the Treasury. 1983. *The Operation and Effect of the Possessions Corporation System of Taxation.* Fourth Report. Washington, D.C.: U.S. Government Printing Office.

U.S. Government Accounting Office (GAO). 1997. "Tax Policy: Puerto Rican Economic Trends." Letter Report, 05/14; GAO/GGD-97-101. Washington, D.C.: U.S. Government Printing Office.

Villamil, José J. 1976. "El Modelo Puertorriqueño: Los Límites del Crecimiento Dependiente." *Revista Interamericana de Planificación* 10: 64–86.

Weisskoff, Richard. 1985. *Factories and Food Stamps: The Puerto Rico Model of Development.* Baltimore: Johns Hopkins University Press.

World Bank. 1991. *World Development Report 1991.* New York: Oxford University Press.

———. 1993. *The East Asian Miracle.* New York: Oxford University Press.

———. 2003. *World Development Report 2003.* New York: Oxford University Press.

Index

About the Book

In the midst of significantly changing economic and political relations with the United States, Puerto Rico is struggling to find a new—and effective—development path. James Dietz examines the island's contemporary development trajectory, providing a comprehensive and up-to-date analysis.

Dietz considers where Puerto Rico's economy is today, and why and how its challenging state of affairs might be improved. Throughout, building on his acclaimed *Economic History of Puerto Rico,* he explores the historical, social, and political forces that have accompanied Puerto Rico's course from the 1940s to the first decade of the twenty-first century.

James L. Dietz is professor of economics at California State University, Fullerton. His numerous publications include *Economic History of Puerto Rico, The Process of Economic Development* (coauthored with James Cypher), and *Latin America's Economic Development: Confronting Crisis.*